REAL TALK
IN ELEMENTARY CLASSROOMS

SOLVING PROBLEMS IN THE TEACHING OF LITERACY
Cathy Collins Block, Series Editor

Recent Volumes

Real Talk in Elementary Classrooms

Effective Oral Language Practice

MAUREEN P. BOYD
LEE GALDA

Foreword by Don Rubin

THE GUILFORD PRESS
New York   London

© 2011 The Guilford Press
A Division of Guilford Publications, Inc.
72 Spring Street, New York, NY 10012
www.guilford.com

Printed in the United States of America

This book is printed on acid-free paper.

Last digit is print number: 9   8   7   6   5   4   3   2   1

Library of Congress Cataloging-in-Publication Data

Boyd, Maureen P.
  Real talk in elementary classrooms: effective oral language practice / Maureen
P. Boyd, Lee Galda ; [foreword by] Don Rubin.
    p. cm. — (Solving problems in the teaching of literacy)
  Includes bibliographical references and index.
  ISBN 978-1-60918-158-1 (pbk.) — ISBN 978-1-60918-159-8 (cloth)
  1. Oral communication—Study and teaching (Elementary) 2. Interaction
analysis in education. 3. Classroom environment. I. Galda, Lee. II. Title.
  LB1572.B69 2011+
  372.62′2—dc22

                                                            2010051819

For my two sons, Liam and Griffin, with all my love;
for my father and seven siblings;
and in memory of my mother,
who had a rare way with words
—M. P. B.

To the teachers present in this book—
you know who you are
—M. P. B. and L. G.

About the Authors

Maureen P. Boyd, PhD, is Assistant Professor in the Department of Learning and Instruction at the University at Buffalo, The State University of New York. Prior to receiving her doctorate, she taught English language arts and English language learning in K–12 English language learner and mainstream classrooms in the Middle East, Asia, and the United States for 15 years. Dr. Boyd is a member of the Literacy Research Association, the American Educational Research Association, the International Reading Association (IRA), and the American Association for Applied Linguistics, and is a participant in subgroups related to talk, literacy, and literature. She has written book chapters and articles in *Research in the Teaching of English, Journal of Literacy Research*, and *The Reading Teacher*, among other journals. This is her first book.

Lee Galda, PhD, is Professor in the Department of Curriculum and Instruction at the University of Minnesota, where she teaches courses in children's and young adults' literature. Prior to receiving her doctorate, she taught in elementary and middle school classrooms. Dr. Galda is a member of the IRA, the American Library Association, and the United States Board on Books for Young People (USBBY). Formerly, she was Children's Books Department editor for *The Reading Teacher* and a member of the Newbery Award Selection Committee and the USBBY Bridge to Understanding Award Committee. Dr. Galda is chair of the 2010–2012 IRA Children's and Young Adults' Book Awards Selection Committee. She sits on the review boards of several professional journals and on the editorial board of *Children's Literature in Education*. The author of numerous articles and book chapters on children's literature, Dr. Galda was lead author of the first chapter on that subject to appear in the *Handbook of Reading Research* (Volume III).

Acknowledgments

Particular thanks to four wonderful teachers—Lisa, Charlotte, Michael, and Sarah—for the real talk in your classrooms. Thanks to Dr. Don Rubin for writing the foreword and teaching us both much of what we know about talk. Special thanks to Arthur A. Schomburg Fellow and master's student Govindan Kartha for his careful reading and feedback and to Katharine Bartelo, Maureen's graduate assistant, for her cheerful support. Thanks to Maureen's colleagues Dr. Erin Kearney and Dr. Mary McVee for feedback on Chapter 1, and to Maureen's doctoral students for the illuminating conversations in the fall 2009 seminar on classroom talk. Thanks also to our three reviewers for their insightful feedback, and to the supportive staff at The Guilford Press: Chris Jennison, Craig Thomas, Louise Farkas, and Marie Sprayberry.

We have spent many hours of real talk in the writing of this book. We have truly practiced what we preach. "I am a part of all that I have met." Any shortcomings are our own.

MAUREEN P. BOYD
LEE GALDA

Foreword

In Chapter 3 of the extended conversation on which you are about to embark, you will be delighted to encounter a fourth grader named PD.

"Ms. Charlotte," PD announces, "I got something to say."

I got something to say. I got a self to affirm. I got an identity to proclaim. I got a concept to label. I got a proposition to predicate. I got a hypothesis to postulate. I got an interpersonal network to animate.

I got something to say.

Expressing what you got to say is a fundamental human impulse. We are *Homo loquens*, after all, the speaking animal (Hacker, 2007). To speak is an essential need and source of gratification, not all that dissimilar from corporeal impulses to ambulate or to reproduce. When you arrive at Chapter 8, you will find our authors speaking about an essential impulse of classroom discourse that is too infrequently invoked in educational theory and research: joy. My goodness, we could use more joy in our public schools, couldn't we? We could use more student talk, don't you think?

Yet so many factors militate against student talk in the PreK–12 classroom (Rubin, 1986). Classroom talk is noisy, and your colleague on the other side of the accordion room divider doesn't appreciate competing with the buzz from your classroom during her oh-so-important disquisition on prime and nonprime numbers. And some assistant principal (none reading this book, of course) prowling the halls seems ineluctably drawn to noisy classrooms like an ambulance chaser perversely hoping to witness a gruesome accident. As the authors of *Real Talk in Elementary Classrooms* acknowledge, a more important reason why silence so often prevails in our schools is that allowing students to talk means that you the teacher must be willing to relinquish some control. Voluntarily turning over the reins to your students requires guts—and also trust. Good news for readers of this book: The educators profiled in the following chapters offer strong and varied models for judging when, how, and to what degree to relinquish control. (In this book, guiding students to nominate and develop topics is called "contingent" teaching.) A final reason why talking to learn too often languishes in our schools pertains to the difficulty of assessing student talk. What is not assessed literally does not count in the current milieu of accountability.

Don't you sometimes wonder, though, whether so many schools and educators devalue and suppress student talk precisely because of the joy factor? After all, if students are having fun—if they are engaged at a visceral and ego-gratifying level—well, they couldn't be learning much, now could they? To the contrary, the book in your hand testifies in each chapter that learning must be effortful, but it need not be painful.

Yet, I am going to support the education killjoy skeptics to this degree: Joyous engagement in speaking is surely necessary for students to develop as articulate communicators, but it is hardly sufficient. With an estimated 286 million cell phones in use and 2.3 trillion minutes of talk during 2009 (CTIA, 2010), there hardly seems to be a dearth of speech in the United States. So while plentiful and exuberant talk is much to be desired, merely increasing the volume of talk cannot in itself constitute the aim of oral communication instruction. Apropos the issue of sheer verbosity, in Chapter 6 you will hear a master teacher named Michael say to Herbert, a student in his third-grade class who is about to share a longer-than-usual reading response, "Well, quantity isn't, you know, the goal here. But when you do write a bunch, sometimes you say more too. Let's hear it!"

The book you are reading is not about just getting students to talk a bunch, however. It is about *real* talk, the kind of talk that results when students are engaged in thinking and learning. At the same time, real talk is the very mechanism by which students think and learn. Real talk is thus both educated talk and educational talk. Concrete thinkers like me can learn to recognize real talk when we hear it by associating it with the tangible utterance type that our authors call "student critical turns."

We learn in this book that real talk—like a student critical turn— is linguistically elaborated. Generally, real talk consists of more than single-word interjections or elliptical replies (though the authors of this book do point out that even brief phatic exchanges can bolster the social spaces in which real talk thrives). Rather, the real talker predicates some quality or action about some subject. Maybe the talker modifies, qualifies, or intensifies the predicate. Maybe the talker links two or more propositions in some way. When a student predicates something about a subject, by the way, the speech act is successful only if the information is somehow new, nonobvious, or consequential to the other members of the class (Michaels, 2006; Searle, 1969). So when a student creates a linguistically elaborated utterance that works as real talk—even just a single sentence—the achievement is inherently a social-cognitive (listener-adapted) accomplishment as well as a syntactic one.

Real talkers also build coherence in a classroom discussion by shaping their conversational turns to respond to one another's earlier statements or questions. A student who persists in injecting isolating ego-centered topics rather than developing (or evolving) the flow of the collective conversation is not engaging in real talk. The coherence in real talk links one student's conversational turn to the next student's and also links one classroom discussion to another. Thus, real talk is intertextual (Allen, 2000). Our authors recount a remarkable instance of that kind of cross-episode intertextuality. Three months after a class discussion of *Arthur, for the Very First Time* and about "what it meant to look through the faraway end," second grader Abeo reinitiates that exact topic, seemingly out of the blue. Abeo has accomplished quite a feat of intertextuality.

Now here's a trait it won't take long to discover about the authors of the book you are about to read: They *really* love literature and, especially, children's literature. As you might expect, the idea of intertextuality is quite consonant with literature study. It was born of the study of literary allusion and tradition (Vergova, 2007). Real talk, student critical turns, intertextuality, and contingent teaching are all hallmarks for learning in *every* subject, and they work for learning both in and out of school. This book offers a glimpse of how real talk works outside the realm of literature study by introducing us to Sarah's second-grade classroom, where real talk emanates from students crocheting together. If you consider how apprentice physicians learn how to diagnose (Blatt, Confessore, Kallenberg, & Greenberg, 2008; Markert, 2001) or how novice architects learn to design (Lasserre, 2010), you'll see that literature study is certainly not the only learning process that depends on real talk.

The third characteristic of student critical turns—and, therefore, another signal that real talk is taking place in a classroom—is substantive engagement. Real talkers are answering a question, evaluating a comment, or extending or qualifying a statement. They are contributing substance to a conversation. Michael, the teacher highlighted in Chapter 6, offers his students an explicit menu of techniques for substantive engagement. At various times he reminds them they may reflect, compare, retell, or directly address an audience. In coaching his students about how to speak substantively, he is in many ways promoting the very classical technique of deploying *heuristics*, such as Aristotle's *topoi*, to help students think of things to say (Enos & Lauer, 1992). In Lisa's second-grade classroom, Charlie has clearly internalized most of the journalist's heuristic. He reflects, "We really get deeply into a story. We read about *what* happened, and think about *why* did that happen . . . *who* made it happen, and all that other stuff." Equipping students with the journalist's habit of commenting on *who, what, when, where, why,* or *how* is just one way to cultivate real talkers.

The verb "cultivate" is especially fitting in conjunction with students learning real talk. The process is a natural one, but not one that should be left to occur haphazardly. Real talk needs cultivating, especially if it is to be accessible to all students across the myriad dimensions of their heterogeneity. The teachers featured in this book model how to cultivate real talk. There's nothing haphazard about it.

Another good verb for talking about talk is "articulate." Real talk articulates; it *connects* in many different ways. Envision with me for a moment a society comprising citizens who had learned to articulate real talk throughout their school years with their families, in their community institutions, and even with their political leaders. How would talk in an articulating society like that operate? Speakers in an articulating society:

- Render their meanings transparent. They don't obfuscate.
- Use codes that are accessible and inviting to their listeners.
- Connect talk, writing, and other media of expression.
- Gravitate toward collaboration and dialogue rather than monologue.
- Help listeners connect with sources of power.
- Draw connections with prior conversations and textual traditions.
- Connect fields of inquiry. They share knowledge rather than hoarding it.
- Connect diverse communities.

Cultivating an articulating society is what this book could be about. Talk about *Real Talk* with your students, teachers, friends, and fellow citizens. See what kind of society you can articulate.

DON RUBIN, PhD
Professor Emeritus,
University of Georgia

REFERENCES

Allen, G. (2000). *Intertextuality: The new critical idiom*. London: Routledge.

Blatt, B., Confessore, S., Kallenberg, G., & Greenberg, L. (2008). Verbal interaction analysis: Viewing feedback through a different lens. *Teaching and Learning in Medicine, 20:4*, 329–333.

CTIA—The Wireless Association. (2010, March 23). CTIA semi-annual wireless industry survey. Retrieved July 20, 2010, from *www.ctia.org/advocacy/research/index.cfm/AID/10316*.

Enos, R. L., & Lauer, J. M. (1992). The meaning of *heuristic* in Aristotle's rhetoric and its implications for contemporary rhetorical theory. In S. P. Witte, N. Nakadate, & R. D. Cherry (Eds.), *A rhetoric of doing: Essays on written discourse in honor of James L. Kinneavy* (pp. 79–87). Carbondale: Southern Illinois Press.

Hacker, P. M. S. (2007). *Human nature: The categorical framework*. Malden, MA: Blackwell.

Lasserre, B. (2010). Theory and practice: Reconciling design as analogies with "real" talk in design education. *Journal of Writing in Creative Practice, 3*(1), 17–21.

Markert, R. J. (2001). What makes a good teacher? Lessons from teaching medical students. *Academic Medicine, 76*(8), 809–810.

Michaels, S. (2006). Narrative presentations: An oral preparation for literacy with first graders. In J. Cook-Gumperz (Ed.), *The social construction of literacy* (2nd ed., pp. 94–116). New York: Cambridge University Press.

Rubin, D. L. (1986). Conflict and resolution in teaching oral communication. In M. Farmer (Ed.), *Consensus and dissent: Teaching English past, present, and future* (pp. 47–56). Urbana, IL: National Council of Teachers of English.

Searle, J. (1969). *Speech acts*. Cambridge, UK: Cambridge University Press.

Vergova, M. (2007). Dialogue, pluralism, and change: The intertextual constitution of Bakhtin, Kristeva, and Derrida. *Res Publica, 13*(4), 415–440.

Contents

Talk is the sea upon which all else floats.
—BRITTON (1993)

CHAPTER 1

Real Talk

What It Is and Why It Is Important

> Students develop their language and literacy capabilities
> by using real language in real situations to accomplish
> real goals.—CHARLOTTE

In this book, we examine talk in the classrooms of four teachers: Lisa, Charlotte, Michael, and Sarah. These are teachers who purposefully and successfully connect students' personal experience and exploration with academic expectations, achieving meaningful transformation and retention of school knowledge. *Real talk* is their primary mediating tool. These illustrative cases show students talking as they form and connect with ideas, personal understanding, and text, while their teachers respond in ways that extend the students' thinking and understanding through talk. This unscripted talk is contingent on the moment and depends on the context and content of the talk. This kind of talk also requires flexible, informed teachers such as these four.

Lisa is a second-grade teacher who plans her reading/language arts instruction around book discussion groups. She uses real talk as a way to help her students understand how literature works; they also develop greater understanding of themselves and others. Charlotte teaches fourth- and fifth-grade English language learners (ELLs). In her classroom, real talk is the vehicle through which students not only inquire about the content they are learning, but acquire proficiency in English. Michael teaches third grade and creates structured opportunities for his eager students to engage in real talk as they pursue literacy learning. Sarah, in her second year of teaching second grade, is delighted when the real talk that grows around an end-of-the-day crocheting experience becomes the basis for developing a close-knit classroom community as students talk to process and plan. All four of these teachers use literature as a springboard for classroom talk, and through contingent instructional practices they create opportunities for real talk. These four teachers all understand that learning, and indeed all aspects of our lives, "float on a sea of talk" (Britton, 1993).

In this book, we do not present a formula for *real talk,* nor do we offer a blueprint for successful teaching and learning. We do, however, provide multiple examples of good teaching practices in varied contexts, while also pointing out consistent markers of effective practice. This book is grounded in the understanding that "each classroom must find its own way of working, taking into account both what each member brings by way of past experience at home, at school, and in the wider community—their values, interests, and aspirations—as well as the outcomes that they are required to achieve" (Wells, 2001, p. 173). We present glimpses into classrooms where teachers and students are finding their own way of working, through what members say to each other and how it is said. We show how teachers exercise *pedagogical content knowledge* (Shulman, 1986) with discernment, and how their content mastery enables *agentive flow*—the freedom, space, time, and willingness to plan lessons and then to make flexible in-the-moment decisions about pacing, materials, foci, and process. Through their use of real talk, these teachers can take the time and attention to extend and transform talk into educationally productive discussions. Classroom talk patterns illuminate how these teachers support students as they learn through talking. In these four classrooms, students are encouraged to talk-to-know, to connect information to real contexts, and to reason together. These four teachers, each deeply aware of their students and committed to learning that goes beyond mere recitation, expertly harness the resource of real talk in their classrooms. They lead discussions from behind and alongside their students in the service of the students' understanding. Unlike scripted curricula, real talk costs nothing, but its value is immeasurable.

WHY TALK?

Why does talk matter? Classroom talk shapes and is shaped by the classroom learning environment. Through talk patterns, teachers demonstrate and discover what they expect and value, just as students discover and demonstrate what counts in terms of learning, knowledge, and knowing. Classroom talk can support students to take risks publicly, explore ideas, and compose creatively and critically in the moment; at the same time, teacher talk can regulate their participation. Examining classroom talk sheds light on what is actually taught and on the ways learning opportunities are either enhanced or repressed. Awareness of how and why teachers generate particular classroom talk patterns helps us become more purposeful in our own teaching.

Classroom talk provides all participants with opportunities to learn and talk together, and thus to tap into the social and cognitive functions of language. When students share ideas and perspectives, and practice articulating insights, questions, and connections, they are also producing their best guesses; as such, they are offering concrete cognitive markers of understanding, which afford teachers opportunities for dynamic assessment. As students listen and respond to others, consider other perspectives and connections to what is said, and reason together to construct new understanding, they are sharing the *cognitive load*— generating, extending, and connecting ideas. Teacher and students alike are transforming their understandings.

However, teacher–student interaction does not happen by itself. Nor can it be imposed or assumed. Rather, it is a process of accretion— a gradual building up of knowledge, confidence, expertise, and trust— and it requires contextual anchoring. That is, it can only happen when real talk occurs in real situations for relevant purposes. Like classroom talk in many popular descriptions over the years (Barnes, Britton, & Torbe, 1990; Eeds & Wells, 1989; Gambrell & Almasi, 1996; Daniels, 1994; McMahon, Raphael, Goatley, & Pardo, 1997; Soter et al., 2008; Nystrand, 1997; Wilkinson, & Son, 2011) real talk in the elementary classrooms described in this book is shaped by talk about children's literature. But it does not have to be. Real talk can occur in all disciplines when teachers create a classroom environment that supports it.

In a safe and supportive classroom environment where the teacher adopts a *contingent* stance—a willingness to listen attentively, and then to influence and be influenced by the unfolding talk—literature can be a wonderful stimulus to engender real talk, but many other stimuli can sustain real talk as well. As a teacher manages, listens, and responds, he or she casts ideas forward for students to select from; the teacher nudges, challenges, invites, and makes room for students to think more deeply, elaborate more explicitly, and take risks as they explore ideas together. This *dialogic teaching* (Alexander, 2006; Nystrand, 1997; Wells, 2001), encouraging real talk, results in engaged student learning.

DESCRIBING REAL TALK

Real talk occurs when conversants adopt varied participant roles as they speak extemporaneously to connect with what they already know and to build knowledge together. What, then, is *real talk*? Real talk is vocalization in the moment, with audience members providing immediate feedback through their own vocalizations. It does not result in tidy conclusions; what one conversant says influences what others think and say (Bakhtin, 1981). In fact, the inconclusive and unpredictable nature of real talk opens possibilities and breeds more questions. Real talk is often messy, hesitant, recursive, incomplete, and choppy, as speakers strive for coherence and fluency. It is often marked by *elaborated utterances* (extended turns of talk) and extended student-led exchanges. As talk-in-use, real talk is meaningful, exploratory, and engaged. By its very nature, real talk is ephemeral, but it need not be insubstantial. It looks different at various times, in varied situations, and for differing purposes; its properties vary according to local context. It can be both individual and collective, hesitant and fluent, social and cognitive, planned and digressive, creative and critical, and everything in between. But the property of *contingency*—of woven dialogue—is recurrent, as speakers adopt varied participant roles to connect, communicate, think, and do.

Through real talk, students talk to learn and learn to talk. The practice of real talk is a continuous bridge from ways of talking at home to ways of talking at school. Thus encouraging real talk enables students to access and use what they know. From birth, human beings are surrounded by talk as caregivers respond to infants' needs with words, songs, and comforting sounds, and infants cry and coo both in response and to communicate needs and feelings. The role of talk in children's lives continues as they develop *linguistic competence,* or knowledge of sounds, meaning, and syntax or word order, as well as *communicative competence,* or the understanding of how to use language to communicate.

Linguist Michael Halliday (1978) argued that early language serves either a *mathetic* or *learning* function or a *pragmatic* or *doing* function. As children develop linguistic and communicative competence, these two basic ways of using language evolve into seven separate functions. The *instrumental* function serves to communicate needs to others; the *regulatory* function consists of commands to others; children use the *interactional* function as they develop relationships with others; they use the *personal* function to talk about themselves. As children learn about the world around them, the *heuristic* function (or asking "why?") comes into play, just as the *imaginative* function becomes apparent in pretend play and other imaginative endeavors. Lastly, the *informative* function, in which children display knowledge to others, develops. By the time children reach school age, they are using language to perform all seven of these functions with ease. They are ready to continue employing their skills at using language to get things done and to learn in an academic setting. Certainly, by the time most children arrive in school, they are both linguistically and communicatively competent—adept at using language in varied contexts and for different purposes.

Virtually all children do go to school with a mastery of how to communicate verbally in their home communities, but school does not necessarily reflect these communities (Heath, 1983). Nor does school necessarily build on children's facility with language. In many cases, the only kind of language function sanctioned in the classroom is the last one to develop: the informative function, in which children are asked to display their knowledge for evaluation by the teacher. Furthermore, in every classroom there are "rules" for communication—that is, norms for participation in the classroom community. These rules can be, and often are, quite different from the rules of children's home communities (Au & Carroll, 1997; Florio-Ruane & McVee, 2000; Philips, 1982). The discordance can be even greater for ELLs, who have the double task of learning another way of using language (with new expectations for participation and engagement with information and text) while also thinking about and learning in English.

Successful teachers build on the knowledge of talk that children bring to school with them, and structure their classroom talk in ways that help children develop as speakers, as listeners, and as thinkers. They develop shared "rules" for classroom talk with their students and in response to the students' strengths and needs. They foster a safe learning climate, where students are taken seriously and where there is space for student ideas, conjectures, and connections. They provide opportunities for children to do what they have been successfully doing for all of their preschool years: using talk to get things done and to find out about the world. Real talk becomes a bridge between home and school.

Effective teachers provide opportunities for real talk that is contextualized by classroom practice and that is both meaningful and exploratory in nature—talk, as Charlotte describes it, that is "real language [used] in real situations to accomplish real goals." By its very nature, real talk is unfolding and responsive; it cannot be scripted. Rather, it is a product of thoughtful planning by the teacher, eager involvement by the students, and contingent practice based on what occurs in the moment of the discourse, as talk is happening. Real talk allows participants to think, to build relationships, and to develop literacy. As Rubin (1990) argues, "We internalize talk and it becomes thought. We externalize talk and it becomes our link to social reality. We elaborate talk and it becomes our bridge to literacy" (p. 3).

In the sections below, we explore some of the theoretical and research bases for the importance of real talk in classrooms. First, we discuss the functions of language-in-use. Second, we examine the contextualized nature of real talk; that is, we discuss how situations for talk are both shaped by and shape classroom discourse. Third, we explore how relevant purposes for classroom talk vary according to context and content.

THE FUNCTIONS OF LANGUAGE-IN-USE

> What a great discussion! [When Charlie said that] "some books are better than others and some books you read more deeply, like we read more deeply than most. We think about what happened, but also why it happened," I tried to act calm and cool on the outside, but I was bursting with joy on the inside.—LISA

How teachers utilize students' language in their classrooms has direct implications for both short- and long-term educational outcomes for their students. Although the important role of talk in student learning for both native English speakers and ELLS has been demonstrated by a variety of research over the past 40 years, a persistent pedagogical focus on literacy solely defined as reading and writing, and occasional listening, has masked this role in actual classroom practice.

Halliday's (1978) seven functions of language constitute one way of describing how language is used in our lives. Another way to look at language is from a more global perspective. Rubin (1990) posits two basic functions of talk: *communalizing* and *epistemic*. The communalizing function is social, as talk defines relationships between participants, and varies from intimate to formally articulate. Talk that is epistemic varies from reproducing to transforming knowledge. We can think of talk, then, as having both social and cognitive dimensions.

Communalizing talk establishes a mood of sociability. Anthropologist Bronislaw Malinowski's (1923/1994) study of the communalizing function of language indicates the important role of this "small talk" in establishing and maintaining relationships and creating a safe and welcoming environment. Seemingly meaningless exchanges such as "How are you?" (along with tone and accompanying nonverbal cues, such as body language and facial expression) are important cultural practices that help meet the needs of individuals, communities, and society. Malinowski calls such exchanges *phatic communion*. However, the communalizing function of language extends through and beyond pleasantries to establishing trusting relationships and an accepting environment for conjecturing, developing ideas, and sharing connections to experience.

The epistemic, or cognitive, function of talk includes both the reproduction and transformation of knowledge. When we are reproducing knowledge, we are reciting or telling (as best we can) someone else's ideas. We are performing. When we are transforming knowledge, we are synthesizing ideas and thoughts, or recasting an idea in an alternative framework in another context, and producing a new insight. We are creating. Reproducing and transforming are at either end of the continuum that constitutes the cognitive function of talk. In our talk, we move freely along this continuum as we make sense of our new experiences by relating them to what we already know (and can reproduce), and this "retrieving and transforming what we already know is a crucial part of learning" (Barnes, 2008, p. 3).

We learn our ways of talking and thinking. Through the process of *language socialization* (Ochs & Schiefflin, 1982; Garrett & Baquedano-López, 2002), we acquire the knowledge, orientations, and practices that enable us to participate effectively and appropriately as members in "communities of practice" (Lave & Wenger, 1991). We not only learn ways to communicate and build relationships; we also learn ways to think and do. As members of many speech communities, we learn discrete ways of talking for particular contexts, speech events, and participants, and in many ways this learned language continues and reproduces cultural norms and expectations. Through recurrent, situated activities, we learn socializing routines as we talk with more competent others and learn the ways of talk and thought embedded in that activity. But talk is not just a cultural tool for communication; it is the means through which we make sense of and organize our world (Vygotsky, 1986). As we apply new frames and contexts, we retrieve and transform what we know, and we both continue and change social, academic, and cultural practices. Our language is not just the words we use, but their meanings and purposes for contexts and relationships.

Talk sounds different in different contexts and when used for different purposes. For example, the process of trying out new ideas ranges from hesitant, choppy, and incomplete turns of talk to elaborated and fluent utterances and extended exchanges as we compose in the moment. Exploratory talk-in-use makes transparent how the meaning of each utterance [and idea] both responds to and anticipates another utterance (Bahktin, 1981). The social nature of talk combines with the cognitive so that people can talk and think together (Vygotsky, 1986), but the influence of audience and immediate feedback can either arouse or repress thinking. The level of comfort for taking risks to apply new ideas or frames to what we already know varies across contexts, speech communities, and purposes. To take the example of a classroom, exploratory talk in small groups about whether something could have actually happened in a story contrasts with the more polished presentational discourse of giving a book talk about that same story.

In classrooms where the social and cognitive functions of language are encouraged through relationships and coherence across conversants, ideas, and utterances, school knowledge can be connected meaningfully to what is already understood. When students are given the opportunity to activate and explore personal links to school knowledge in a safe and supportive environment, talk is likely to consist of engaged, connected exchanges rather than fragmented recitations, and thus is far more likely to forge meaningful and lasting understanding. Whatever scheme we apply to the multiple functions of talk, it is beyond question that children bring a remarkable language facility with them to school. What we do with that facility in the classroom makes all the difference in how and how much our students learn.

How Situations for Talk Shape and Are Shaped by Classroom Discourse

> I truly feel that it [the discussions students had with each other] helped create a classroom community that was based on stronger friendships, for the simple reason they were given opportunities to get to know each other; they were able to *talk* to each other. So often our students are shushed throughout the day, and we wonder why our students feel disconnected or don't feel comfortable sharing their ideas. Midway through the year I noticed that when we had a class discussion, even my more reserved students were sharing their ideas and providing their input.—SARAH

In a collaborative classroom where ideas are respected and real talk is encouraged, students can experience all seven of Halliday's language functions as they build communicative and academic competence. But such classrooms are not the norm. Genuinely reciprocal and dialogic talk is not always permitted in classrooms.

When we examine "lived" classroom talk, we see enacted rather than intended (Cazden, 2001) talk practices, and we see how opportunities for learning are shut down or opened up. A body of research on classroom talk agrees on what constitutes good teaching across the curriculum and which classroom conditions engender and arise from such teaching. Dialogic inquiry and instruction are crucial (Alexander, 2006;

Nystrand, 1997; Wells, 2001) to encourage an exploratory and reasoning focus among conversants (Mercer, Wegerif, & Dawes, 1999; Mercer & Hodgkinson, 2008). There is both room for student elaboration and exchanges as they take turns and shape the scope of the talk (Soter et al., 2008), and an expectation that talk is respectful of community norms, is substantive, and is held accountable to ideas and text (Michaels, O'Connor, & Resnick, 2008). One recent overarching framework for quality talk (Wilkinson & Son, 2011) positions authentic teacher questions (Nystrand & Gamoran, 1991) as pivotal, as they can lead to more elaborated student utterances and thus provide opportunity for more student reasoning. However, Wells (2001) asserts that a real question is one that the student wants to answer; real talk is an answer to that question and to the further questions that the answer generates.

The Role of the Teacher's Instructional Stance

As teachers and students, we bring to the classroom our learned ways of thinking, talking, and learning. A teacher's *instructional stance*, or way of teaching, is evident in his or her talk. This stance encompasses a coherence and resonance across patterns of interactions; it embodies what a teacher counts as knowledge, teaching, and learning. It is manifested in the amount of time students have to talk, the type of talk required (exploratory, presentational, discussion), the subject of talk, turn-taking norms, who determines the scope of the talk, and who has interpretive authority (Barnes, 2008; Chinn, Anderson, & Waggoner, 2001; Gutierrez, 1994; Soter et al., 2008). But talk is more than the sum of its parts. In the speech community of the classroom, talk has a coherence and a history that is built over time; there is a recognizable pattern informing how the students read the moment and respond. The patterns of interaction associated with an instructional stance influence how comfortable students are with inquiring, sharing, or taking risks.

Several terms from learning theory have been used to describe instructional stances or frames. For example, in regard to discussing literature, Chinn et al. (2001) offer the *recitation* instructional stance and the *collaborative-reasoning* instructional stance. They show how these differ in terms of classroom talk patterns about literature and in identifying who holds interpretive authority, who controls turn taking, and who controls the topic of the discourse. One recent meta-analysis of nine approaches to literature-based discussion (Soter et al., 2008; Murphy, Wilkinson, Soter, Hennessey, & Alexander, 2009), posits three possible instructional stances that determine what is privileged in terms of student response: an *expressive* stance, which privileges the reader's personal affective response to the text; an *efferent* stance, which encourages a focus on information; and a *critical-analytical* stance, which encourages various opinions and perspectives about texts. Different instructional stances were shown in both the Soter et al. and Murphy et al. studies to engender different amounts and types of student talk. In both these studies, as in many others (see, e.g., Applebee, Langer, Nystrand, & Gamoran, 2003; Boyd & Rubin, 2002; Nystrand, 2006), there were strong relationships among expectations that students would interpret text, amount of classroom dialogue, and amount of high-level reasoning.

As we listen to and respond to the patterns of talk and the schooling expectations these patterns signal in the classroom speech community, we learn ways of "doing" school. For us as teachers, providing opportunities for real talk mediates the extent to which we value the communalizing and epistemic (reproducing and transforming) functions of talk. For our students, opportunities for real talk mediate the extent to which they develop these functions of talk. Students learn ways to participate in speech events such as class discussions or read-aloud time, as well as ways to perform specific speech acts such as responding to teacher questions. Inquiry and elaboration only occur when the context is supportive and the conversants are attentive.

To bring students from recitation to exploration and elaboration, effective teachers extend the purpose of their talk to go beyond providing information and assessing recall of that information, and develop the role of teacher talk as dialogue. Effective instructional talk provides recursive and repeated bridges to students' contributions, taking their talk and connecting it with ideas and instructional goals. Their path to learning is through classroom discussions engendered and sustained through planful and in-the-moment contingent instruction (Boyd & Rubin, 2006). The intricate interweaving of how teachers use talk, what teachers and students talk about, and how teachers set up routines that encourage student participation demonstrate a shared purpose, a thoughtful adaptiveness on the part of the teachers as they listen and respond to students, and a focus on the outcomes and functions of such talk.

Classroom Discourse Characteristics That Facilitate or Discourage Real Talk

Talk is the action component of interaction (Barnes et al., 1990; Rubin, 1990), and yet consistently, over the years and across classrooms, students make fewer than a third of the utterances. Often their participation is limited to recitations, and short, unconnected ones at that, even though we know that not all student talk is equally efficacious.

Dialogue facilitating students' exploratory and elaborated utterances in classrooms is essential if the students are to use talk to learn and to explore new ideas.

Researchers and educators have argued for over half a century for a new view of classroom discussion (see, e.g., Gambrell & Almasi, 1996; Barnes et al., 1990; Eeds & Wells, 1989; Hynds & Rubin, 1990; Nystrand, 1997; Wells, 1999) in which students adopt traditional teacher participant roles, such as initiating, facilitating interaction, facilitating interpretation, and evaluating. In this view, in other words, students use talk in ways that go well beyond Halliday's (1978) informative function of displaying knowledge. What does this look like in the classroom?

The Importance of Exploratory Talk

Exploratory talk (Barnes et al., 1990; Mercer & Hodgkinson, 2008), an individual and group exploration of ideas, is at the heart of a good discussion. Students use exploratory talk and the ability to think together—to *interthink,* as Mercer (2002) puts it—as they publicly and often collaboratively explore knowledge and test new ideas. As they are "trying out" both how to say something and what to say, students manifest their thinking in exploratory talk. This talk is necessarily hesitant, incomplete, and recursive. Furthermore, if students are encouraged to explore together and to share the cognitive load, then turn taking will be at times appropriately overlapping as students generate ideas and add to them, counter each other, and reason together. For educationally effective talk to happen, teachers and students need to know how to highlight and facilitate exploratory talk.

The research of Mercer et al. (1999) focuses on elementary classroom contexts where students work in small groups and have been supported in their use of conscious markers of exploratory talk and reasoning words such as conditionals ("could," "might") and qualifiers ("maybe," "I think," "I believe") to highlight the possibilities in meaning making together, and where they are given opportunity to practice this without teacher monitoring. These researchers found that these contexts supported growth in both individual and group understanding (individual test scores and group work in classrooms). The social and cognitive functions of talk worked together, as "both the shared construction [of knowledge] and the individual struggle to interpret are essential" (Barnes, 2008, p. 10). Here again, these results highlight the consequential role of teacher talk, to make explicit and available the kind of talk students might use. Of course, exploratory talk can only occur in a safe and supportive environment, as it requires students to take risks.

Patterns of Discourse and Their Effects

Effective teachers provide opportunities for, and challenge, students to apply in the classroom what they already know about using talk to getting things done and to foster learning. Starting with interesting and relevant content is essential, but the patterns of discourse, not the content or the group size, are what will shift teacher and student participant roles. Routines are firmly grounded in the norms for the particular speech community, so to shift discursive patterns—to expect students to negotiate changing participant roles—there needs to be a classroom culture where this is safe, where there is an ethos of respect and involvement, and where students' contributions are taken seriously (Christoph & Nystrand, 2001). Moving beyond recitation to talking openly and sharing ideas involves risk: There is the real likelihood of stumbling and making grammatical and linguistic mistakes (in both first- and second-language contexts), as well as the possibility of someone's ignoring or challenging an insight, not understanding an explanation, or interrupting an elaboration. In real talk, or in-the-moment thinking and response, there will almost definitely be hesitancy and recursiveness as the speakers grapple with word choice and idea exploration.

If we are to move toward real talk, then we must attend to the norms of participation in our classroom speech communities. We must consider: Who controls the floor? Who determines the scope of the talk? Who has interpretive authority? We must make time and space for exploratory and elaborated student talk.

Who controls the floor? In most classrooms, students must raise their hands and be acknowledged before gaining the floor to make their contribution. Granting permission to talk is the domain of the teacher, who also enforces space between turns of talk to limit overlapping speech. For the most part, what this looks like in classrooms is more performance than discussion. Other research has endorsed turn-taking norms as indicators of students' opportunities for holding the floor (Cazden, 2001; Chinn et al., 2001). If there is to be real talk, then the teacher must allow for more loosely chained turn taking. There needs to be space for students to develop ideas; to grapple together; and to add to, rebut, and yes, in the excitement of the moment, to speak over others. Real talk is messy, but turn-taking rights also constitute a proxy for who gets to control the discussion. A teacher who relinquishes control of turn taking frees up linguistic and cognitive discussion space for students and invites more of a collaborative-reasoning stance (Chinn et al., 2001) in discussion.

Who determines the scope of the discourse? In real talk, the topic evolves and grows as students contribute. Each participant adds to and shapes the scope of the conversation, as each utterance responds to and anticipates the next. Teachers who want to promote real talk in class allow room for student talk. When students contribute, these teachers do three things: They listen attentively; they allow time for other students to contribute; and when students contribute, these teachers build on what they offer and connect these offerings to the curricular focus. They sanction digressions and realign lessons when appropriate, often by extrapolating from what has been discussed. In real talk, there is joint authority in shaping what is talked about. In consequence, what can be learned is enhanced, because we learn in connection to what we know. If a concept can be concretized, made local, and connected with personally through student-initiated talk (Boyd & Maloof, 2000), we have a coming together of spontaneous and scientific concept formation (Vygotsky, 1986), and thus real learning.

Who has interpretive authority? In traditional classrooms, the teacher is the primary knower, and as such he or she holds interpretive authority (Chinn et al., 2001). A food or banking metaphor is helpful here (Freire, 1993): The teacher holds all that is needed, and to "cash in" or "feed their hunger," students should invest in the teacher for nourishment. However, a teacher who routinely practices *uptake* (Collins, 1982) (i.e., selectively directs and supports student meaning making) can, if desired, place the students as authority or primary knowers.

Who has time to talk? More student talk, in terms of frequency and length of student utterances, is a classroom practice that supports student learning. However, given the long and ingrained tradition that teacher talk should dominate classroom talk, teacher utterances are considerably longer and more controlling of the scope and rhythm of the discourse. Moreover, teachers typically think that more student talk is occurring than is actually the case (Marshall, Smagorinsky, & Smith, 1995). Soter et al.'s (2008) review and reanalysis of literature-based discussions found that the too-infrequent practice of granting students extended time on the floor—time to talk—is necessary for effective discussions. Students need time on the floor to explore and elaborate ideas. Although we know that the size of a group affects opportunities for time on the floor, we also know that simply establishing small groups will not shift patterns of discourse (Nystrand, Gamoran, & Heck, 1992). These more effective patterns have to be deliberately developed by teachers.

How students are positioned as participants in classroom talk—their control of the floor, their input into the focus of discussion, their interpretive authority, their time to talk—matters. If they have time and shared authority for, and control of, the discourse, then they have the opportunity to engage in talk that can transform their understandings of whatever subject they are discussing.

Types of Teacher Questions and Their Effects

The features of effective discussion are not "natural" in any classroom; rather, they are the work of a planful teacher. Creating a collaborative environment, valuing students as knowledgeable and interesting human beings, and providing opportunities for extended exploration of ideas through talk are all necessary for effective discussions. Among the most powerful tools that any teacher can use to shape the discourse in a classroom are teacher questions.

Much of the early research on classroom talk (Barnes et al., 1970; Cazden, 2001; Dillon, 1984; Mehan, 1979) documented how teachers structured "discussions" in such a way that they controlled both the topic and direction of the talk, and how more exploratory talk might generate higher levels of student thinking. One outcome of this early research was the explication of the prevailing discourse norm in classrooms: the IRE pattern, in which teachers Initiate through a question; a student Responds; and the teacher Evaluates that response, then initiates another question.

Mehan's (1979) seminal explication of the IRE pattern captures how the teacher's evaluation in the third turn makes explicit the performance nature of IRE talk in the classroom. In exchanges *A* and *B* below, the teacher question and student response are the same, but the teacher's follow-up recasts the function of the question as *authentic* (i.e., wanting to know the time) or *evaluative* (i.e., assessing whether Denise can tell the time). In both cases, the exchange is terminated by the teacher's third move (Mehan, 1979).

	Exchange *A*	Exchange *B*
TEACHER:	What time is it, Denise?	What time is it, Denise?
STUDENT:	It's three o'clock.	It's three o'clock.
TEACHER:	Thank you.	Very good.

In exchanges such as exchange *B*, when a student is expected to fill in the semiotic blank with information already known by the questioner, the utterance becomes one of retrieval, not creation. Moreover, the turn-taking sequence is so clearly delineated (teacher–student–teacher) that when one student is called on or starts to speak, other students can "switch off," because the turn taking is such that they will not "perform" until called upon in a future sequence. It follows, then, that the teacher makes two-thirds of the utterances and that the students make short and choppy utterances.

This is a pattern most of us have experienced and instantiated: the efficient review of content to ensure that "we are all on the same page." If we stop with just the IRE question, response, and evaluation exchange, student talk is limited to fill-in-the-blank recall recitations, and learning is limited to the reproductive end of the epistemic talk continuum. When a teacher chooses *not* to evaluate in the third-move slot, but instead follows up with a question or comment, there is an opportunity for students to move beyond performance talk. Wells (1993) documented the potential of the teacher's third move. In recasting this third turn as a Follow-up move that in fact might either end an exchange or encourage further exchanges, he raised awareness of how to extend this tight exchange into more conversation-like discourse. Thus this teacher third turn has continued to be the focus of research (Boyd & Rubin, 2002, 2006; Nassaji & Wells, 2000; Lee, 2006, 2007), because it is in this move that we see a teacher's pedagogical expertise and flexibility (or the lack thereof). This recent research reveals that teacher-directed talk in classrooms is not thoroughly described by the default IRE/IRF norm. The function of the follow-up move is crucial; we must consider how teacher talk is wielded and what learning results because of it. The focus must extend beyond the utterance to the question event or topical episode (see Boyd & Rubin, 2006; Nystrand, Wu, Gamoran, Zeiser, & Long, 2003).

In particular, we know that if the teacher's follow-up actually builds on a student's contribution—in other words, if the third turn in the default IRF pattern is changed or expanded—then this teacher uptake (Collins, 1982) can encourage further student thinking and elaboration. When uptake is included in the teacher third move, an exchange is transformed, as the teacher can then "lead from behind" (Wells & Chang-Wells, 1992). By selectively building on parts of student responses—that is, by providing specific and clear connections with what has been said, and not simply offering vague praise—the teacher is validating a student contribution, extending student thinking, and sharing the authority to direct the scope of the exchange (Bloome & Egan-Robertson, 1993; Boyd & Devennie, 2009). Though contingent, this third move is in fact crucial, as it can either build coherence and scaffold student elaboration or shut down exchanges.

For decades, teacher questions have constituted what Dillon (1982, 1984) has called the "presumptive practice" of classrooms. He uses this descriptor because teachers use questions widely, presuming that they automatically open discussions and extend student thinking. Dillon argues that this is not the case. Certainly how questions are wielded, and to what end, have long been the subjects of much research and commentary (Boyd & Rubin, 2006; Cazden, 2001; Dillon, 1984; Hunkins, 1970; Lee, 2006; Mehan, 1979; Nassaji & Wells, 2000; Nystrand & Gamoran, 1991; Wells, 1993). One review of questioning and comprehension reported that in some classrooms, 90% of teacher utterances were questions (Nystrand, 1997). Nystrand noted that sometimes there were as many as 100 questions an hour, 80% of them to elicit simple recall. For the most part, researchers talk about types of teacher questions, but, as in understanding the "third turn," it is also important to understand teacher questions in terms of what they produce.

Researchers and practitioners typically agree that there are two types of teacher questions. *Display* (or *closed*) questions are those to which a teacher already knows the answer and is expecting a performance of knowing from the student; *authentic* (or *open*) questions are ones to which the teacher does not know the answer and so is expecting to learn something new from the student. This typology (see Figure 1.1) is useful because it addresses whether the questioner is inviting multiple or convergent possibilities of response, and, by extension, whether it functions to assess student knowledge or to invite student exploration and articulation. However, a question can and does do more, as it also can encourage or shut down student talk.

To be sure, the question prompts the student response. The dialogic nature of talk means that students form answers both in response to and in anticipation of a teacher question. In other words, students not only respond to the question; they answer the question in a way they think is appropriate. Students' perceptions of how teachers are likely to respond to student answers—based on the students' sociocultural/ historical experiences across the speech community of classrooms and

---

Traditionally, teacher questions have been categorized as dichotomous:

Open or Closed Questions

- *Open:* There is more than one possible and accepted answer.
- *Closed:* There is one expected right answer.

Authentic or Display Questions

- *Authentic:* The teacher does not know the answer and wants to know it.
- *Display:* The teacher knows the answer and is asking the student to display that she or he knows it too.

FIGURE 1.1. Typology of teacher questions.

within this particular classroom community—factor into the students' response to the question. These predispositions, in addition to the students' funds of knowledge (Moll, 1992) and the classroom environment, shape how the students respond to the type of question a teacher asks. Thus, in the example above, Denise might presume that her teacher is asking an open or a closed question because of her experience in that teacher's classroom.

Just as a student's answer to a teacher question responds to and anticipates other utterances, so too does the teacher question. If the teacher question is intended to promote more conversation-like exchange in the classroom, or to extend student thinking, then it must be contingent on what has gone before; and, having anchored itself in that previous utterance or idea, it anticipates casting itself forward. This may not be immediately apparent, as often it takes several turns of talk in an exchange to support and develop a thought.

Most research advocates the effective use of authentic questions to "open" the scope of the discourse and encourage student elaborations, and disparages the restrictive use of display questions, which "foreclose" student talk opportunities. However, recent research such as Wells's work on IRF (discussed above), and that of Boyd and Rubin (2006) and Lee (2007), demonstrates that the shaping factor is not the type of question, or whether the question or comment occupies the "third turn." Rather, it is the function of the question, what it asks students to do, and, as Wells (2001) puts it, whether or not students want to answer the question. If the question, whether open or closed, is contingent on student contributions and positions the students for further exploration and articulation, then it functions to assist student elaboration rather than to foreclose it. We call such questions *contingent* questions.

The Importance of Contingent Questions

Within the specific speech act of questioning and response, questioning restricts and directs the nature and scope of the response. Dillon (1982, 1984) argues that conventional teacher questions "disrupt and depress" student thinking, as they are perpetuating teachers' rather than students' ways of thinking. Certainly the purpose of many teacher questions, especially when combined with IRE sequences that assess fast-paced recall of information, is to elicit recitation rather than to promote thinking or reasoning. Furthermore, the power structures in classrooms are such that most students comply.

Authentic questions ask for information that is not already known and open the response to the possibility of more than one acceptable answer. Such questions elicit greater elaboration, as students can share from their own experience and articulate their own opinions. Authentic questions position students as *primary knowers* (Berry, 1981)—participants who can provide needed explanation, assume interpretive authority, or feel empowered to give an opinion. Authentic questions often open up or initiate a topical sequence of talk. Contingent questions (Boyd & Rubin, 2006) can take this inquiry one step further, as by definition they ground a new contribution in what students have already contributed to the conversation, in order to extend the students' thinking. Contingent questions, even if not seemingly authentic or open, continue the scope and depth of inquiry, facilitating students' thinking and exploration as they offer coherent bridges across ideas and contributions. Contingent questions and statements signal the importance of, and support students toward, going beyond retrieving information to transforming understanding.

To understand the full scope and outcome of contingent questioning, it is important to consider what Nystrand et al. (2003) call the *question event*. In some cases, the teacher may have to review what a student knows, and may use the IRE/IRF discourse norm to do this quickly, in order then to assist the student in going beyond what he or she already knows. Using the IRE/IRF patterns for this purpose (and contingent questioning would be one choice for the third turn in the IRF discourse norm) may be in the service of subsequent student articulation. Other critical contingent talk practices include the teacher's explicitly valuing student talk, listening carefully to student contributions, and giving contingent responses in ways that both model and scaffold elaborated thinking and sharing for the students. This contingent talk includes uptake and frequently employs the dominant instructional tool of the question, but as contingent questioning—extending student exploration by either specifically asking for clarifications or more information, or opening up the scope of the conversation and eliciting divergent responses.

Unscripted contingent questioning is formulated in the moment. It acts as scaffolding for students as they talk their way toward greater understanding that is both educationally and personally relevant. It builds a coherence, a connectivity across what is said. Effective teachers consider what students contribute, anchor the questioning scaffolds in student contributions, and provide necessary support within the questions they ask—support that acts as a bridge to an appropriate learning or educational purpose. This kind of teacher talk directly supports student exploration and elaboration, and it reminds students to access their entire funds of knowledge by using all seven functions of language. It also underscores that student ideas are socially significant (Bloome & Egan-Robertson, 1993) and cognitively worthy of being extended.

The notions of contingency and contingent questions anchor the ideas presented in this book.

It is through elaborated utterances engendered by contingent questions that each student more fully explores ideas, exploits the potential of talk to raise awareness of linguistic and grammatical structure and choice, and indicates what he or she knows (in terms of content, structure, and delivery) so that others (teacher and students) can respond. Sometimes longer turns of student talk are sharings or retellings as students tell about their experiences. These have the additional value of providing and building shared referential knowledge that can be evoked and built upon. At other times, talk may be exploratory monologues (Thompson, 2008); on these occasions, students are prompted to talk-to-learn in pairs and small groups. Boyd and Rubin (2002, 2006) have shown how contingent questioning (along with a reluctance to evaluate) was a consistent shaping presence for linguistically extended, structurally coherent, and socially engaged student utterances, which they called *student critical turns*. These elaborated utterances are markers of social and cognitive ability. They build confidence and a facility with public communication—an additional long-term outcome of a classroom culture where student ideas are encouraged and where students feel safe in their exploration.

To enable real talk, therefore, teachers must actively construct a classroom learning culture that welcomes ideas and either ignores or responds to mistakes calmly. Moreover, they must construct this culture with no expectation of "getting it right" or relying on one clear path. In real talk, there are many "right" answers—answers crafted by engaged students who consider the knowledge they are acquiring through exploratory talk in the safe space of their classroom discourse community.

REAL AND RELEVANT PURPOSES FOR CLASSROOM TALK

> . . . they have to listen and I have to listen, and if I do listen . . .
> I will be inundated with teachable moments . . . —MICHAEL

The boundless sea of talk on which we float at home, at work, at school, and in our social worlds is not only rich and varied, but also purposeful. Whereas purposeful uses for talk in the world are almost infinite, within the classroom they are closely related to the interests and needs of the students, the goals of the teacher, and the requirements of the curriculum. Although purposeful learning takes many forms, we focus here on literacy learning. Furthermore, just as effective instructional practices vary across content, goals, and situations, we are concerned with the relationship between the oral language practices described above—effective discussion—and literacy learning. Thus we focus on the learning that occurs when students talk together about a shared experience related to literacy.

Purposefulness goes well beyond tapping student interest; it includes the learning outcomes that discussion can provide. Although real purposes may begin outside of discussion (in shared experiences surrounding books or projects, for example), discussion increases student interest, thus enhancing these purposes. As students learn from one another and the teacher, and as they think deeply about the subject at hand so as to be valuable members of the discussion group, purposefulness increases. When students are invested in the conversation, talk becomes both a product of and a means to real purpose.

Dialogic classrooms (Alexander, 2006; Nystrand, 1997; Skidmore, 2000) demonstrate this reciprocal relationship. In these classrooms, teachers model expectations and language patterns for students; students take on traditional teacher roles as they question, facilitate interpretation, and shape the scope of talk with their own contributions. They are socialized into how to use language to learn, to explore ideas, to question, and to communicate in other ways within the classroom setting. They appropriate language as they hear the teacher and others using applicable terminology, while exploring concepts that are particular to a subject matter. Knowing how to use language to learn, finding out what language to use, and discovering that their ideas are central to what is known allow students to take risks—to use exploratory talk to question and elaborate tentative notions. In turn, this kind of talk spurs students to learn (Alexander, 2006; Barnes et al., 1990; Boyd & Rubin, 2002, 2006; Mercer & Hodgkinson, 2008; Nystrand, 1997).

The acts and processes of talking about the content of learning, and learning to be facile users of talk, help children develop as learners and thinkers across three dimensions (based on the work of Swain, 1995). First, talk as exploration or elaboration is sought after in and of itself, and this process of *composing in the moment* pushes thinking and requires cognitive activity. Second, talk performs a *noticing* function: It heightens the speaker's awareness of structures, patterns, and vocabulary that are part of the content being discussed. Third, talk provides *immediate feedback* on both what is said and how it is said. Talk, when done well, is both social and cognitive—a bridge across literacies, communities, materials, and content. Real talk is indeed both "the verbalization of experience and the experience of verbalization" (Wilkinson, 1970; p. 71).

To do talk well enough to enhance student learning, teachers must provide demonstrations of and opportunities for students to do more than fill in the blanks, or share and describe. Students must think in the moment and, through their participation in conversation, offer, support, and extend connections across speakers, materials, and experiences. In this way, students share the cognitive load and construct meaning together. As we have seen, teachers can scaffold this type of learning by asking questions that are grounded in what students say, and then supporting them as they push them to further articulation. In other words, they ask questions and make comments that are contingent on what the students have offered. Also described as "leading from behind" (Wells & Chang-Wells, 1992), this process of restating, clarifying, and reconceptualizing student contributions through contingent talk is a vital part of learning. This might feel uncomfortable at first, as students have become accustomed to teachers' accepting their initial response, without expecting them to elaborate and support their thinking. Yet this kind of reasoning and exploratory talk is what we need to support and extend student cognitive activity in any content area.

Facilitating such talk also requires teachers to rely on a deep pedagogical content knowledge base (Shulman, 1986) and on passion for this knowledge, from which to pull the appropriate connections. They must develop a deep reservoir of strategies, experience, and knowledge to make those connections relevant and engaging. Moreover, they must enact the principle of *equifinality* (von Bertalanffy, 1968)—that is, the idea that there are many ways to reach the same outcome in any productive discussion. Teachers can negotiate which of the many possible paths created through talk they will direct students to follow.

When teachers model this exploratory talk, they make space for students as knowers. A shared authority in the classroom (Oyler, 1996) is negotiated as students and teacher use talk to bridge school and home practices and experiences, and to make relevant connections between and among them. Through this kind of talk, students come to see themselves as having interpretive authority, as being primary knowers. This transfer of authority is empowering for students; the content to be learned becomes theirs to know and share, rather than the property of the teacher alone. This helps make learning more purposeful.

In literacy learning and teaching, language is both the vehicle for learning and the content of learning. As students learn language in the literacy classroom, whether they are learning English as a second language or learning the language of literate talk, they are also learning how to use this language to articulate and share their ideas. Simultaneously, they are learning the content of literacy—language as it is used, or, more familiarly, reading and writing, listening and speaking. They are also engaged with the consideration of the ideas inherent in what language use (both written and spoken) produces. Real talk, then, is central to learning language, learning about language, and learning through language; as such, it is central to literacy learning and teaching.

Just as talk is central in literacy classrooms, so is text—most often in the form of children's literature, either repackaged as part of basal readers or in its original trade book form. Fortunately for language arts teachers, children's literature is inherently interesting for most students, as its stories, poems, and nonfiction texts offer experiences that children can relate to and information that they hunger for. Children's books are a primary means to developing purposefulness. When children read engaging texts, they are willing to grapple with the ideas presented there, especially when they are allowed to read and respond freely.

Research and theory on how readers process texts of all kinds echo many of the descriptors of real talk—describing reading as dynamic, social, and dialogic, with readers as primary knowers. *Transactional theory* (Rosenblatt, 1978/1994) describes how a reader's experiences, abilities, predispositions, preferences, knowledge, and attitudes all influence the meaning that is created when the reader meets a text. Rosenblatt terms this meeting a *transaction,* to highlight the mutual contributions of reader and text; she argues that readers use text to create meaning by infusing the words on the page with meaning. In other words, meaning is created not only by the words on the page (put there deliberately by the author), but by the reader of those words. Reading researchers describe a reader's active role in comprehension similarly (Pressley, 2006): Meaning is generated in a dialogue between text and reader.

The type of text and the *intention,* or *stance,* of the reader influences this dialogue between text and reader. Rosenblatt (1978/1994) describes this dialogue as varying on a continuum from primarily *efferent,* in which reading is being done to gain knowledge to use in the real world, to primarily *aesthetic,* in which reading is being done to participate in a "virtual" experience. A more efferent stance is *convergent* (Langer, 1995), as readers try to make sense of the particular point or concept presented in the text, whereas from a primarily aesthetic stance, readers focus on the various possibilities that a text might offer (Langer, 1995). A more efferent stance is effective for reading various types of nonfiction for information; a more aesthetic stance is effective for reading stories and poems that present visions of the possibilities of life. Rarely, however, is reading purely either efferent or aesthetic; rather, readers move along a continuum from one to the other as they read. Furthermore, how students read is affected by the norms and expectations in the classroom: What they are asked to do with books influences how they will approach reading those books. Thus, what teachers expect in discussion influences how students approach books, and how students approach books affects what they bring to discussions. In the case of reading stories and poems, allowing students the space for an aesthetic experience while reading means that they can bring this experience to the discussion table. They can share ideas generated with others, confirm and extend those ideas, and learn from the ideas of others.

This kind of reading positions readers as primary knowers, as the meaning is not fixed in the text, but rather is the product of the act of reading by a reader. As such, what each reader builds with any text is in fact a "valid" reading, at least for that moment in time. The ideas that readers generate as they read—ideas constructed from what they bring from their lived experience and the text they are reading—become the basis for a teacher's instructional decisions. These instructional decisions are rooted in the demands of the curriculum and the goals of the teacher, but are also contingent on student responses, student-constructed meaning. This creates relevant purpose.

Reading is also dynamic in that it occurs over time and changes over time, as a reader both anticipates and looks back upon the meaning being created as reading progresses. Furthermore, reading does not end when the covers of the book are closed, as thinking about and talking about the book continue to deepen or alter the meaning created. In school, this continued development of meaning is often rooted in the social experience of reading and talking together about books—not only during any one literacy event, but over the course of the school year.

There have been many iterations of how classroom practice can enhance students' reading and responding to literature. Among these are Short and Pierce's (1990) *literature discussion groups,* Daniels's (1994) *literature circles,* Eeds and Wells's (1989) *grand conversations,* and McMahon et al.'s (1997) *book clubs.* All of these approaches involve talking about text. As noted earlier, Soter et al. (2008) recently analyzed nine approaches to literary discussion, categorizing them in terms of text, discussion routines, and instructional task. These researchers concluded that effective literary discussions look much like the effective conversations described above: They include authentic questions, extended student talk, and a high degree of uptake. However, the research they were able to review did not explore the role of contingency that marks real talk as presented here.

Alexander's (2006) five criteria for dialogic talk offer a more general way to think about purposeful classroom talk:

1. Do participants learn and talk together (*collective*)?
2. Do they listen and share (*reciprocal*)?
3. Is this an environment where students feel safe to take risks (*supportive*)?
4. Do participants build on each other's contributions (*cumulative*)?
5. Does the teacher direct the talk toward some educational purpose (*purposeful*)?

These criteria extend beyond literature discussion to a wide variety of real talk—about lives, about ideas, about text, about content. When we look closely at classroom talk, we see both the constancy and variety of pedagogical practice: Real talk makes transparent routines and variations, the messiness of digressions, and the power of teachable moments.

Teachers who engage in real talk with their students take risks. Real talk is messy, substantive, and noisy. It is difficult to predict, because it is not scripted but contingent on the responses of students. It requires a great depth of teacher knowledge about teaching and learning, about students, about the content of the curriculum, and about ways to support students as they engage in the process. It requires a faith in the importance of the teachable moment, the fruitful digression, the in-the-moment decision making that makes teaching an art. In the next six chapters, we describe four teachers and their students learning through real talk, in all of its messy glory.

REAL TALK IN FOUR CLASSROOMS

This book is about four very effective teachers who use talk in very different ways, yet with similar foundational assumptions, as they orchestrate language arts instruction and other classroom activities. Our focus is on talk with a teacher present rather than in independent student groups, although a lot of talk does occur in student groups—talk that is a direct reflection of the structures these teachers have created. In all cases, these teachers respect and make connections to the knowledge and insights of the students in their classroom and make space for their students to use language to form and share their own ideas while also learning from the ideas of others (the teacher and fellow students). In all cases, there is real talk—talk that spans a range of functions well beyond the informative, talk that positions students as primary knowers, talk that is truly dialogic.

In the next six chapters, we see four remarkable teachers working in very different ways with very different children. In Chapter 2, we watch Lisa, a teacher with 10 years of experience in a public school in a small city in the southeastern United States, as she works with her second-grade reading group (all students' names are pseudonyms) to develop routines that allow collaborative talk about books. We see how Lisa transforms her reading group across the school year from a group that reads into a group that is engaged deeply with texts, through creating conditions that support an aesthetic reading of stories and poems, consistently modeling good discussion behavior, making astute use of questions, and explicitly discussing expectations for student participation.

Chapter 3 explores how Charlotte (a pseudonym, as are the names of her students), a public school teacher with 15 years' teaching experience in the same small city, uses literature to inspire language and content learning for her fourth- and fifth-grade ELL students. Charlotte uses a wide variety of trade books to shape her instructional units, both as shared, in-class reading and as independent reading at home; she scaffolds connections within and across texts to promote content learning, critical and literate thinking, and English language development in her students. We follow her again in Chapter 4 as we explore how she uses contingent questioning to encourage her students to develop their own ideas, while at the same time they gain practice in using English to learn.

In Chapter 5, we visit Michael (a pseudonym, as are the names of his third-grade students), a public school teacher with 31 years' experience, during afternoon read-aloud time in a small city in the northeastern United States. Michael feels strongly about establishing a love for reading in his students before they begin to focus increasingly, in fourth grade and beyond, on reading-to-learn in many subjects. He uses reading aloud as a vehicle for allowing students to choose the books and at the same time offering opportunities for book talks and peer recommendations. His interactive read-aloud structure offers opportunities to build vocabulary, teach literary concepts, highlight and practice comprehension strategies, and make textual connections. We see a different part of the daily routine in this classroom in Chapter 6, during Michael's morning meeting. We watch how he articulates very particular overarching goals and expected behaviors for his students, redirects student comments to ask for elaborated thinking, and allows students choices, all with great humor.

Michael, Lisa, and Charlotte are all experienced teachers, but new teachers can also effectively use talk to help their students learn, and we see second-year teacher Sarah do just that in Chapter 7. Eager to help her semirural second-grade students (once again, all student names are pseudonyms) develop the fine motor skills needed for handwriting, Sarah introduces crocheting as an end-of-day activity—something calming for the students to do while they wait for their buses. This activity develops into much more, as the talk that surrounds it leads to student problem solving, the development of a classroom community, and the generation of opportunities for literate talk and authentic literacy activities.

We use transcripts of classroom talk and of interviews with teachers, teacher lesson plans, literacy artifacts (poems, letters, drawings, reading logs), and field notes to create rich portraits of these four teachers with varying backgrounds and experience as they talk with their students in different contexts. As we document what they do and how they do it, we demonstrate how their practice reflects fundamental principles of effective talk in classrooms. We also highlight the vast (and necessary) variation in how effective talk occurs across learning events, differing student abilities and needs, and multiple goals.

In Chapter 8, we examine some pedagogical assumptions about what constitutes rich classroom talk. We do this by providing examples of very different kinds of effective conversations between teachers and students, and among students with the teacher present, in diverse literacy events: book discussion group (Lisa); small-group discussion during ELL instruction (Charlotte); selecting books to read aloud and sharing reading journals in morning meeting (Michael); and crocheting as a vehicle for classroom talk that extends the reach of English language arts time (Sarah). Although this book focuses on the language arts, the practices we document are effective in other content areas, as talk is critical for learning in all contexts. Furthermore, the teaching practices that we document are effective with a wide variety of students; we present here students in second through fifth grades, ELLs, international students, and mainstream students of varying abilities and interests, as well as both urban and rural students from the northeastern and southeastern United States. All of these focal classrooms highlight the potential of real talk to support and extend learning.

As you read the next six chapters, you will see how these four different teachers use talk to help their students learn. You will also see multiple examples of the development of a shared purpose, the impact of routines, and the importance of teachers' thoughtful adaptiveness. As you read about what these teachers and their students say and do, notice both the diversity of practice in these various contexts and also the consistency that these four teachers demonstrate as they seek to help their students use real talk to develop linguistic competence, literate thinking, content knowledge, and a sense of themselves as primary knowers. These teachers are seeking what Britton (in Barnes et al., 1990, p. 91) has described: "We want children, as a result of our teaching, to understand; to be wise as well as well-informed, able to solve problems rather than have learned the answer to old ones; indeed, not only be able to answer questions but also able to ask them."

CHAPTER 2

Exploring the Aesthetic

Talking the Way from Unconscious Enjoyment to Conscious Delight

LISA: Think about your book. . . . You open a book and . . .

LYNETTE: It starts making sounds. Opening a book is like opening a door to a house.

LISA: What happens?

CURTIS: We are turning into characters. We are imagining that we are in the book.

By mid-October, the 12 culturally diverse second-grade students in Lisa's reading group are sharing the books that they have been reading individually. Many are still enjoying picturebooks, but some are already reading chapter books, enjoying their new ability to read and understand books that look so "grown up." Maya, discussing Ursula LeGuin's (1988) *Catwings*, tells her peers that she knows the story isn't true, because "cats don't talk and cats don't have wings." The group has been discussing the differences between fantasy and realistic fiction, as well as between fiction and nonfiction. Maya goes on to say, "I wonder how the cats got their wings?" This opens the conversation to the group, and several of them respond simultaneously with "Maybe Santa went down the chimney." This, of course, reflects their growing understanding of what is real and what is "make-believe." Lynette comments that "The author should have told you," and Susan agrees: "Yeah, at the end, like a surprise." Charlie joins in with a comment about another book when he says, "This book kind of reminds me of Horton [Seuss, 1940], the elephant who has the egg, because the baby was half elephant and half bird." Finally, Lisa asks Maya a question: "Maya, did it bother you that you didn't know how cats got their wings?"

This vignette represents just a few minutes of an extended conversation about books and reading that the children conducted with little intervention from Lisa. This was possible, however, because she had worked with her group to get them to this point in the 8 weeks since the beginning of school. Just a month after this Lynette and Curtis spoke of entering into books—and it was only November! What was happening in this classroom?

In Lisa's classroom, effective book discussions took place because of the structures that she was building with her reading group—structures that gave her students clear directions and support for selecting books, reading and responding to books, and talking about books in their book discussion group. Not all the conversations were brilliant, and not all students were engaged all of the time; over the course of the year, however, they all learned how to use talk about books to support their own developing ideas about reading and understanding children's literature. By the spring, they were having hour-long discussions of commonly read chapter books in which they considered sophisticated ideas about life, literature, and the connections between the two.

This chapter traces that development. We look first at how Lisa worked with her group to develop their discussion skills—including the rules they crafted together; the approaches to discussion that she demonstrated through her own contributions; and the talk about discussion that she had with students as they developed these skills. We then see how Lisa also taught her students how to read and think about books as she expanded their possibilities for response and their knowledge about how literature works.

LEARNING HOW TO TALK ABOUT BOOKS: "JUST JUMP RIGHT IN"

One prerequisite for learning through talk (Barnes, Britton, & Torbe, 1970; Halliday, 1982) is, of course, learning *how* to talk in particular situations. Although most children know how to have conversations with others long before they enter school, knowing how to have conversations about books in a school setting is not something most students bring with them to the classroom. Even though the 12 members of Lisa's book group were reading at or above grade level, Lisa's students were no exception. The group, 5 boys and 7 girls, came from diverse socioeconomic and cultural backgrounds. These African American, African, Indian, Asian, European American, and multiracial children, from working-class to middle-class homes, and from one- and two-parent families gathered together each day to talk about the books they were reading. Although several of them had been ELLs, they were all relatively fluent in English by the time they entered second grade.

Furthermore, although she had taught for 10 years, this was only the second year that Lisa was attempting to shape her language arts instruction around talk about books, so she was still learning about successful practice. The previous year she had had some success, but she knew that she needed to work on her own skills in a more deliberate fashion, and asked for help in doing so. The transcripts and descriptions presented in this chapter are the results of field notes and audio- and videotape recordings of most of the 70-minute language arts periods from that academic year, recorded by Lisa and her two university colleagues. A fuller description of this research can be found in Galda, Rayburn, and Stanzi's (2000) *Looking through the Faraway End: Creating a Literature-Based Reading Curriculum with Second Graders.*

In standards-based classrooms like Lisa's, conversational skills are central to students' ability to use talk to shape their ideas and to explore ideas relevant to them. Across the year, Lisa's students learned both to share their own ideas and to expand their own understandings through considering the ideas of others. Thus, as the year progressed, student talk in Lisa's classroom reflected a developing understanding of how literature works—an understanding that was shaped by their talk about text with others. Over 50 years ago, Early (1960) proposed that literary appreciation develops from pleasure to understanding to conscious appreciation as children mature. Here we see how the same growth can occur in the space of a single year, when children are engaged with literature in classrooms full of purposeful, effective student talk about text, and when they are supported by a knowledgeable teacher.

Lisa already understood how important literature could be in the lives of students (Galda, 1998; Galda, Cullinan, & Sipe, 2010; Rosenblatt, 1995). She had already read a great deal about classroom talk, and she was familiar with the sound research base indicating that discussion could be an effective way of learning from text and developing response. She had read descriptions of how talk about text might work. Because she had studied transactional theory (Rosenblatt, 1978/1994), Lisa was also aware of the differences between approaching a text from a primarily aesthetic stance and doing so from a primarily efferent stance, and she knew that what teachers ask students to do with a book affects the stance students take. She also understood how important stance is to both engagement with and understanding of text (Langer, 1995; Rosenblatt, 1978/1994), and how important narrative thought is in our lives (Britton, 1993; Bruner, 1986). She realized that she had two tasks ahead of her: guiding her students toward effective talk about text and helping them understand how to approach different texts for different purposes. She planned to spend the majority of the year supporting their facility in responding from a primarily aesthetic stance. Lisa thus began this year with a fund of knowledge about oral language and reading. An avid reader, she also knew a great deal about literature and how it works, and about the children's literature that could engage her students.

Lisa set out to establish turn-taking patterns that would encourage students to respond to one another; to respond to student talk when necessary with positive evaluations and contingent questions; and to ask questions that positioned herself as a seeker of knowledge, rather than as the primary knower. In addition, Lisa sought to become a better listener, so that she would be able to request elaboration when helpful and to build on student comments as opportunities to convey knowledge about literature and how it works. She worked as both coach and scaffold (O'Flahavan, 1995) as she taught her students how to participate in discussions, while also giving them an array of ideas to bring to the table.

From the beginning of the school year, Lisa instructed her students about how their book discussion time would operate. In early September, the day before the first book discussion circle, she introduced some broad parameters. First, she discussed how to choose books to read and then share with the group. She began by asking her students how they selected books; she received answers ranging from "Browse," to "Look at the covers," to "I already read it and liked it." She then told them that they each should choose a book, take it home to read, write a response in their journals (another new procedure that she had already explained to them), and share the response the next day. She continued:

"Share time is time to talk about books that we're reading. That's an important way to discover books that you want to read. Talk with a friend about books. The teachers have a bulletin board that tells about books they like, and someone has already asked me to lend them the book I read this summer. Not that we all have the same taste, but talking with others in one good way to find out about books we want to read."

Note that Lisa began by asking her students how they selected books, and then framed the next day's sharing discussion as another resource for them to use, thus setting a purpose for the discussion that was relevant to their needs. She also reminded them of comprehension strategies that they were familiar with, asking them to "preview and predict."

Lisa was working within a thematic framework shaped by the themes in the district-required second-grade basal reader, so the many picture-books, easy-to-read books, and transitional chapter books that she had on her classroom bookshelves in September all centered around the initial theme of "friends, family, and neighbors." This helped to establish a coherence in sharing time that might not have otherwise occurred. The next day, as the students finished a spelling lesson and gathered for their first book discussion group, she told them: "Put your spelling on the table. You need your blue journal and the book you read last night ready to go." They then placed their chairs in a circle and began their first conversation, with Lisa asking each student to "tell the name of the book and what you wrote about it." Many of the students needed her to remind them to tell the title, and all of them were looking at their blue journals, reading aloud what they had written the night before. Occasionally Lisa mentioned that they "all need to be listening" so that they could ask questions; asked them questions about their books that reflected the "preview and predict" strategy; and gave them ideas about things they could notice as they read, such as how authors describe characters and how the books fit into the overarching theme.

When Lisa asked Amanda how she knew that the characters in *Henry and Mudge Get the Cold Shivers* (Rylant, 1989) were friends, Amanda answered, "Because in the book it said that every day they shook hands." Lisa commented: "I like the way Amanda went back to the book. Amanda found the words that told her [about the friendship]." This brief comment allowed Lisa to begin to help students "go back to the book" during discussions. In this initial conversation, Lisa coached students in how to perform ("tell the title," "be a good listener"), how to build on known skills ("preview and predict"), how to use journal entries ("bring your blue journals"), and how to consider themes and return to the text for evidence. Returning to the text, of course, is not only a procedure that makes for better conversations, but also an effective strategy when responding to literature.

Lisa ended this initial session with a discussion of some predictions that the students had made regarding a book she had read to the class the day before. When Charlie said that his prediction "was absolutely right," she asked him how he knew what was going to happen. When he indicated that he based his prediction on what he and his friends did themselves, Lisa built on this idea by clearly restating (and implicitly appreciating) what Charlie had said and then linking it to an earlier comment:

> "So you're using what happened in your life to predict. Someone else told me that they knew what was going to happen because that's what usually happens in stories. Stories do have a certain structure, include a problem, and that helps us predict and know what's happening."

This exchange, in which Lisa seized a "teachable moment," allowed her to expand her students' ideas about prediction. Prediction strategies for the group included previewing pictures, looking closely at text, relating the story to their lives, and using what they knew about story structure. All that was written on her lesson plan was to remind them of the "preview and predict" strategy; everything else came about because she was listening closely to what her students were saying, using their words to expand her lesson.

Listening closely, creating supportive structures while also being flexible, and teaching toward multiple goals marked Lisa's instruction on this day and on the days that followed. She harnessed her knowledge about her students, reading comprehension, literature, and discussions, so that she could build on the students' comments to shape a lesson that encompassed much more than simply reviewing a comprehension strategy.

Lisa's planful coaching of students as they learned to be members of a discussion group was evident in almost every book discussion event during the fall. Although she was sometimes frustrated in the early part of the year, she knew that increasingly meaningful discussions would develop over time, and so she consistently demonstrated good discussion practice and explicitly taught it. In September, just a few weeks into the school year, Lisa noticed that her students were beginning to understand that she really did want them to talk to one another about books. Since school began, Lisa had encouraged her students to join in real conversation, trying to wean them away from the traditional pattern of recitation that they had learned during their first 2 years at school. This was difficult for these 7-year-olds; they wanted to play by the rules they already knew and did not yet trust that their new teacher really meant what they thought she was saying. This changed dramatically during one particular discussion. It began with the usual stops, starts, and looking toward Lisa for direction and affirmation, which had characterized all of the discussions thus far. However, on this particular day, after two students began to talk simultaneously (resulting in an embarrassed silence), Curtis piped up with "Just jump right in," repeating verbatim the words that Lisa had used for weeks. With Curtis's utterance of Lisa's words, the group relaxed and began to talk in a less formal manner than they had before.

This change, however, was only superficial until the group learned how to enter into a conversation; how to take turns without explicit permission from Lisa; and how to listen to each other so that they could move from individual contributions without much uptake to talk that was truly conversational, with students responding to one another's comments. To do this, Lisa spent a great deal of time in the first few months of the school year directing the children's behavior and scaffolding ways to discuss literature through both demonstration and explicit instruction. She began with basic conversational courtesy, such as not interrupting. The group discussed body language, particularly how looking at the person speaking demonstrates that you are paying attention to the speaker and are interested in what is being said. Lisa offered them different ways to enter a conversation, and how to sustain discussions by commenting on others' ideas rather than offering something not linked to prior conversation.

In early September, she discussed the basic guidelines for conversation that she wanted the students to follow. These were stapled onto the blue response journals that students brought to the discussion group with them, and the students discussed them until Lisa was sure that they understood them (see Figure 2.1). Notice how she built on these guidelines in the discussion of "how to do book group," below.

1. LISA: One—Stay on topic. What does that mean?
2. CHARLIE: Stay on task. You don't just start talking about something else. Talk about the story, not what happened last night.
3. LISA: Yes, we should be talking about the story. Stay on the

---

1. Stay on topic.
2. Be active in discussion.
3. If you don't understand something, ask someone to explain.
4. Listen carefully to what others have said.
5. Don't be afraid to disagree, but do it politely.
6. Give everybody a chance to share their ideas.
7. Be ready to support your opinions with evidence from the story.

FIGURE 2.1. Early fall guidelines for discussion in Lisa's book group.

story. Number two—Be active in discussion. What does that mean, Tom? Susan? Cong?

4. SUSAN: Talking about something.

5. LISA: Yes, I want you to talk about something.

6. CURTIS: You can use the front page. (*Holds up his journal.*)

7. LISA: Excellent idea, Curtis! If you don't know what to say, you can look at your sentence starters [in the journal] for a way to start. Number three—If you don't understand something, ask someone to explain. What can you do?

8. CATERINA: Ask nicely.

9. LISA: Who would like to do this for me? Caterina? Pretend I just gave a response and you don't underdstand.

10. CATERINA: Could you please discuss it again?

11. LISA: Perfect. Can you please say it again? (*Caterina repeats it.*) Okay, number four—Listen carefully to what others have said. It's important that you be a good listener as well as a talker. Number five—Don't be afraid to disagree, but do it politely. Look back in the book. Number six—Give everybody a chance to share their ideas. Number seven—Be ready to support your opinions with evidence from the story. If you think something, you should be able to go back and say, "I think that because of words or pictures."

Notice how Lisa first stated the suggestions in turns 1, 3, and 7, and then elicited explanations from her students. She acknowledged their contributions (turns 3, 5, 7, and 11), and asked for an example of a good behavior in turns 7 and 9. By turn 11, she was running out of time, so she quickly reviewed the last four rules, while also giving her students language that they could use in subsequent conversations—which they did. The final rule, supporting a comment with evidence from the story, was something the students had begun doing after they heard Lisa praise Amanda for doing just that in the very first discussion they had. Her students wanted to please her, so they diligently tried to do as she asked them.

Before the students left for winter break, their conversational skills had improved considerably. They had learned to listen to one another and respond to others' comments rather than only introduce their own (often unrelated) ideas. They had begun to explore books deeply, discussing genre, characterization, and theme, while also remembering to return to the text for evidence. These students had come a long way since September—but, of course, they were not having classroom-based book discussions during their winter break, and their discussion skills had faded a bit by the time they returned to school in January. Noticing this, Lisa planned a lesson to remind students of what they already knew about being good members of a book discussion group, and then to help them apply that knowledge to a critique of their current discussion behaviors. She decided to videotape a book discussion and then ask students to reflect in systematic ways on their conversation. She began by telling students what they would do with the conversation that was being videotaped:

> "The purpose of doing this is to reflect on ourselves and the tone of our voices. We should also think about 'What did I add to the discussion?' or 'Am I really saying something interesting?' Also, focus on the positive. 'What do we do well? What and how can we improve?'"

The students then engaged in their discussion, which Lisa videotaped. After the discussion was over, the students viewed their participation, and wrote down "what things we did well" or "things we need to improve." The students, after a few giggles, were generally attentive. When they finished, Lisa began the conversation:

1. LISA: What did you notice?
2. BETH: We need to know what we want to say before we say it. Susan started saying, "Ummmm." We need to know. [This was something Lisa had stressed in the fall.]
3. CHARLIE: (to Susan) We are not saying you are doing a bad job.
4. LISA: That's a good point. We need to be rehearsed. Not only are you doing your response, but what relevant things can you bring to the group—the most interesting things? What's going to provide and promote discussion?
5. AMANDA: I don't think we should talk at the same time.
6. LYNETTE: We can improve on controlling our talking.
7. LISA: Not only can we improve on talking, but also on listening. Let's focus on what we are saying.
8. SUSAN: Tom didn't understand it.
9. BETH: He's not understanding.
10. AMANDA: And lots of people were correcting Susan.
11. BETH: Think about what you say before you say it.
12. LISA: What else?

13. CATERINA: Everybody was talking at once.

14. LISA: What did we do well?

15. BETH: We were speaking up.

16. LISA: Yes.

17. BETH: The person who we are talking to, we need to look at that person.

18. CURTIS: You can be shy, but you have to speak up. *(Plays more of the videotape and stops again for discussion.)*

19. LISA: Who is doing the majority of the talking?

20. STUDENTS: Susan.

21. LISA: Why, do you think?

22. CATERINA: Everybody did the same amount.

23. LISA: Everybody? You may want to think about that some more. Who is an active listener? Are you really participating in the discussion? Why am I not saying anything? Why do people choose to not say anything?

24. HAO: We still have to wait for someone to stop talking, or it wouldn't be clear.

25. BETH: We should try not to correct people.

Charlie and Amanda then agreed with Beth, and Lynette recalled being corrected; several others nodded. Lisa summed up their ideas: "Maybe we need to be more sensitive to one another. Keep thinking about how you can improve. How are we going to improve?" Notice that Lisa asked students for their opinions about the discussion they viewed (turns 1, 4, 12, 14, 19, 21, 23), thus making it clear that she wanted them to critique, but that she also had certain outcomes in mind. This balance of preplanning and responsiveness worked well.

The next day, Lisa began by reminding everyone of what they had discovered the previous day, as she asked students to recall that conversation.

1. LISA: We are going to be working on. . . .

2. AMANDA: Don't speak when someone else is speaking.

3. LISA: Yes, watch the overlaps.

4. HAO: Speaking up.

5. CATERINA: Listening.

6. BETH: Have [eye] contact.

After this brief recall, discussion resumed. Over the next few weeks, students continued the discussion, with Lisa also asking them to assess their processes and discuss what was working and what was not. A few weeks later, she showed them another video clip of one of their discussions, and asked them to look at themselves individually and evaluate their behavior.

1. TOM: I am fumbling around.

2. LISA: Do you notice that certain people are talking more than others? Are you aware of it?

3. LYNETTE: We're responding a lot.

4. LISA: Did anyone else notice anything? Some of you really are not aware. Seeing the video helps. You can bring it to a conscious level.

5. LYNETTE: Do not interrupt each other.

6. LISA: What else?

7. CHARLIE: People kept interrupting each other.

8. LYNETTE: We kept three conversations going.

9. SUSAN: Abeo didn't talk.

10. LISA: Amanda asked Abeo a question: "Did you read that book yesterday?" In order to know when to jump in, you have to be in [the conversation].

11. LYNETTE: Everybody might just sit there.

12. LISA: Anything else? What were you doing right?

13. CHARLIE: We were being polite.

14. LYNETTE: We were staying on task. We responded to questions.

15. LISA: Give me an example.

16. LYNETTE: When Beth said she liked Howie.

17. CHARLIE: I disagree with that, because you [Lisa] had to come out and ask.

18. LISA: Based on what we have seen, what do we need to work on?

19. BETH: We need to speak up.

20. CATERINA: Keep the conversation going.

21. LISA: I think we need you [Caterina] in it. You weren't with us. Did you notice that?

The students and Lisa worked together to understand what they did well and what needed to be improved. Notice how in turns 2, 4, 5, 12, 15, 18, and 21, Lisa either asked students what they noticed, or asked whether they noticed a specific behavior. It might have been more efficient simply to tell them what she wanted them to notice, but she understood that their awareness had to come from within themselves.

These "metadiscussions" seemed to be turning points in how the group functioned in discussions. As students became more aware of their own behaviors, the conversational skills that they had developed before winter break reemerged, and they could articulate what they needed to do to improve. Lisa took their articulation of the "rules" for good discussions and made a new chart, based both on the guidelines that had been stapled to the students' response journals since early fall and on their new awareness of what they needed to do to be productive members of their discussion group. She then posted the new chart (see Figure 2.2) so they could see it easily from their discussion circle, and she often encouraged the students to look at the chart, self-monitor, and reflect.

By thus sharing the responsibility for good discussion behavior with her students, rather than simply telling them what to do, Lisa helped them polish their participation in the practice of book discussion in a school setting, particularly in her classroom. She also helped them develop a habit of self-monitoring and realize that they were responsible for their own learning. Wanting to live up to their responsibility as good members of the group, most of the students worked hard to do what they knew they should do. In this manner, Lisa gradually and increasingly freed herself of discussion management duties; she could thus focus on how her students were understanding the books they were reading, and what they revealed about themselves as people and as readers as they participated in the discussions.

1. Keep the conversation going.
2. Stay on task.
3. Include everyone in the discussion.
4. Take turns.
5. Don't interrupt.
6. Respond to questions and ideas from others.
7. Be polite.

FIGURE 2.2. Midyear student-generated "rules" for discussion in Lisa's book group.

DEVELOPING CONSCIOUS DELIGHT:
"IN THIS CLASS WE THINK ABOUT WHAT WE READ"

When Charlie announced to the group that "in this class, we read differently. We think about what we read," Lisa was delighted, for "thinking about what they read" was the primary goal she had set for her students as they made the transition from recently independent readers to fluent and engaged readers. Getting them to think about what they read was the reason she was committed to group discussion, as she knew that talking with others about books not only would force her readers to articulate their own thoughts, but also would provide them with new ideas and understandings as they listened to their conversational peers (McMahon et al., 1997). Setting the expectation that their responses—and their comments in discussion—would be thoughtful was just the beginning of Lisa's quest to help her students grow as readers.

Learning to Return to the Text for Evidence

Lisa began to help her students learn behaviors specific to good book discussions, in addition to procedures that shape good discussions in general, on the first day—as we have seen above, when she praised Amanda for returning to the text to support her comment, and as she discussed the rules for discussion under which she and her students operated. Later that week, Curtis told others about his book, Donald Crews's *Bigmama's* (1991).

1. CURTIS: I liked the part where they called their gramma Bigmama.
2. LISA: They called their grandma Bigmama? What's the name of the book? Who's the author?
3. CURTIS: *Bigmama's* by Donald Crews. They called her Bigmama not because she was big, but because she was special. It sounds like someone loves that person.
4. LISA: You know, what I liked about Curtis's response is that he's not only telling us what he liked; he's giving us a good reason. That's important.

Curtis then read aloud a bit, and Lisa responded, "I like again how Curtis went to the book to share the author's words. That's a good thing to do."

In the course of the first week of book discussion group, Lisa made explicit her desire to have students anchor their responses in the texts they were reading. Returning to the text pushed them to support their comments with the author's words (or illustrator's art)—reminding them that their ideas originated during the act of reading, and that response and book are linked. During the discussion excerpted above, two other students, Susan and Lynette, immediately adopted this strategy, imitating Curtis by reading from their books to support their points.

As they grew comfortable with participating in book discussions, Lisa's students increasingly returned to the text with zest, often finding that different people noticed many different things. In a discussion of *The Bossy Gallito* (González, 1994), three students cited the text to explain how they knew that a previous statement was true:

1. CURTIS: They tell us it's a parrot. On this page it says, "of his uncle, the parrot." That's how I found out it was the parrot.
2. AMANDA: That's how I knew.
3. LISA: Did anyone know in a different way?
4. ABEO: The border of the page. Look in the corner, and you can see the word *parrot.*

Notice how Lisa expanded the discussion in turn 3 by asking for different perspectives. In this brief exchange, she pushed her students to recognize that evidence can be found in many places, and Abeo rewarded her in turn 4 by drawing attention to another part of the "text" of picture-books, the illustrations. The idea that different people notice different things in the same books continued to develop as the year progressed. Of course, returning to the text to justify their responses was not the only response strategy that Lisa offered her students. Across the course of the year, she also demonstrated varied response options, gave students specific assignments that asked them to respond in a variety of ways, and questioned students so that they would elaborate on their responses. As returning to the text did, these practices, once introduced, became part of many different book discussions.

Thinking about Craft to Develop Literary Understanding

Another idea that Lisa introduced early in the fall was to think before speaking. This was initially presented as part of good book discussion behavior, but thinking about books is also obviously an important aspect of being a thoughtful reader, and nurturning thoughtfulness was Lisa's main goal. During their fall exploration of the theme of friendship, the students discussed *Pink and Say* (Polacco, 1994), and Lisa reminded them that thoughtful responses do not necessarily occur immediately. Notice how often she used the word *think* in her turns.

1. CURTIS: I didn't like the part when Moe Moe Bay got shot. They were mean soldiers, and I think Pink and Say should have gone with the soldiers to Andersonville, because then Moe Moe Bay wouldn't have died and no one would have died.

2. CHARLIE: That's a good point.

3. LISA: (*to all*) What do you think?

4. CHARLIE: I have a point to make. How would we know that they wouldn't have died? Pink and Say were just kids. Moe Moe Bay was old. She had lived most of her life already.

5. LISA: (*turning toward Curtis*) What do you think about that?

6. CURTIS: That's a really good point, Charlie. But I don't know what to say.

7. LISA: That's okay. Sometimes we need time to think.

Looking at this brief exchange, we see that these students were already beginning to learn to support their responses with specific reference to the text (turn 1), to be polite (turns 2 and 6), and even to admit that they were at a loss for words (turn 6). Lisa made this acceptable with her explicit response, reassuring Curtis and reminding the group that everyone needs time to think (turn 7).

One of Lisa's goals was to have her students really engage with texts so that they would think deeply, so she added many reading experiences to those offered in the basal reader, stretching the thematic structure of the reader with thought-provoking books. During the exploration of friendship in September, she nudged her students to move beyond the comfortable contribution that began "My favorite page was . . ."—a frame that had structured earlier conversations. In the second week of September, she offered them two new ways to explore books with her comment: "Can you think of how your book relates to other books? Have you thought about how the characters change in the book? Let's go beyond 'My favorite page.'" The next week, Maya demonstrated that she had taken Lisa's challenge to heart when she discussed her independent reading, *Henry and Mudge and the Careful Cousin* (Rylant, 1994). Notice how Lisa's talk first clarified and then affirmed Maya's point:

1. MAYA: I noticed that Annie was really quiet, just like me. It's a changing story.

2. LISA: What changes?

3. MAYA: Annie.

4. LISA: I liked how you didn't just say your favorite page, but talked about a character and the character's changing in the story.

Lisa, in turn 4, chose not to comment on the third thing that Maya did, which was to compare herself with the character of Annie; nevertheless, the idea of comparison, of looking at characters in terms of similarities with self, was one that she intended to explore. Here she reinforced Maya's successful attempt to go beyond sharing her favorite page, and she restated the idea of character change—an idea that continued to surface across the course of the entire school year.

In October, during the science spy theme, Lisa introduced something new to think about: genre. Students began making genre distinctions as they read books that were nonfiction, books that were fiction, and books such as *The Magic School Bus* series by Joanna Cole (a blend of fiction and nonfiction, with facts woven into a fictional story). They discussed, sorted, argued, and learned how authors make choices that best suit their purposes. For example, they came to understand why a book about dinosaurs might be written as a fantasy voyage to the time of the dinosaurs, instead of as a forthright presentation of facts.

As they discussed genre issues, Lisa gently introduced other literary concepts—concepts that would help the students develop a more robust understanding of how literature works. They considered design and format in picturebooks, and eventually moved to a consideration of authorial style that developed and continued across the school year. For example, during a discussion in late October, Lisa asked a simple question: "Who was telling the story?" She then encouraged students to "think about who is telling the story" when they were reading. She followed up by explaining:

> "It was the narrator. If the boy had been telling the story, you would only know the thoughts of the little boy. Usually you can tell by the use of the pronoun. It's called *third person* when the narrator tells the story."

Lisa thus simplified a complex concept—point of view—for her students, expanding their ideas about how literature works by introducing the notion. This is yet another example of how she began unpacking a new concept quite simply (asking a brief question, in this case), and then bringing it up over and over throughout the school year until it became part of how her students thought about text.

A few days after the introduction of point of view, students' comments during discussion provided the opportunity to introduce them to metaphor and imagery. Lisa had just read *Hello, Tree!* (Ryder, 1991). When one student commented, "Light doesn't dance," the group began a long, discursive discussion about how tall trees grow, how much they liked climbing trees, how branches were sturdier at the bottom than at the top, and so forth. Eventually Charlie asked a wonderful question:

1. CHARLIE: How does a tree have secrets? In the beginning of the book, it said that trees have secrets.

2. BETH: Maybe because the tree has lived so long and has felt so many things.

3. LYNETTE: Maybe people have told about secrets to the tree.

   (The conversation continues until eventually Charlie goes back to the initial idea of light dancing.)

4. CHARLIE: I wonder how sunlight can dance on the ground, and I have a guess. Maybe the sun shines on the ground and just dances around.

5. MAYA: The light, the sun, goes under when the wind blows the branches, and it seems like it's dancing.

6. LISA: All words are chosen very carefully. The words just flow right off of your tongue.

Together these students created meaning, figuring out the poetic ideas offered by the author. All Lisa needed to do then was offer them words with which they could discuss these techniques. A bit later in the same conversation, Maya, the same student who called a story "a changing story" when she shared a book as they were exploring the theme of friendship (excerpted above), offered: "I like the way she [Joanne Ryder] writes stories that make you feel like you are dreaming." Lisa asked what she meant, and Maya referred to Ryder's (1988) *The Snail's Spell*, another book that blends poetic fiction and fact. In the course of this conversation, they returned to the text for specific words, discussed metaphor and personification, linked one book to another by the same author, and identified one aspect of this author's style—writing stories that "make you feel like you are dreaming." The idea of an author's having a recognizable style continued to be discussed when the students embarked on an author study of Patricia MacLachlan later in the school year.

During the same time that these young readers discussed genre and style, Lisa moved from sharing picturebooks—either read independently or read by her to the whole group—into reading chapter books aloud. The first book she selected was *Arthur, for the Very First Time* (MacLachlan, 1980), a piece of fiction that nicely expanded the science spy theme they were exploring in their basal readers. During a discussion of this book, one of her students wondered why Arthur, the protagonist, liked strawberries—a seemingly random comment. Notice, however, how Lisa used Hao's comment to help her students think more broadly about life, and how she redirected the talk to offer them insights into how authors develop characters.

1. LISA: Let's stop there, Hao. Let's give people a chance to respond. You brought up a lot of "don't knows" and "I wonders." Think about that. Why would he like strawberries?

2. BETH: 'Cause they're good.

3. LISA: Hao, through this book, I hope you're realizing people aren't all the same. That we're different. Arthur's probably a very different person than you are, right? I'm a different person than you are. Maya's different than I am. What Maya likes, I might like some of the same things; sometimes we don't like the same things. And that's okay.

4. TOM: Like my sister loves tomato and I don't like it at all.

5. LISA: Exactly. So are you having trouble understanding why a character would like strawberries?

6. HAO: Yeah.

7. LISA: Why not? Should all characters in the world be like Hao?

8. CURTIS: No.

9. LYNETTE: People are different from each other.

10. LISA: That would be boring, wouldn't it?

11. CURTIS: Yes. Because some people are different.

12. SUSAN: Some people are active. People act in different ways.

13. CURTIS: Some people don't like animals; some people do.

14. LISA: But by knowing, do you understand, or by Patricia MacLachlan telling us that [Arthur] does like strawberries and Moira likes strawberries, it helps build a character. It makes them real if we know their likes and dislikes. Do you understand that? That by knowing all those details, he becomes real. Moreover, we don't know all those details. He is not a main character; he's a flat character. We don't know that much about his personality. So, by knowing all those details about Arthur, I feel I know him really well. Like he's a friend. Authors do that. They give you all that information, so you do know them like a friend.

15. CURTIS: It's like Arthur just jumped out of the book!

In this conversation, Lisa took a seemingly random comment—"Why would he like strawberries?"—and turned it into an opportunity to discuss life. She introduced the idea that it would be boring if people were all alike (turns 3, 7, and 10), and she also introduced ideas about the author's craft of characterization (turn 14).

In the excerpt on the previous page, and in that below, notice how students' conversational skills had developed—although Lisa was still quite present in both discussions, asking questions and drawing attention to interesting ideas. She was still coaching her students in how to manage a productive discussion, but was also freer to scaffold their ideas about literature and how it works than she had been earlier in the year.

1. LISA: And at the end, when he says, "Why, she looked almost pleasant," why does he think she [the pig] looks pleasant?

2. HAO: Because she likes having babies. Oh, yeah, he wouldn't know that [an idea they had previously discussed].

3. TOM: It didn't tell us in the book. There's not enough information, really.

   (Several students agree with Tom. Someone suggests looking in the text for clues.)

4. CATERINA: She is clean.

5. LISA: He likes her because she's clean, Caterina?

6. CURTIS: That doesn't make sense.

7. LISA: You're right, Tom. It isn't spelled out for you. It's a gap. You have to go back and figure it out. What experience did he have? What might change his perspective on how the pig looked?

8. SUSAN: I know.

9. LISA: Let's everybody take 5 seconds and reflect on that. *(They pause.)*

10. SUSAN: When he first got there, maybe he'd never seen a pig before and they just looked—you know, sometimes pigs look gross the first time you see them. [The school was actually not far from the university pig farm.] But then, after a while, they don't seem gross. He's been at Uncle Wrisby's farm for a while, and now he actually gets close to her.

11. LISA: Ooooh. I like that word *close*, a good descriptive word. Before, he made an impression based on what he had seen from a distance, So now he's getting close to something. It's a different perspective.

12. SUSAN: Now he's doing things.

13. LISA: Yes, he's doing things.

14. SUSAN: He's changing.

15. LISA: He's changing.

16. CHARLIE: Now he's learning that all the stuff on the outside really doesn't matter. He's learning that she may look ugly, but that doesn't mean she really is ugly on the inside. She's really nice on the inside.

Notice how, even though Lisa took 7 of the 16 turns, she spent those turns both supporting and extending what students were saying. In the first turn, she asked an open-ended question, really wanting to know what they thought about Arthur's change of heart. Her second turn (turn 5) asked Caterina to elaborate, although she chose not to as Curtis made his comment (turn 6). Lisa's third turn (turn 7) affirmed Tom's position that the book didn't really tell them why, and gave him a term for that openness in a text by saying, "It's a gap." She also introduced the term *perspective* in that turn—something that they had been discussing across the fall, and something that was at the heart of the thematic structure in the book. When Lisa asked them to pause and think (turn 9)—still a frequent suggestion—Susan explored this with her long turn (10) in which she offered the idea of "getting to know someone," which Lisa immediately validated (turn 11) with her praise for the word *close*. She then echoed what Susan said as a way of validating Susan's response (turns 12–15), and Charlie summed everything up with his long comment (turn 16), offering up the idea of differences between appearances and inner quality. This insightful comment about characters' seeming one way "on the outside" and being different "on the inside" echoed throughout the rest of the school year as the students explored characterization, what authors do to create their characters, and what impact getting to know these characters might have on how the students thought about their own lives.

PUTTING IT ALL TOGETHER: RELATING LIFE AND THE AESTHETIC EXPERIENCE

When the students listened to Lisa read *Arthur, for the Very First Time* in the fall, they were stretched to the limit to understand the story. They were clearly engaged by it, and eager to hear more each day, but could not quite grasp the ideas that MacLachlan was exploring. When school began after winter break, they asked to hear the story again, bringing their lunches into the classroom and giving up their lunch recess to do so. This book—the first chapter book that the whole group shared—became a touchstone book for them, as they repeatedly returned to it and some of the themes it raised across the year.

By April, the students were discussing character change and the distinction between internal feelings and external manifestations with increasing sophistication. They were also frequently putting themselves in a character's position or even imagining themselves as characters in a book. They made causal inferences and predicted future behavior as they read Sid Fleischman's (1986) *The Whipping Boy*. Notice how rich the following discussion was, and how Lisa's statements affirmed, clarified, and extended the responses the students were offering.

1. CATERINA: If I was Jemmy, I'd just do it.
2. LISA: You can imagine yourself there and doing something?
3. CATERINA: Yeah.
4. CURTIS: I would distract his . . . if I just got sucked into the book, I would start distracting Cutwater and giving Jemmy and Prince Brat time to run away.
5. AMANDA: I was really thinking about would Prince Brat go with the plan or would he not? And I thought he would not go with the plan because he didn't want to leave, because before he said he didn't want to leave.
6. CATERINA: Yeah. He just seemed like he didn't want to go.
7. LISA: That's interesting, Amanda. So you're saying that he's almost thinking it's better to stay where he is than to get this freedom and to have to risk it on the streets, or possibly go back to the castle.
8. SUSAN: I think the Prince didn't want to go back.
9. CHARLIE: I think [the Prince] likes [Jemmy].
10. BETH: I think they're gonna be friends.
11. CURTIS: In the inside he likes him, but on the outside he's just mean.
12. LISA: Mmmm. What does that mean, Curtis? I understand what you're saying about the inside is different from the outside, but why do you think that is?
13. SUSAN: You can always be good on the inside, but be bad on the outside.

14. CURTIS: Like a good heart, but on the outside there's a bad heart.

15. LISA: Why would we only be seeing the outside of him?

16. BETH: I don't think he likes anyone to know that he likes Jemmy.

17. LYNETTE: Maybe he just wants people to know that on the outside. Like he likes him on the inside, but he actually doesn't know how to tell everybody he does.

18. SUSAN: When Lynette said he was changing a little, he was opening a little bit . . . he's inside out, meaning that he's nice.

The discussion began with Caterina putting herself in the protagonist's (Jemmy's) shoes (turn 1), and with Lisa quickly supporting her in turn 2. Curtis took up Lisa's implicit invitation to "become" the character in turn 4, making explicit that his comment was contingent on getting "sucked into" the book. Amanda changed the focus in turn 5 by offering a prediction that she made, while also disclosing that she was "really thinking" about what Prince Brat (the antagonist) would do. Caterina agreed, and Lisa picked up on the idea in turn 7, as she supported, clarified, and elaborated on Amanda's comment. Her turn led to Charlie's speculation on how Prince Brat feels about Jemmy, which led to Curtis's comment on the difference between internal feelings and external actions, adding to the months long discussion of the inside–outside theme. In Lisa's next turn (turn 12), she asked Curtis to explain his reasoning, and the rest of the comments were a mixture of statements about the way people are (turns 13 and 14) and why (turn 15) they only "see" the "outside" of Prince Brat (turns 16 and 17). Susan's final comment pulled the discussion together with a reminder that characters change—something they had encountered in many of the books they had read this year. This conversation was part of a rather sophisticated discussion in which students spoke of entering the story's world, linked what they knew about life to the text, and made inferences about characters' motivations.

As students continued their focus on why Prince Brat acts as he does, and Lisa offered them a way to understand him when she asked, returning to the text, about what they had read the night before.

1. LISA: What did we learn, though, in Chapter 14 about the relationship between Prince Brat and his father?

2. CURTIS: That his father never really noticed Prince Brat before.

3. LISA: There was a line that Prince Brat said while having a discussion with Jemmy, and it was like a window into the relationship between Prince Brat and his father. And when I was reading that, I thought, "Hmmm, maybe that's why he doesn't want to go back."

4. CHARLIE: Because his father never does anything. His father never notices him. He's, like, he's a shadow.

5. LISA: What does that mean, *notice*?

6. SUSAN: He didn't, like, really play with him or anything like our dads do.

7. LYNETTE: Like when he wanted to play something, his father tells him he's busy or "Not right now" or something.

8. CHARLIE: Prince Brat knows how to play stuff, like pulling off people's wigs.

Notice how in turn 3, Lisa demonstrated how she anchored her understanding of Prince Brat's behavior in the text, precipitating Chris's comment about the king in turn 4. Lisa then asked (turn 5) for elaboration of Chris's term *notice,* which brought three examples from the text in turns 6, 7, and 8. The conversation then continued with Lisa's perceptive question in turn 9:

9. LISA: So then what is he missing?

10. CHARLIE: His father.

11. SUSAN: He doesn't quite have a real father.

12. BETH: His father is [the] King and he has too much to do, and he can't do much with the Prince.

13. CHARLIE: He's a real father, but . . .

14. SUSAN: He doesn't seem like what a father would be.

15. LISA: Okay, so are you saying that Prince Brat is just spoiled and he's expecting too much out of his dad?

16. CURTIS: Yes.

17. BETH: He's too busy to pay attention.

18. CHARLIE: I guess the reason that he's always being a brat is because he . . .

19. SUSAN: He wants attention.

20. CURTIS: He wants to get attention.

21. BETH: He never gets any love from his father.

22. LISA: What did you say, Beth?

23. BETH: He never gets any love from his father.

24. LISA: So it's not that he's a spoiled brat?

Lisa's provocative question in turn 15 was phrased as a request for clarification, but also functioned as a catalyst for students to articulate their
reasoning, thus setting up Lisa's next question (in turn 24), and creating
some dissonance among her students. Notice next how Lisa's provocative questions and comments in turns 26, 28, 30, and 34 helped them
make sense of what they were thinking but couldn't quite articulate.

25. SUSAN: No.

26. LISA: He's missing something?

27. SUSAN: He never gets cuddles like we do from our dads and
    moms.

28. LISA: That's affection, isn't it? So are you thinking that Prince
    Brat thinks that no one cares about him?

29. SUSAN: He doesn't care about anybody else because nobody else
    cares about him.

30. LISA: I see. So you're saying that if we didn't get love and affec-
    tion, then it would be hard for us to care about other people.

31. CHARLIE: And I think the reason that Jemmy is [the] opposite
    of Prince Brat is he had a father. His father was never, like, "I'm
    way too busy to do anything with you."

32. SUSAN: Yeah, they catch rats together.

33. LYNETTE: But the Prince [and] his father didn't really do that
    much.

34. LISA: What do you mean? He had everything he wanted!

With her clarification in turn 30, and the clarification question and comment in turn 34, Lisa helped her students get to the heart of the characters of Prince Brat and Jemmy, after Charlie introduced the difference
between the two in turn 31. Notice how adamant the students were
about the importance of love, and how they brought their own experiences and feelings to their understanding of the characters.

35. SUSAN: Except for love.

36. LYNETTE: He had everything he wanted, but everything he
    wanted wasn't enough to satisfy him.

37. CURTIS: He just wanted his dad.

38. LISA: You mean all the clothes, all the toys, having a whipping boy, all that stuff?

39. CURTIS: He wanted love from his dad.

40. LYNETTE: That stuff is nice, but he needs his father more than he needs all that.

41. LISA: So you're saying that Jemmy had more than the Prince did?

42. SUSAN: Uh-huh. He had more love.

43. LISA: He was poor. He didn't even get anything to eat.

44. SUSAN: Love, attention.

45. CURTIS: He gets more attention from his dad, the rat catcher.

46. LISA: Wait a minute. Are you saying that the love overruled even the hunger and the food? He didn't have toys and he didn't have a mom and all that stuff?

47. LYNETTE: You need your dad more than you need all that junk.

48. BETH: You need your parents.

49. SUSAN: And Mom.

50. LYNETTE: You need Mom and Dad.

51. SUSAN: You need love, cuddling, attention.

52. LISA: You could just have one [referring to Mom and Dad]. It could be one or the other.

53. LYNETTE: Like I could just have my mother. [Lynette's mother is a single parent.]

54. CURTIS: My mom's a single mom.

55. LISA: Exactly. And you're very empathetic to other people. That means you've gotten lots of love and you love other people.

56. LYNETTE: Like, you love your whole family.

57. LISA: Interesting. Abeo, what do you think about all this?

58. SUSAN: I say I think it's cool.

59. LISA: What's cool?

60. SUSAN: The way we just explained about . . .

61. BETH: You [Lisa] were trying to convince us that all the toys were enough, but we changed [it]. That was better.

62. LYNETTE: It is better.

63. SUSAN: We're some kids.

64. ABEO: I agree, because my mom keeps on saying that love is the greatest thing that you could ever get.

This lengthy discussion, which continued well after turn 64, demonstrated the depth with which these students read, thought about, and discussed books. In this excerpt of talk Lisa did what she had done from the beginning of the year: listened closely, asked questions to clarify, elaborated on student answers, and posed challenging questions and ideas. Her students knew what she was doing, as Beth made clear in turn 61—and they clearly enjoyed the challenge, congratulating themselves on being "some kids," as indeed they were.

When these students entered Lisa's classroom, they already were "some kids," and she knew that. She built on their own ideas uttered in book discussion group, while also bringing her own expert knowledge to the table in a purposeful manner. Because she clearly respected her students' contributions to the discussions, they also respected hers and were willing to learn from her—about how literature works, about how to talk about books in this particular classroom setting, and about their own thoughts as she pushed them to think deeply. In turn, they taught each other new ways of thinking and being as readers and new ways of looking at the world, as they moved from unconscious enjoyment to critically conscious delight in their books and in their own ideas.

Through discussion, these students learned how literature worked, how to think about texts, and how to relate texts to the world (Cochran-Smith, 1984). They developed their ability to use what they knew and had experienced in order to understand what they read, and to use what they had read to understand a little more about the world. They also developed their reading skills and strategies. By the end of the year, every one of them had gained grade levels on the routinely administered informal reading inventories. The smallest gain was three grade levels (one student); four students gained four grade levels; the biggest gain was six grade levels (two students). Although none of these students began as struggling readers, as they were all reading on grade level or above, most of them were not avid or engaged independent readers. By the time the school year was over, they all were both avid and engaged. Through judicious choices of children's books, careful scaffolding of conversational strategies, attentive listening, and carefully planned instruction coupled with flexible and contingent questions and comments, Lisa guided these students as they became "some kids."

THINGS TO THINK ABOUT

- As you read about the kinds of literary understanding that Lisa explored with her students, stop and think about your own practice. What books do you routinely share with your students? What are the literary qualities that make them worth sharing? Make a list of how these books can help students understand how literature works.

- Using a transcript of a conversation between you and your students that you have recorded, analyze the talk for ways in which you validate students' responses and support their tentative ideas.

CHAPTER 3

Productive Digressions

When Best-Laid Plans Give Way to Student-Led Discussions

> PD: I wonder how they [the whales] communicate. . . .
> I want to know how they communicate.

Sitting and leaning into the center of a kidney-shaped table are six fourth- and fifth-grade ELL students, four boys and two girls—each clearly focused on *Seven Blind Mice* (Young, 1992), a picturebook that their teacher has just finished reading out loud. These students discuss the text, at times cutting each other off in their urgency to make their points. You can tell from their accents and language usage that English is not the first language of these students. As you look closely, you notice a small unopened picturebook, *Dear Mr. Blueberry* (James, 1991), on the table in front of the teacher.

You look around the classroom, noting that it is divided roughly into halves by a free-standing, decorated notice board. Your eyes are drawn back to the right side of the room, where the discussion about *Seven Blind Mice* is taking place. You notice a lot of student work pinned on the walls, and many books displayed and in stacks on the counter space. All the books are about whales—dozens of reference books about the sea or whales, and both fiction and nonfiction picturebooks. Some books are lying open on the counter space, and you can see sticky notes that the teacher has added to draw attention to particular illustrations or facts. A 6-foot-wide poster of a northern right whale adorns one wall. In the middle of this space, just next to the teacher's chair, is a red stand with a large sheet of poster paper clipped to it. The heading on this sheet is no surprise: WHALES. Two of the three columns below this heading are filled in: "What we know" (this column extends to a second poster sheet and touches the floor) and "What we want to know." The third column, "What we learned," is thus far blank.

When you listen for a moment, you hear the two girls in the group enthusiastically build on each other's ideas and ignore the teacher: "The blind mice, the white blind mice did the right thing. He went all over the place. Oh, he did the right thing." (Teacher: "Oh, so the white mice . . .") "Like a rainbow color. Every color makes white, so he know every colors. And he just feeled the thing and the other colored thing there by itself. But the white every color, rainbow colors, and rainbow colors make white." You smile and wonder how these blind mice fit into a study of whales.

These ELLs left their fourth-and fifth-grade mainstream classrooms every day to have a 40-minute class with Charlotte, their ELL teacher. Like many ELL teachers, Charlotte traveled between two schools, taught across grades, and shared a classroom. This group was her first of the day at her second school, and after this class was lunch. The students typically got to the ELL classroom before Charlotte did, so before she left at the end of each day, Charlotte wrote notes describing particular tasks for her students to do when they arrived at her classroom the next day.

There were four boys and two girls in this class, including two sets of brother–sister siblings. These students were from mainland China,

Taiwan, Pakistan, and Mexico. Their family backgrounds ranged from parents who were studying at the local university and were literate in at least two languages, to parents working in a local restaurant who were not able to read or write in any language. These students had been learning English with Charlotte for more than a year, and each could express age-appropriate ideas.

Charlotte had been teaching for about 15 years. She was bilingual in English and Spanish. She knew these students well; she knew their family histories and what was happening in their daily lives. She was mindful of these dynamics as she planned lessons and taught class.

In this chapter, we explore the decisions and revisions underlying an unplanned discussion about a picturebook fable, *Seven Blind Mice* (Young, 1992); discuss how such detours could be productive in an instructional unit on whales; and describe how "going all over the place" was "doing the right thing" for effective and engaging instructional practice.

TALK IN ELL CLASSROOMS

Promoting student talk is an explicit instructional objective in every ELL lesson. Talk in the target language is both process for learning content and expressing ideas, and the sought-after learning product. From first-language mainstream contexts, we know that extended time "on the floor" in student-centered exchanges, exploratory talk, and elaborated utterances promotes communicative competence, individual reasoning, shared understanding and knowledge, substantive engagement, and high-level comprehension (Applebee et al., 2003; Hymes, 1971; Mercer et al., 1999; Murphy et al., 2009; Murphy, Wilkinson, & Soter, 2011; Nystrand, 1997, 2006; Resnick, 2010; Soter et al., 2008). For ELL students, student talk plays an even more critical role in providing practice in, awareness of, and immediate feedback in using the target language. If their talk is limited to recitation, then ELL students do not experience the necessarily varied participant roles needed to communicate. Talk confined to social interactions is equally limiting, as ELL students do not then acquire the elaborated code of schooling and associated ways of thinking. Moreover, many ELL students do not participate fully in mainstream classrooms because they lack confidence, feel self-conscious, or are simply overwhelmed.

In contrast, an ELL classroom can be a context in which language is played with, rehearsed, and applied, and in which student talk in English is a sought-after outcome in and of itself. When students grapple with language and content in a classroom context, compose at the point of utterance, and negotiate meaning together, the students are not simply learning the grammar and vocabulary of a language. They are learning to communicate effectively and to sustain age-appropriate thoughts and ideas. In Charlotte's classroom, the talk also revolved around selected literature that introduced and extended specific content, and classroom discussions of these books provided opportunities for her ELL students to rehearse and practice content vocabulary and concepts in context.

This kind of talk, in which students experience varied participant roles as they explore ideas and construct knowledge with others, does not just happen. It unfolds in a classroom environment where students feel safe enough to take risks and are encouraged to do so. The teacher plays a critical role in structuring opportunities for real talk and defining what it looks like in her classroom community. In the act of teaching, Charlotte decided what to encourage and what to let go. Her contingent moves, her responses shaped what counts. Why, then, did Charlotte set aside her planned lesson to spend time (re)reading and discussing *Seven Blind Mice*, a book that did not extend content about whales? Understanding why Charlotte pursued this digression from her lesson plan sheds light on what constitutes real talk and contingent instructional practice.

PLANFUL LITERATURE-BASED INSTRUCTION

Because there was no formal ELL curriculum in place, Charlotte developed and tailored what she called "integrated units of study." These units, as she described them, encompassed "not only the language my students need, but also the content and skills"; the material was chosen to be "challenging and interesting enough that all will benefit," and "most importantly, [to] provide an atmosphere in which my students are willing to take risks."

Every 2 years, Charlotte taught an integrated unit on whales toward the end of the academic year, because the entire fifth grade went on a week-long whale-watching trip where content knowledge about whales was valuable social and academic capital. Charlotte framed her units with open-ended "essential questions" (Tomlinson & McTighe, 2006) that reflected the most important issues, and she carefully selected literature to stimulate inquiry, debate, and further questions. The following questions framed the planning and implementation of the whale unit:

1. What is a whale?
2. What sources of information can be used to find out about whales and other topics?
3. What are the interactions between whales and mankind?

Charlotte wanted her students to know content; to know how to access additional content resources; and to understand why this content was relevant and how it affected them and their community.

To address the essential questions, Charlotte determined her lesson objectives and then planned and presented the instructional content and learning focus through purposefully selected children's literature. In planning an instructional unit, Charlotte considered texts for their content, their illustrations, and their potential to resonate with (contrast with, extend, "zoom in" on) other texts. In fact, all types of books were fundamental elements in this classroom curriculum. There were reference books, to enable students to check out a particular item or simply to browse; there were picturebooks that had been read in class, and others that had not yet been read but were displayed in ways that called out for them to be picked up; still more books were available for students to take home and to peruse before, during, and after class. For this particular unit, over 100 books were readily available in this small classroom. In addition, this class reviewed web articles to address and research particular questions; used interactive computer programs, such as *The Magic School Bus: Whales and Dolphins* (Scholastic, 2001); and visited websites set up by classes in other schools exploring the subject of whales.

While all of these texts were on hand and students were encouraged to share what they were reading independently, the instructional unit was shaped in large part by the picturebooks that Charlotte read aloud to the class as a group. For example, Charlotte selected texts to read aloud to highlight content (*Orca Song* [Armour, 1994]), to present contrasting perspectives (*The Whales* [Rylant, 1996] and "Killer Whales" [Yolen, 1996]), or to offer ways of presenting and reading for information (*Dear Mr. Blueberry* [James, 1991] and *Kayuktuk: An Arctic Quest* [Heinz, 1996]). The order in which books were read aloud was influenced by students' interests as expressed through discussions in the classroom; feedback on the students' needs as articulated by their reading, writing, and speaking performances in the classroom; and informal communications with the students' mainstream teachers. Charlotte's pedagogical content knowledge was extensive. The more she knew, the more flexible she could afford to be with her instruction.

MULTIPLE PATHS: OF MICE AND WHALES

The discussion about *Seven Blind Mice* presented below occurred during the second lesson of the whale unit. Charlotte had begun the unit by reviewing what students Knew about whales; then they had brainstormed what they Wanted to know more about; and toward the end

A KWL chart is a graphic organizer that the teacher and students commonly complete together (as a class) on a large sheet of poster paper.

- **K** stands for <u>K</u>now.
  Students list what they already know on the topic.
- **W** stands for <u>W</u>ill or <u>W</u>ant.
  Students list what they think they *will* learn about this topic.
  Students list what they *want* to know about this topic.
- **L** stands for <u>L</u>earned.
  Students list what they *learned* about this topic.

FIGURE 3.1. A KWL chart.

of the unit they would review the important aspects of what they had <u>L</u>earned (KWL; Ogle, 1986; see Figure 3.1). During the first lesson, the class as a group had completed the first two columns of the KWL chart, and this large sheet would be displayed, added to and referred to throughout the unit. Charlotte's main content objective for the second lesson was to review how students could access information and thus research what they wanted to learn about the topic of whales. The lesson plan was to read *Dear Mr. Blueberry* (James, 1991), a humorous

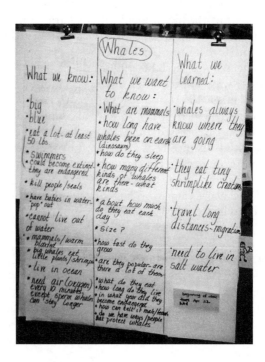

text that Charlotte noted in her plan book as being, "built on a child's curiosity and misconceptions about whales. It was a good book to discuss where we could find information about whales, or different ways of knowing, which I wanted to be part of this unit." It was a plan that aligned well with the KWL activity from the first lesson and with the essential questions for the instructional units.

Since these students often arrived before their teacher got to class, it was common practice for them to read and comment about the books on display and to share books they were reading independently. One student, Steve, had brought in information about Ed Young, the author of *Seven Blind Mice*. Young, like Steve, had been born in China. This conversation was continuing when Charlotte arrived, so as she was waiting for the rest of her students to arrive, she logged onto the Internet to learn more about Ed Young. The students wanted to reread *Seven Blind Mice* (which they had read in class months before). When Lucy asked, "Are we going to do that first or the whale thing first?", Charlotte responded, "We will do both because you want to do both." And so the class began with Steve haltingly reading from *Seven Blind Mice*. Notice, as you read the transcript below, how Charlotte positioned herself as a reader and teacher, and how this influenced the roles that her students were able to assume for themselves. Notice also how she managed to shape the discussion so that she addressed her planned intention for this lesson.

1. ROSEY: Can you read that again? No, um . . .
2. CHARLOTTE: The last one?
3. ROSEY: Colorful thing, color thing.
4. CHARLOTTE: It's to discover colors.
5. ROSEY: Uh-huh.
6. CHARLOTTE: ". . . the days of the week." Everybody understands those two parts; you learn the colors and the days of the week. But what does he mean when he says, "And one of the truest paths"?
7. ROSEY: Does he mean that, um, to go around the thing and see what it is?
8. PD: No.
9. ROSEY: Maybe.
10. ZACH: I give up.
11. CHARLOTTE: Okay, maybe. You're going around the thing. Do I know the answer? No!
12. PD: Yes!
13. CHARLOTTE: No, I don't!

14. ROSEY: Maybe.

15. CHARLOTTE: "One of the truest paths." What do you think? Steve? What is he saying; what does he mean? What is a path?

16. ZACH: A path?

17. CHARLOTTE: A path.

18. PD: A path, like a road.

19. CHARLOTTE: Like a road. So what would be the truest road, do you think? What does that mean?

20. PD: (unclear, overlapping) To the right.

21. JORDAN: The real path.

22. CHARLOTTE: The what?

23. JORDAN: The real path, or, yeah, like when you go the real way. The right way.

24. CHARLOTTE: Oh, going the real way. Do you think that is what he is trying to teach us, the real way, to learn the . . . ?

25. ROSEY: The blind mice, the white blind mice did the right thing. He went all over the place. Oh, he did the right thing.

26. CHARLOTTE: Oh, so the white mice . . .

27. LUCY: Like a rainbow color. Every color makes white, so he know every colors. And he just felt the thing and the other colored thing there by itself. But the white every color, rainbow colors, and rainbow colors make white.

In this discussion, we see evidence that these ELL students were comfortable adopting varied participant roles as they engaged with ideas and each other, and we see how their contributions shaped the scope and pace of the discussion. In turn 1, Rosey initiated with the guiding question for this exchange, "Can you read that again? No, um . . ." She then responded to the teacher's clarification question with, "Colorful thing, color thing," and articulated her inquiry: "Does he mean that, um, to go around the thing and see what it is?" She was leading. Her peers were following along, and it was PD (not Charlotte) who responded to Rosey's question. Only when Zach purported to "give up" did Charlotte weigh in, but not to provide the answer; rather, it was to distance herself repeatedly from interpretive authority. Her "Okay, maybe" left room for possibilities. Her "Do I know the answer?" and immediate, emphatic "No!" explicitly rejected authority status, as her question to Steve did implicitly: "What do you think? Steve? What is he saying; what does he mean? What is a path?" She gave the students space to stretch, and positioned them with authority for response-ability (Rubin, 1990). They could take risks, they could build on each other, and they could elaborate. We can see from this discussion how these students talked their way to understanding: PD's "A path, like a road" led to Jordan's "the real path," which was elaborated to "The real path, or, yeah, like when you go the real way. The right way." Rosey built on that to conclude, "The blind mice, the white blind mice did the right thing. He went all over the place. Oh, he did the right thing." And this culminated in a remarkable *student critical turn*—a linguistically extended, structurally coherent, and socially engaged utterance that was a marker of cognitive activity (Boyd & Rubin, 2002): "Like a rainbow color. Every color makes white, so he know every colors. And he just feels the thing and the other colored thing there by itself. But the white every color, rainbow colors, and rainbow colors make white."

These students were making sense of this notion that it takes all the perspectives to see what is there—and they experienced that in the process of getting there. This behavior of Charlotte's, her willingness to get out of the way, is not common. Charlotte was there, directing when needed, but willing to be talked over or even ignored at times as these students took ownership of making sense together. Six out of every 10 utterances here were made by the students; when Charlotte did talk, it was to give the students back their own words, or to ask questions that were contingent on what had been said. Contingent practices were consistent across the patterns of talk and learning decisions in this classroom. In Chapter 4, we look at contingent questioning in more detail.

So why did Charlotte digress from her planned lesson? She recognized that lessons are not "discreetly packaged, stand alone entities" (Nunan, 1996, p. 44); she did carefully plan each lesson to build on the preceding one, but she recognized that while this planning helped her to know where she wanted to go in terms of lesson objectives, there were multiple paths to get there. Her experience had also taught her that if she chose her path in response to the students' interests and contributions, she could foster student-led discussions. Charlotte knew what her learning objectives were. She could teach ways to get information by exploring how to learn more about Ed Young; she could illustrate the much more sophisticated notions of the impact of incomplete information and perspective through a discussion about *Seven Blind Mice*; and in the process of these engaged discussions, her students would be building linguistic, communicative, and academic proficiency. So she decided in the moment to realign her instructional plan. *Dear Mr. Blueberry* could wait for another lesson.

CONTINGENT DECISION MAKING: IN THE MOMENT

Teaching involves decision making. Although many important decisions (such as which books to read) are usually made before the lesson begins and are articulated in lesson plans, two-thirds of teachers' decisions are made in the moment (Bailey, 1996). In the opening vignette, Charlotte adjusted her plan to align with the students' interest in Ed Young, but continued in pursuit of her instructional goal. When other students joined with Steve to express interest in knowing more about Ed Young, Charlotte built on that interest.

1. ZACH: Is he dead or alive?

2. CHARLOTTE: He's still alive.

3. ROSEY: He's alive.

4. PD: You can tell his (*unintelligible*) on (*unintelligible*).

5. CHARLOTTE: Where might we find his address, I wonder?

6. ROSEY: In the computer.

7. ZACH: Computer.

8. JORDAN: Yeah.

9. ZACH: Dictionary.

10. CHARLOTTE: Where would we look in the computer? In the dictionary?

Charlotte's question in turn 5—"Where might we find his address, I wonder?"—set up this student-selected content to become the means through which the lesson objective was accomplished. The students' answers provided her with the feedback she needed to appropriately support, review, and direct sources and ways to search for and check information. The students were engaged, the research process was reviewed, and there was lots of student talk along the way, so the underpinning lesson objective of promoting real talk in the target language was also realized. *Dear Mr. Blueberry* would be read on another day.

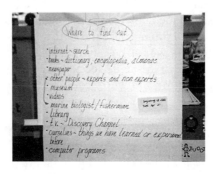

For the most part, in-the-moment instructional decisions do not involve changing texts in midstream. Effective teachers prepare lesson materials that set up conversational opportunities, and in the act of teaching, they decide which "teachable moments" to build on and which to let drop. Charlotte's practice of making reference books freely available for perusal before class, and occasionally marking a page with a sticky note with the words "Look familiar?" to draw attention, set up such conversational opportunities. Often these conversations began as students gradually arrived, and then continued into class time. These conversations captured the social and cognitive nature of real talk, demonstrating both the students' growing confidence in talking about what they knew, and their deeper knowledge about whales.

1. CHARLOTTE: (*reading*) "The white whale has a huge head and is about 50 feet long."
2. ZACH: That's the ugliest you see.
3. PD: I hate the white whale.
4. CHARLOTTE: The right whale?
5. LUCY: Oh, that's pretty, the (*unclear*) white.
6. ROSEY: That's the right, not white.
7. PD: Okay, the white whale.
8. ZACH: It's the ugliest.
9. ROSEY: The white whale is pretty.
10. STUDENTS: (*Unclear mumbling as students look at book.*)
11. ROSEY: That's not the white. That's the right.
12. LUCY: Well, the thing that I hate about white whale is that . . .
13. ZACH: It's too fat.
14. LUCY: . . . is that it has a hole up here, it has all that bumpy and red stuff on the top.
15. ZACH: And so fat!
16. ROSEY: What is—what is it called again (*pointing to part of whale*)?

In this exchange focusing on a reference book students had been reading before class started, Charlotte's talk role was minimal. She read one line of text and made one clarification request ("The right whale?"); her students carried the conversation. Through talk that was unrehearsed, composed at the point of utterance, recursive, hesitant, overlapping, and important to them, these students learned not only how to hold the floor, but how to add to, repair, and end conversations. They learned confidence in the target language and in the content discussed. Charlotte structured these opportunities for real talk, and she made room for students to select and develop them. Moments such as these, when Charlotte built on a student contribution, were common in this classroom community. In facilitating these explorations, Charlotte, like all teachers, balanced achieving "well executed, spontaneous learning opportunities" against the potential danger of "fuzzy, floundering digressions" (Bailey, 1996, p. 15). Student learning is enhanced when teachers risk digressions—and even when these are not fully successful, it is better than sticking to a plan when that plan is not working. Certainly it can be tricky to decide how long to spend on an aside, and what to exclude from a lesson because of the time spent "sidetracked" by digressions. But in an ELL class, a successful lesson must include talk in the target language, and not all talk is equally efficacious. Talk where students are reciting fill-in-the-blank content answers, or talk that is lacking in a content focus, is of limited value to ELL students when they return to their mainstream classrooms. However, talk that allows varied participant roles and engages with content—talk that combines the social and the academic, as in this unit on whales—is productive and sought after. When it occurs, effective teachers foster it, even when it digresses from the focus of the lesson. Note the quotation that opens this chapter: "I wonder how they [the whales] communicate. . . . I want to know how they communicate." A student was articulating what he wanted to know more about. The students were concerned about how the whales communicate, and Charlotte was concerned about how her students communicated. These concerns did not need to be at odds with each other.

For most teachers (and administrators), a successful, productive lesson would be one that went as planned and that covered the expected content. For Charlotte, "sometimes successful is just that they are able to share and generate ideas . . . to be able to say something [so] that the others are able to go with that thought, or build on that thought, a little bit of scaffolding with each other . . . but not to water down material." Charlotte explicitly planned a variety of materials, across genres and at different levels of difficulty. She then took the amount of time her students needed and maintained a focus on *the process of making sense* of the text rather than on quickly covering the material. Sometimes Charlotte's planned strategies to scaffold student understanding were not as successful as she intended. In these moments, which happen to all of us, Charlotte did not hurry her students toward an answer, or quickly provide one for them; rather, she patiently supported her students to think in and through their use of English. The talk practices in this classroom did not shut these students down. They empowered them to challenge what was presented to them and articulate their reasoning; to ask for further clarification and lead a search for understanding; and to share and elaborate on connections across texts and experiences.

CHALLENGING WHAT WAS PRESENTED: A PICTURE WORTH A THOUSAND WORDS

Almost all of the shared read-alouds Charlotte selected were picturebooks. In her written reflections on why she selected each text, Charlotte noted that "clear visuals can be used as a springboard for engaging students in discourse" and that "visuals also form the basis of linkage between prior knowledge and new labels." When Charlotte typed up the poem "Killer Whales" (from a book of poems titled *Sea Watch*; Yolen, 1996) and added a clip art picture of a whale at the bottom, she meant for it to be helpful. Certainly it became a springboard for engaging students in discourse, and it linked previous readings to this poem, but not quite in the way that Charlotte expected (see clip art picture below).

Growing content knowledge and the confidence that such knowledge brings, coupled with a classroom culture where students commented and held each other publicly accountable, resulted in these students' being highly critical of their teacher's selection of clip art to accompany the poem "Killer Whales." The following talk occurred after Charlotte passed out sheets of paper with the poem typed up and the clip art pasted below.

1. LUCY: This doesn't look like that.
2. CHARLOTTE: Well, this is from the computer, and this is a drawing, an illustration that someone did.
3. LUCY: Doesn't look like killer whales.
4. CHARLOTTE: Well . . .

5. ZACH: Look like a . . .

6. CHARLOTTE: It's just the computer drawing. But wait a minute, we haven't answered Rosey's question. What did you say?

Here we see that Charlotte acknowledged her students' point (twice, turns 2 and 6); then, however, she did not spend much time discussing the choice of illustration, but moved the focus forward. Nevertheless, these students were clearly distracted by the clip art and commented on the inappropriate selection on three separate occasions throughout the lesson. In addition, Jordan felt sufficiently empowered to fold the paper over so that the illustration was removed from his sight. Charlotte did not appear to feel undermined by her students' response to her clip art selection, and in an interview after class, she was very matter-of-fact:

"I was putting it there so I would have a reference because I didn't have a picture. . . . They [the students] argued a lot about the clip art I had put at the bottom of the poem because it did not look realistic. The colors were right but it looked more like a blue whale in shape. . . . Some of them folded it [the page] because they got so upset with the picture."

Charlotte knew what the role of illustrations could be, and acknowledged that her selection had fallen short. She was pleased that her students were clearly building knowledge about whales and were well able to apply and articulate this learning.

Lucy later selected the killer whale as her focus for an assignment. She illustrated her poem with a more accurate drawing than the clip art.

ASKING FOR CLARIFICATION: FIVE AND FIFTY WAYS TO TALK ABOUT POETIC LANGUAGE

It was not always the case that understanding came easily to these ELL students. Charlotte selected a range of genres for shared reading for this unit, including poetry. One poem in particular, "Killer Whales" (the one with the ill-chosen clip art), proved to be very challenging. Charlotte had planned a lesson wherein two poems, "Killer Whales" by Jane Yolen (1996) and the picturebook poem *The Whales* by Cynthia Rylant (1996), would provide content and context for her students to contrast the roles of whales as hunters and nurturers. But the "Killer Whale" poem was difficult for these students to make sense of—not because it contained hard words, but its poetic language and use of pronouns made it difficult for these students to figure out to whom "we," "he," "you," and "ours" referred. As these ELL students grappled with the meaning of phrases such as "five and fifty" and "Put your babe upon your back," Charlotte supported their struggle rather than removing the need for it.

The following excerpt is merely part of a long and recursive search for the identity of the parent with the baby on its back (the full discussion continued for over 15 minutes and some 300 utterances). Notice how, as students nominated successive candidates, they assessed their answers by returning to the text to test their ideas in context. Notice also how students used exploratory language to construct a narrative that made sense for this poem. Finally, think about what the students' focus was and how Charlotte followed their lead. In the excerpt below, Charlotte began by summarizing what the students had just figured out.

1. CHARLOTTE: The top side is black and the bottom side is white. All right, what does this mean?
2. PD: Put your baby upon your back.
3. CHARLOTTE: Okay, put your baby upon your back, "Or he is ours today."
4. PD: Ohhhhhhhh, ohhhhhhhhhhh . . .
5. JORDAN: They might eat him.
6. PD: They might eat him.
7. LUCY: Or maybe might eat him.
8. CHARLOTTE: They might eat him . . .
9. PD: If you don't put upon your back, somebody will get him or eat him.

10. CHARLOTTE: Who is the somebody that's gonna get 'em?

11. LUCY: Shark, shark, shark!

12. PD: Sharks or octopus.

13. ZACH: Another killer whale, another killer whale.

14. LUCY: Killer whales don't eat another killer whale.

15. CHARLOTTE: Okay, so are they talking to—are they talking to other killer whales, or are they talking about sharks coming to get them?

16. ZACH: Yeah, the sharks.

17. PD: No, but I read this book. It says killer whales don't have any enemies.

18. CHARLOTTE: Okay, killer whales don't have any enemies, so who is doing the talking, then? Who is talking here?

19. ROSEY: People.

20. LUCY: People might get them.

21. CHARLOTTE: People?

22. ZACH: No.

23. CHARLOTTE: Would people put their babes upon their back?

24. STUDENTS: (*in unison*) No!

25. LUCY: Whales put their babies upon their back.

26. CHARLOTTE: Okay, so you think that people are saying to them that they're going to get their babies if they don't protect them?

27. LUCY: Yeah.

As these students tried to make sense of "Put your babe upon your back/Or he is ours today," they turned to the lines before and after this one to move slowly toward an understanding of who put whose baby on its back. The inquiry process was messy, but the reasoning belonged to the students. There was room for conjecture as they explored what "might" have happened. Charlotte's job was to give students back their own words and reasoning; to revoice (O'Connor & Michaels, 1996) and refocus; and to scaffold student exploration—all of which she did in turns 8, 10, 15, 18, and 21. The student talk was short, choppy, incomplete, and recursive, but it was talk to construct meaning. Together, these students were teaching each other and applying what they knew about pronouns and referents. They were thinking in and through the target language, safely offering their best guesses.

Students' talk provides feedback that their teacher can use to assess language learning and frustration and to inform instructional decision making. Following her students' cues, Charlotte continued to support the line-by-line search for understanding of the narrative of the poem. As the following excerpt shows, when the students explored ideas for meaning, some of these ideas would not align with the text. Charlotte did not shut down exploration; instead, she allowed time for self-revisions as meaning was constructed together.

1. CHARLOTTE: Okay, but who are we talking about eating here?
2. LUCY: Dolphins, sharks.
3. CHARLOTTE: Okay.
4. PD: Sharks.
5. ZACH: I say killer whale, I say killer whale.
6. CHARLOTTE: You say they're killer whales? You say they're— you say there's dolphins that are eating . . .?
7. PD: They're gonna kill the baby whales!

PD's epiphany in turn 7 was explored, not corrected. Eventually, over 30 turns of talk later, he understood who kept whose baby on its back and who's "gonna kill the baby whales."

1. CHARLOTTE: Put your baby upon your back.
2. LUCY: No shark . . .
3. CHARLOTTE: Or be . . .
4. LUCY: There's another animal, was it?
5. PD: Maybe the dolphin's baby?
6. CHARLOTTE: Okay, so there's . . .
7. PD: The killer whale is coming to get it!
8. CHARLOTTE: Okay, so the killer whale is saying, "Put your," to the dolphin—"Put your babe"—or to the other animal, "Put your babe upon your back/OR he is ours."

After being directed toward the poem title, and negotiating contextual cues, the students had at last reasoned out that the killer whales were the ones coming to get the babe—that the whales were hunting baby dolphins.

The talk focus for this lesson ended up being very different from what Charlotte had intended. Much of the lesson was a student-led focus on a line-by-line deconstruction for meaning (such as in the "Put your babe upon your back" excerpts above). At the beginning of the lesson, Charlotte proposed her planned lesson: "I want you just to think about what the person is trying to tell you when you read this poem. Okay. How does it make you feel?" However, her students remained intent on making sense of the meaning of the poem. Charlotte recognized that without understanding the poem, her students could not meaningfully extend its themes to further reading, so she supported this student-led digression from her planned lesson. Surely it must have been tempting simply to provide these students with the correct answer. Just telling them would have been efficient; after all, it took them almost 300 utterances to arrive at understanding. Charlotte did not. Instead, her talk scaffolded their inquiry. Almost 400 turns later, she reminded her students of her lesson plan: "Okay. How does this—now that you've thought about this poem, how does this poem make you feel about killer whales?" A short exchange followed in which Charlotte bid for this "feeling agenda" lesson, but her students were not engaged.

After the lesson, Charlotte noted that deconstructing this poem for literal meaning was "the last thing I wanted to do"—but since it was clearly what the students needed to do to understand the poem, she tried to support them to the point where they could figure it out. Charlotte's ultimate objective was not efficiency, but rather promoting learning in and through the English language. She was successful not simply because of the amount and variety of student talk, but also because the talk enabled her students to transfer their new understanding to another text, as occurred in the excerpt below.

1. ROSEY: Okay, I guess over here—they say out in here, like, keep your baby on your back thingie.
2. CHARLOTTE: Okay, all right, what is he doing here?
3. ROSEY: I think protecting—I guess they're protecting your, um . . .
4. CHARLOTTE: Okay, is that a way of protection?

In this case, Rosey appropriated—unsolicited—the very phrase that these students did not understand and applied it to another text. Not only did she understand the phrase, but it was now part of her repertoire. In this class she could "try it out," even though she had just learned it.

The tension between efficient and effective instructional practice is an ongoing one. Listening and acting on student cues and taking time to risk uncharted digressions, require pedagogical flexibility and confidence. It is not simply a matter of giving the floor to a student who is taking a long time to share a story. A good teacher learns when to build on student utterances and when to move on, and how and when to extend student thinking and connect contributions back to instructional objectives. Teachers make these judgments daily, as they create or suppress opportunities for productive student talk with coherent coverage of material.

ELABORATED UTTERANCES: MAKING CONNECTIONS TO THE TEXT— A DOMINO EFFECT

Sometimes a text resonates with a group of students. This certainly appeared to be the case with one text, *The Whales' Song* (Sheldon, 1991)—a beautifully illustrated story, chosen in this instance for its poetic, fable-like quality rather than for its informational content. As indicated above, an undergirding learning objective for this class was to promote talk in the target language of English. This kind of talk was evident in a discussion of *The Whales' Song*. In the story, Lilly's grandmother tells her about her own childhood, and about leaving small gifts (shells or stones) for the whales that came into the bay; if they took the gift, they would give something in return. Her unpleasant great-uncle scoffs at this belief, saying that Lilly shouldn't be "dreaming her life away" listening to "silly old stories." Moreover, he is skeptical that the whales have spoken to Lilly when she recounts her experience. Two students related to this skepticism, and their line of thinking was expanded by one or two questions from the floor. However, when Charlotte asked an open question ("Have your parents or has anyone else, or have you ever—has anyone ever—told you a story that maybe other people wouldn't agree with?"), there was a cascade of sharing. This ranged from talk about video games, to stories told by various relatives, to stories read in other classes. As one student after another shared their stories, time to talk was granted to them. They simply told their anecdotes. Charlotte did not extend their tellings in any way. At times, she did not even comment as one student's story ended and another's began. The students shared; the teacher listened. Although she did not "rush" the conversation, she deliberately ignored opportunities for digression, thus keeping this conversation to an appropriate length.

THE WHOLE IS WORTH MORE
THAN THE SUM OF THE PARTS

Ed Young:

• we need to see the "whole" not just the parts to understand something or someone

• sometimes we see things or people and compare them with ourselves or our ways of seeing, doing, or acting

This chapter explores productive digressions in an ELL classroom setting, but our reasoning is applicable to every classroom where student learning is privileged. We know that encouraging real talk—talk that unfolds in context, where students construct extended exchanges and so initiate, extend, challenge, repair, and end conversations; talk where students elaborate as they compose in the moment, to push both their understanding and their linguistic repertoire; talk where students are exploring concepts and constructing meaning together—is not an easy matter. There is no script; there is no "one way." Furthermore, the whole picture emerges only as we "go all over the place" and then step back, as it does for Ed Young's seven blind mice. Examining classroom talk helps us do that.

We plan lessons, and then we make decisions in the moment of teaching that enact and adjust those lessons as we respond to student cues and privilege particular learning goals. The lesson, and the moment, do not stand alone. What tells the tale is the pattern of interaction, the instructional unit—the elephant, as it were. In the moment, it can be difficult to tell the difference between success and failure. But it is in those instances when teachers digress from their lesson plans to follow students' own ideas that teachers learn the *in-the-moment* expertise needed to enhance learning opportunities and enact real talk. This means learning how to get out of the way and to give space to students, and to do so in a conscious, conscientious way. When we talk as teachers is as important as what we say (Boyd & Rubin, 2002).

Relinquishing control of the floor—getting out of the way and allowing students time and space to talk—is a daunting prospect. When teachers give students some control over turn taking, the scope, and pace of the discourse, there may be more student engagement, but there will also be more digressions and less efficient coverage of material. But the "whole" will be a shared authority (Oyler, 1996)—a shared understanding and a shared agenda of what counts as knowledge or learning. The sense that students have a say in the instructional focus of a lesson cannot be simply given at the beginning of the school year along with new schoolbooks. It is earned and learned as students experience the teacher's *gradual release of responsibility* (Pearson & Gallagher, 1983). If the process of student articulation is a goal (Skidmore, 2000), then as teachers we model and support providing guided participation. But we also need to remove that support and allow students to experience grappling with language and fumbling through exchanges. To support student thinking and learning, teacher talk can build a reciprocal scaffold anchored in, and contingent on, what the students have contributed to support their intended explorations (Dyson, 1990). The teacher can make the scaffold larger or smaller to provide whatever is needed to support student elaboration and can position the scaffold wherever along the digression or planned curricular objective is appropriate. If teachers want to promote student thinking and learning, then their planning and in-the-moment decision making must be subservient to goals for student learning; they must come to view digressions as potential opportunities to encourage real talk in the classroom. Good teachers are responsive to their students. In the act of teaching, they know how to ask good questions, how to listen and to follow up, how to alter the direction of the conversation, and how to use language in ways that assist and not just assess language use and comprehension. Good lesson planning prepares materials that set up these conversations; it identifies core questions that direct inquiry in particular and appropriate ways, but it does not impose a script.

For student-led discussion to take place, students need to be placed in roles where they feel and are considered expert. If the teacher is always the interpretive authority, then students will go on a "treasure hunt" to provide the teacher-determined answers instead of reasoning for themselves. Often students' expert status is expressed in digressions—moments when the talk diverges to showcase a particular student's knowing. It is our experience that teachers who respond to student cues, who risk "teachable moments," and who even realign lessons in the moment are propagating productive talk. Such pedagogical flexibility cannot be scripted, but it is critical to engendering student cognitive activities; to working within the *zone of proximal development,* that dynamic and individually negotiated learning space (Vygotsky, 1986); and to pushing students toward further exploration and articulation. Through questioning, we can redirect, reengage, and enhance student-led classroom discussion. The next chapter looks closely at how Charlotte facilitated classroom talk that encouraged students to negotiate and explore their own lines of reasoning. We show how this was not a laissez-faire instructional practice and how Charlotte employed consistent, principled questioning and uptake strategies.

THINGS TO THINK ABOUT

- A central component of Charlotte's ELL curriculum was a literature-based instructional unit. Shared readings of a range of picturebooks provided common knowledge on a particular topic for reference and discussion. Select six picturebooks for a particular ELL classroom community. Identify ways these books complement, build on, or resonate with each other. Consider genre, accessibility, content, and order of reading.

- Teachers talk *a lot*. One of the remarkable things about Charlotte's classroom is her consistent practice of making only about a third of the utterances. As you reread the transcripts of the *Seven Blind Mice* and "Put your babe upon your back" discussions, consider how Charlotte invites and then makes room for student contributions. In your own words, list three ways she accomplishes this, citing at least two supporting examples for each.

CHAPTER 4

The Contingent Third Turn
Listening to Scaffold Response-Ability

> JORDAN: Wow, I found something on the news . . .
> there were seven whales that were coming
> into the Pacific Ocean.

When Charlotte arrives one day, she is not surprised to see that all six of her students are already busy in the ELL part of the classroom. Rosey and Lucy are discussing which whales they like best, poring over pictures in one of the reference books that Charlotte leaves for this very purpose; Steve, PD, and Jordan are writing in their journals; Zach is poised in front of the extra-large note paper on the table, holding a marker in his hand. Before Charlotte can say, "Good morning," Zach reports that they have been "good neighbors" today. Charlotte smiles. Yesterday she left her students a note reminding them that although she was "happy to see their enthusiasm about our whale unit," the reading specialist in the other half of the room had mentioned that they had been "a little noisy" in the time before class, and she wanted them to be sure to be "good neighbors."

Charlotte sits down and is about to take out the "props" in her bag, when Jordan excitedly reports his news about seven whales being trapped. Zach, the other fifth grader, has also heard this news; he is fascinated that it cost "seven thousand dollars to get those whales." Charlotte asks Jordan, "Why do you think they got trapped?" When he responds that there was too much ice, she follows up with "Why do you think there might be too much ice?" The exchange continues to develop, with other class members listening, when Charlotte asks the group: "What about . . . does that remind you of anything that happened in *Orca Song* [Armour, 1994]? Did anything happen there that would sound like . . . " Before she can complete the thought, Rosey picks it up, reminding the class how the baby whale in the picturebook gets caught in netting. Charlotte and her students continue to discuss the whales' predicament as she begins to unpack her bag. When she pulls out her new props—a plastic igloo and a box of sugar cubes—Jordan immediately asks, "Could we study about them people?"

The day before, the class read *Kayuktuk: An Arctic Quest* (Heinz, 1996). The students thrilled to the story of Aknik's quest and became fascinated by Inupiat traditions. There was almost complete silence as Charlotte read aloud, and then so much discussion about the illustrated borders paralleling the story that she has decided to continue with this book today. Aknik lives in a tent, and as a class they begin to talk about how in the Arctic people live in different structures in different seasons. As Charlotte passes the igloo around the table, Lucy asks, "How come they speak a different language, those people in Alaska?" The ensuing discussion about how people speak different languages leads them to talk about cave paintings and then about how igloos are built; it finally spills into a resumption of the previous day's discussion about the border art in *Kayuktuk*. Without Charlotte's ever having announced that it is time to "begin class"—but, rather, through her listening and then responding with questions that invite extensions and connections across schooling foci and student contributions—Charlotte and her students have organically unfolded the lesson plan for today.

It was common for these students to ask questions, and it was not unusual for them to run out of time and continue exploring a topic the next day. The 40-minute assigned time for the ELL class routinely began early and ran into lunch, but these students wanted even more time. One student, Zach, cajoled Charlotte to "write a note. Excuse Zach and Jordan to the ELL when we have social studies and science." As her use of the toy igloo and sugar cubes demonstrated, Charlotte actively planned building on student interest, but she also opened space for student questions and for in-the-moment exploration, and allowed students to assume expert status. Such was the culture of this class.

In this chapter, we continue to demonstrate the importance of student talk in ELL. We show how the culture of a classroom is created by and demonstrated through the norms for talk—norms that affect opportunities for the amount and type of student talk. We see how Charlotte's particular use of contingent questioning (Boyd & Rubin, 2006) inspired and sustained her students' engagement with learning. Charlotte positioned her students as learners and knowers as they studied about whales and deftly wielded contingent questions to further her students' exploration and articulation. Charlotte's way of teaching, her instructional stance, shaped what could be learned and how it was learned. We begin with a close look at part of a conversation about whales in this fourth- and fifth-grade ELL classroom.

PRESIDENT BOB WHITE: COMMUNICATION, CONJECTURE, AND CONNECTIONS

Like Chapter 3, this chapter focuses on Charlotte's instructional unit on whales. In the following exchange, Charlotte's students discussed the magical elements in the picturebook *The Whales' Song* (Sheldon, 1991). The story begins with the main character, Lilly, listening raptly as her grandmother tells her that if she leaves a gift for the whales, they may leave something in return; her great-uncle scoffs at the story, deriding it as an old wives' tale. At the story's conclusion, a pod of whales calls out Lilly's name. The exchange below occurred after Charlotte had completed reading *The Whales' Song,* and the class was debating whether the story was plausible. The discussion provides dramatic insight into how this class functioned. As you read the transcript below, think about the impact discourse norms had on what type of talk was enacted. As you read, note how Charlotte used contingent questions in different ways to promote and extend engaged student thinking and learning.

1. CHARLOTTE: Do you think—what do you think about this story? Do you think this is something that actually could . . .

2. STEVE: It was a lie.

3. ROSEY: *Could* happen . . .

4. CHARLOTTE: Could happen?

5. STUDENTS: (*overlapping chorus*) Yeah. Yeah. No.

6. CHARLOTTE: Okay . . .

7. STUDENTS: (*overlapping chorus*) Yes. No.

8. PD: You don't . . . you don't . . .

9. STEVE: Part of yes, 'cause someone's grandmother could have told his granddaughter a story, and then his great-uncle doesn't agree. But when the whales [are] saying their names, it's not true.

10. CHARLOTTE: Okay, so you don't think that could actually happen?

11. ZACH: Yeah, yeah, it can.

12. STEVE: No, no, I mean . . .

13. LUCY: You can because, um, because the whale might make a sound. Well, it might be sounded, but . . .

14. CHARLOTTE: Oh, okay, so it could be a sound. Have you ever heard a bird that sounds like this? (*She whistles twice, making a sound that approximates the call of a northern bobwhite.*)

15. LUCY: Yeah, I heard that bird.

16. CHARLOTTE: And people say that that sounds like he's saying, "Bob White, Bob White."

17. ZACH: What is that?

18. CHARLOTTE: "Bob White."

19. LUCY: What Bob White?

20. ZACH: Beer.

21. CHARLOTTE: Oh, just calling somebody's name, "Bob White, Bob White."

22. ZACH: Bob, Bob, it's a President of the United States once.

23. STUDENTS: (*in chorus*) Bob, Bob, Bob . . .

24. ZACH: It's one of the Presidents.

25. CHARLOTTE: So maybe I . . . maybe the little girl wanted it to be . . .

26. ZACH: [He's] 16 [i.e., the 16th U.S. President].

27. ROSEY: It might be Cynthia Light [pseudonym for school administrator].

28. LUCY: No . . .

29. ZACH: I think he was 15 or 16, the President of the United States.

30. CHARLOTTE: Bob White? No, there's never been a White that was a President.

31. ZACH: Well then, Bob.

The excerpt above represents just a few minutes of conversation, yet a close reading of this "lived classroom talk" sheds light on instructional discourse practices that invite and support student thinking. Who controls the floor, who determines the scope of the talk, and who holds interpretive authority are norms apparent in discourse; they reveal how teachers shape opportunities for student talk.

Who controls the floor? As noted in Chapter 1, teachers make two-thirds of the utterances in most classrooms (Nystrand, 1997; Chinn et al., 2001). In part, this is because the talk "goes through" the teacher. Most classrooms have a teacher–student–teacher–student–teacher–student turn-taking pattern, as the teacher modulates contributions and enforces space between turns to avoid overlapping speech. You can tell immediately that Charlotte's was no "traditional" classroom, as the talk did not routinely "go through" her, and there was overlapping speech (including talking over Charlotte) as students made their points. In the exchange above, the teacher–student ratio of talk was reversed, as the *students* made two-thirds of the utterances (21 of the 31 turns of talk); they thus controlled the floor in terms of time on the floor.

Who determines the scope of the talk? Again, teachers typically set the parameters for what and how talk unfolds. Here again, however, Charlotte considered her students' interests and contributions in the *what* of classroom talk. She routinely adapted lesson plans when she reflected on the preceding lesson, and she was open to realigning lessons during the act of teaching to incorporate student interests and contributions (as we have seen in Chapter 3). The format for *how* talk unfolds was already well established in this classroom as the end of the school year approached: Charlotte read a selected text out loud (in this case, *The Whales' Song*), and as a class they periodically stopped both during and after the reading to discuss points of interest. Discussions in this classroom community were also unusual in that students took on traditional teacher participant roles: They asked questions (such as Lucy's

"What Bob White?" in turn 19) and answered other students' questions (such as Zach's answer that Bob White was a brand of beer or a President in turns 20 and 22), in addition to assuming the traditional student role of responding to teacher questions.

Moreover, the scope of the talk unfolded in conversational rhythms. As you read the excerpt, you can hear five of the six students in this ELL class grappling with the story. Charlotte did not even get to finish her set-up for the inquiry—"What do you think about this story? Do you think this is something that actually could . . . " (turn 1)—before Steve responded with "It was a lie" (turn 2), Rosey countered with "*Could happen* . . . " (turn 3), and Charlotte repeated Rosey's articulation of possibility (turn 4). Members of the class disagreed, and when PD started to explore hesitantly with "You don't . . . You don't . . . " (turn 8), Steve overrode him to elaborate on his own thinking: "Part of yes, 'cause someone's grandmother could have told his granddaughter a story, and then his great-uncle doesn't agree. But when the whales [are] saying their names, it's not true" (turn 9). Charlotte tried to clarify the ambiguity: "So you don't think that could actually happen?" (turn 10). Zach and Steve disagreed (turns 11 and 12), and then Lucy put forward her case: "You can because, um, because the whale might make a sound. Well, it might be sounded, but . . . " (turn 13). Charlotte revoiced, "Oh, okay, so it could be a sound" (turn 14). But then in the same turn of talk, she offered another frame for this exploration: "Have you ever heard a bird that sounds like this?", and she whistled the "bobwhite" bird sound that sounds like its name. (This is a bird local to the region.) Lucy responded with "Yeah, I heard that bird" (turn 15).

These students displayed a high comfort level as they immediately indicated they didn't understand the connection (turns 17 and 19). A digression then unfolded as Zach asserted that Bob White was a President of the United States, and this idea was bandied about across several utterances (turns 20–31). Charlotte first attempted to redirect the conversation, ignoring Zach's comment and saying, "So maybe I . . . maybe the little girl wanted it to be . . . " (turn 25). But when Zach insisted that Bob White was the 15th or 16th President (turn 29), Charlotte quickly truncated the unproductive digression by wielding one of her exceedingly rare explicit evaluations; she simply and firmly declared, "No, there's never been a White that was a President" (turn 30). Even at that point, Zach was comfortable enough to insert a final "Well then, Bob" (turn 31).

In this excerpt, therefore, we see that Charlotte shaped the scope of the discourse, although her moves were at all time contingent on student cues for interest and understanding.

Who holds interpretive authority? There was a high level of engagement and conjecture as these ELL students debated *The Whales' Song,* but there was no one right answer. At one point in an earlier lesson, Charlotte had explicitly challenged her students: "Do I know the right answer?" As her students chorally responded with a mixed "Yes" and "No," Charlotte had insisted, "No, I don't." Her patterns of talk reflected this. By the end of the school year, in Charlotte's discussions with her ELL students, fewer than 0.5% of her utterances functioned as evaluations. Instead, she revoiced students' contributions, rewording but giving them back their own words and ideas—for example, "Oh, okay, so it could be a sound" (turn 14). She asked contingent questions to push them further along in their thinking ("Okay, so you don't think that could actually happen?" [turn 10] and presented frameworks for different ways to conceptualize whatever they were considering ("Have you ever heard a bird that sounds like this?" [turn 14].

By consistently replacing the evaluative third turn (the E in the IRE pattern) with contingent "tell me more" follow-up alternatives, Charlotte created a talk environment where students felt safe taking risks as they explored the role of interpretive authority that Charlotte offered to them. The combination and dependability of the patterns of classroom talk in Charlotte's classroom eased these risks and made it more likely that students would engage in talking-to-learn. Exploring ideas during talk in any language involves risk taking, because, by the very nature of talk, ideas are forming and may be incomplete or even inaccurate. Exploring ideas in another language adds the risk of incorrect word usage or inappropriate grammar structure.

EXPLORATORY TALK, ELABORATED UTTERANCES, AND FRUITFUL DIGRESSIONS

In the excerpt above, there was a lot of conjecture as students explored the possibilities in *The Whales' Song.* These students thought aloud and engaged with ideas and each other as they tried to figure out what something might mean. They employed talking-to-learn or exploratory talk (Barnes et al., 1990), marked by their use of reasoning words such as "I think," "I agree," "because," "would," "could," "might," and "maybe," and by the hesitant delivery of in-the-moment processing. Students were not trying to figure out what the teacher wanted them to say. Instead, these students took risks as they interrupted, extended, challenged, and proposed ideas and meaning together. Charlotte stepped out of the way, and only stepped back in when her cultural and historical background knowledge was needed, as it was during the "Bob White" interlude.

Exploratory talk can culminate in elaborated utterances—for example, when Steve (turn 9) articulated his reasoning. This utterance contained markers of reasoning: "'cause," "could have," and "doesn't agree," all within one elaborated turn of talk that qualified as a *student critical turn* (see Figure 4.1). It was longer than 10 seconds; it responded coherently to Charlotte's preceding utterance; and social engagement was manifested in Steve's uptake, which rested on and extended his peers' previous utterances. Steve's opening transition acknowledged their responses ("Part of yes"), and then he explained his reasoning for supporting yes ("'cause someone's grandmother could have told his granddaughter a story, and then his great-uncle doesn't agree"). Steve then followed up with "But when the whales [are] saying their names, it's not true," thus supporting his judgment that the whales did not say Lilly's name. Steve's summary of the two sides of the argument set up the subsequent discussion.

Charlotte validated digressions as she drew upon other resources (whistling bird sounds) to make the point that animal noises can sound like names. Her actual point was somewhat lost, but she too was taking risks in the conversation. Some paths were fruitful and others not, but she recognized and modeled the vital practice of bringing in other experiences to help construct meaning. The exchange illustrates that real talk is not scripted; it unfolds in a messy, recursive, hesitant, and sometimes sprawling manner, as participants revisit shared ideas and introduce new ways of framing.

In an ELL classroom culture where students grapple with language as they explore and negotiate meaning together, students are

Student turns of talk that are linguistically extended, structurally coherent, and socially engaged are designated *student critical turns*. To qualify for this designation, an utterance must meet the following criteria: The turn of talk must be elaborated (more than 10 seconds), coherent (building on the previous three utterances), and engaged (evidence of uptake). SCTs are evidence of students' communicative competence and markers of cognitive activity.

FIGURE 4.1. Student critical turns (SCTs; Boyd & Rubin, 2002).

not simply learning the grammar and vocabulary of a language. They are learning to communicate effectively and to sustain age-appropriate thoughts and ideas. In Charlotte's classroom, talk represented both product and process. As product, it was each student's best linguistic guess and communicated what the student did (or did not) understand. Talk about literature introduced and extended specific content, and it instigated dialogue with the teacher and other students. It was also the process for developing communicative competence and expanding linguistic repertoires (Echevarria & Graves, 2007; Lee, 2006). In classrooms where there are real conversations, the social and cognitive functions of talk are exploited as students learn how to enter, continue, recap, and end conversations, and they practice varied participant roles as they query, respond, initiate, and add to contributions. This does not happen automatically. Rather, it is possible because students feel safe and supported in a classroom where there is an ethos of respect and involvement (Boyd & Rubin, 2006). The environment in Charlotte's classroom included the expectation that the teacher and peers would not shut down student exploration. Instead of a "got you" attitude, there was an exhortation to "tell me more"; students were expected, challenged, and pushed to more fully articulate or reason out their assertions. How students responded was linked to their predispositions, which were shaped by the histories of not just the types of questions Charlotte asked, but also the ways she followed up on their responses. Charlotte's talk practices were consistent instructional moves, neither scripted nor laissez-faire, but selectively contingent on student contributions. Although Charlotte could deftly employ contingent questioning to direct the content of a discussion, she used it primarily to encourage students to tell her more.

TEACHER QUESTIONING

Teachers ask a lot of questions, and students respond to those questions. Students quickly discern what teachers want to hear: a fill-in-the-blank answer or an actual exploration of student thoughts. Teacher questions can *assess* recall of known information or *invite* students to share or elaborate. However, if the teacher never builds on student responses, then students quickly realize that these are viewed as performances rather than as substantive contributions. Teacher questions can also *assist* thinking and articulation; contingent questions anchored in classroom talk can serve to push student contributions further, offering direction for elaboration if students elect to respond.

Like most teachers, Charlotte used the question as her dominant instructional tool, but unlike most teachers, she did not predominantly use her questions for short, choppy recall (Nystrand, 1997). Charlotte used both *closed* or *display* questions, for which the answer was already known and there was typically only one acceptable answer; and *open* or *authentic* questions, which did not have a predetermined answer. Furthermore, she presumably was interested in hearing the answer, because there was more than one acceptable answer. Charlotte asked questions that pertained to students' experience, questions that related to the text, and questions that related the students' experience to the text. Across the unit on whales, Charlotte consistently used contingent questions to support the thinking and understanding of her students. She did this by first listening attentively to what her students offered, and then anchoring her questions solidly within their contributions and nudging them toward greater clarification, deeper thinking, or further elaboration. As noted earlier, this was directly reflected in the teacher–student ratio of talk (one-third to two-thirds). In the following four excerpts, notice how Charlotte's questions made explicit the welcome for and value placed on students' contributions. Also notice how Charlotte's patterns of questioning positioned her students as primary knowers and as having interpretive authority.

Authentic Questions and Increased Student Talk

For the most part, authentic or open teacher questions are associated with increased student talk, because they invite students to express what they think, feel, and know–positioning them as the primary knowers or authorities, and therefore as expected and competent to provide the information needed for others to understand. For example, an authentic question might ask students to connect personal experience to an experience in a text, such as in the following excerpt. Charlottte and her students were discussing the text *Kayuktuk: An Arctic Quest* (Heinz, 1996)—the picturebook mentioned in this chapter's opening vignette. In this story, a young Inupiat boy, Aknik, must prove himself worthy to be a hunter for his tribe. Ultimately, he defies tribal directive but proves his courage and worthiness when he wisely spares an Arctic fox and her whelps. Notice how Charlotte opened the talk with an authentic question.

1. CHARLOTTE: Could that happen to anybody? To have to show that you're grown up about something?
2. STUDENTS: (*choral response*) Yeah, me, uh-huh.

3. ROSEY: See, sometimes you want to prove to, like, your parents and stuff. No, I mean, like, show off, like, you got something and then when you go back, it's gone.

4. CHARLOTTE: And so what happens?

The exchange was almost conversational. Charlotte's questions assumed that these students both wanted to contribute and had something new to contribute. Note that Charlotte's response to Rosey ("And so what happens?") was another open, authentic question, because presumably Charlotte did not know what Rosey's parents' response was likely to be. Unlike a "thanks for sharing" response that would be likely to close down the exchange, Charlotte's contingent follow-up question exemplified the practice called *uptake* (Collms, 1982): It signaled that she was listening and that Rosey should elaborate further.

Authentic questions are not confined to the domains of personal experiences or responses to literature. They are also asked in relation to understanding of literature. Most teacher educational literature recommends that teachers use open questioning, and associates the use of such questioning with dialogic instruction and high-level reading comprehension (Wilkinson & Son, 2011; Mohr & Mohr, 2007). This association is premised on the assumption that authentic questions provide opportunities for students to construct new understandings as they think, explore, connect, and articulate in response to such questions. As research and practice have shown, however, facilitating such student talk is not easy. Opportunities for students to have the floor to talk, the students' sense that they have something to say and that what they say is listened to and valued, and a safe learning environment in which to say it are also critical elements. Charlotte's classroom included all these elements, as well as authentic questions. In the excerpt below, notice how she asked an authentic question inviting student interpretation when she invited Steve to predict what he thought could happen to the young hunter, Aknik, when he does not do what his father has directed. Notice how Charlotte asked questions and made comments that built on what students had said.

1. CHARLOTTE: Okay, Steve, what do you think could happen?

2. STEVE: Maybe, um, um, you can, you want to go somewhere, but your father doesn't want you to go, like . . .

3. LUCY: That can happen.

4. STEVE: He wants to hunt the whale, but his father . . .

5. PD: (*unintelligible*).

6. CHARLOTTE: Okay, you want to go to a place, but your father says that you aren't what?

7. PD: You're not ready for it.

8. CHARLOTTE: Ready for it. Has that ever happened to you, where you wanted . . .?

9. PD: Yes.

10. LUCY: A lot of times.

11. CHARLOTTE: Steve, you want to tell us? You don't want to tell us about it?

12. PD: I got one. This is my mom and my dad have a conversation, and whenever I get in, he say, "You're not ready for this."

13. CHARLOTTE: Oh, okay, so sometimes . . .

Charlotte's initial authentic question—"Okay, Steve, what do you think could happen?" (turn 1)—was very general, and it opened up the space for the students to shape the scope and pace of the discussion. These students did not "go through" Charlotte to bid for the floor, as they confirmed, extended, and jumped in to comment. Steve's response of "Maybe, um, um, you can, you want to go somewhere, but your father doesn't want you to go, like . . . " (turn 2) resonated with the other students; it preceded self-nominated turn-taking norms in action as Lucy validated Steve with "That can happen" (turn 3), and PD, Lucy, and Charlotte prevented Steve from completing his comments (turns 4–10). When Charlotte tried to return the floor to Steve, it was again appropriated by PD (turn 11). By asking an authentic question and allowing the answer to shape the subsequent discourse, Charlotte was giving over, or sharing, control of the scope of the classroom discourse and the opportunity to impose a tighter coherence or connection across utterances. The result was overlapping, messier talk–talk that resulted in an engaged process and an articulation of deep understanding. Steve struggled to articulate how Aknik has to make decisions that are contrary to his father's directions but appropriate for the situation. Aknik's decision reflects a maturity—a "being ready"—and PD's empathetic sharing digression about maturity and not being ready signaled a high-level understanding of the text.

Open, authentic questions also allowed these students to self-nominate and share. In Charlotte's classroom, there were many cascades of sharing. Sometimes student comments were simply uttered one after another and not built upon. At other times, Charlotte asked for clarifications or more detail. Unlinked student comments do not qualify as student critical turns because they stand alone. In the excerpt below, notice how many student comments, all uttered within 5 minutes, were made in response to Charlotte's authentic question "Has that ever happened to you before?" (turn 3). Notice also that Charlotte's question was in response to PD's conjecture about Lilly hearing the whale say her name.

1. PD: Oh, maybe she's having a dream and her mother, um, her grandmother comes up and says, "Lilly, Lilly, Lilly."
2. LUCY: Yeah.
3. CHARLOTTE: Has that ever happened to you before?
4. ZACH: Yes, I got good dream, my mom say wake up.
5. STEVE: See, when I was dreams, someone pushed me, see, my mom she was trying to wake me up, he pushed me, and in my dream I dreamed someone's pushing me.
6. PD: See, when I, like, I'm having a nightmare, see, it's like a computer. I turn on the computer and it says, "Wake up," clicking, I wake up.
7. CHARLOTTE: Oh, well, that's good, so you can wake yourself up when you have a nightmare.
8. LUCY: Ah, um, in my country we didn't had any alarm clocks, and what my brothers do wake me up, they get a glass of water and splash it on people so they could wake up.
9. ZACH: Um, when I'm, like, sleepy and watch, like, scary movie, like somebody jump off the, like, climb the mountain, and then I dream that I was that guy, and "Ahhhhh!" And—that's why my mom don't let me watch scary movies!

These students were comfortable talking about their experiences, and as they shared, they worked within both the cognitive and social aspects of learning. As they talked, they became more proficient in the target language of English, and they learned more about each other in the process. Charlotte listened to their contributions, and she balanced acknowledging and building on what her students shared with prompting other ways of seeing and knowing, and providing other and more elaborated ways to say those ideas.

Display Questions and the IRE/IRF Discourse Norm

One way to lead students into additional meanings is through display questions, which allow more teacher control over topics and turn taking. They get the job done in terms of covering particular material efficiently, but the practice has been disparaged as producing short, choppy, fill-in-the-blank student answers for an already determined teacher response. This is in part because display questions are tightly associated with the default norm of classroom discourse, the IRE/IRF, and the convergent nature of teacher questioning (Dillon, 1984). In an IRE or a conventional IRF exchange, the student is expected to fill in the semiotic blank with information already known by the questioner, and the utterance is one of retrieval, not composition at the point of utterance. Moreover, the turn-taking sequence is codified as teacher–student–teacher; thus when one student is called on or starts to speak, other students can "switch off," because they can be sure that they will not "perform" until called on in a later sequence.

In the following excerpt, notice how Charlotte made use of alternative IRF sequences. This talk occurred as the students were examining the illustrated borders on each page of *Kayuktuk*.

1. PD: Ms. Charlotte? I got something to say.
2. CHARLOTTE: What?
3. PD: In every page there is, like, a picture—it tells you what is happening.
4. CHARLOTTE: Does it? Is it kind of like the borders?
5. PD: Yep.
6. CHARLOTTE: Does that remind you of anything we've seen?
7. PD: Yeah . . . (*unclear, overlapping*).
8. ZACH: Yeah, the drawings.
9. CHARLOTTE: The drawings that show, that tell us, the story.
10. PD: See, look, first there were two (*uintelligible*), the whale, then . . .
11. STEVE: Picturebook.
12. PD: I don't know what this is. This is the sled and he's going. This is the ship; there's the arrows, the spear, or whatever; and I don't know what this is and it goes on.
13. JORDAN: And there's the babies [of the mother fox].

This exchange contains an IRF sequence. Charlotte initiated it with a fill-in-the-blank yes–no question, followed by a question that on the surface asked an opinion but in practice expected agreement: "Does it? Is it kind of like the borders?" (turn 4). PD filled in the expected blank with his response, "Yep" (turn 5). Charlotte followed up with an open question of sorts: "Does that remind you of anything we've seen?"

(turn 6), and the IRF sequence was continued. PD and Zach filled in the blank with "Yeah," and "Yeah, the drawing," (turns 7 and 8), and Charlotte followed up with an elaboration that validated their response: "The drawings that show, that tell us, the story" (turn 9). Although the third-move follow-up ("Does that remind you of anything we've seen?") was structurally an open question, Charlotte had a particular answer in mind, and the question functioned to focus the student's attention on previously shared books and their illustrations. This question could then have resulted in a treasure hunt of sorts, but the students followed along with Charlotte and quickly provided what Charlotte expected: the "drawings" and "picturebook" (turns 8, 11). In fact, PD talked over Charlotte's validation of Zach's response (turn 9) to point out the retelling of the story of *Kayuktuk* in pictures. This IRF sequence, while functioning to recall information, was in the service of assisting PD's exploration after his successful bid for the floor ("Ms. Charlotte? I got something to say" [turn 1] and comment ("In every page there is, like, a picture–it tells you what is happening" [turn 3]). This culminated in further student-directed discussion about the illustrated margins (turns 10–13), including PD's student critical turn: "I don't know what this is. This is the sled and he's going. This is the ship; there's the arrows, the spear, or whatever; and I don't know what this is and it goes on" (turn 12). Clearly, this IRF sequence did not shut down student talk; rather, it prepared the way for PD's elaboration. Charlotte's role here in this excerpt, and consistently across other discussions, was to listen to her students and practice uptake—most often in the form of a question that selectively built on what the students contributed. In other words, she used contingent questioning.

Contingent Questioning

Contingent questions (see Figure 4.2) cannot be scripted. They are necessarily composed in the moment, as they are responses to previous

> *Contingent questions* are questions that explicitly build on contributions made within the previous three utterances. Their form can be open or closed, authentic or display—but they function to facilitate students' thinking and exploration, as they offer coherent bridges across ideas and contributions. They increase the scope and depth of inquiry.

FIGURE 4.2. Contingent questions (Boyd & Rubin, 2006).

utterances. Whereas display questions in most classrooms result in disconnected student talk, Charlotte used them in a different way, challenging the notion that display questions are associated only with fill-in-the-blank or recitative student talk. Charlotte's display questions were posed in direct response to what students offered. Her *contingency*, not the type of question, mattered. In Charlotte's class, there were slightly more display than authentic questions, but 90% of these display questions were contingent on previous utterances. In contrast, about half of Charlotte's authentic questions were contingent, functioning to open up and redirect the scope of the talk.

Authentic questions opened up the discourse and in fact provided opportunities for students to share connections (such as the cascade of personal experiences generated in the discussion of *The Whales' Song*). As teacher, Charlotte decided which contributions were built upon and which were simply left as stand-alone contributions. Display questions were often proffered in clusters, as Charlotte adopted a Socratic stance to prompt and scaffold a student's efforts at further and more specific elaboration. In contrast, authentic questions such as "What do you think?" offered more scope but less support to the respondents, as these invited students to articulate their thinking and reasoning out loud.

The consistency with which Charlotte proposed contingent questions, and the positioning of those questions in relation to elaborated student utterances and extended student inquiries, underscored their role as important scaffolds for student talk in this classroom. Notice the discourse patterns as these students discussed *Dear Mr. Blueberry* (James, 1991), a picturebook organized through letters exchanged by a student, Emily, and her teacher, Mr. Blueberry. Embedded in this humorous correspondence is a bevy of facts about whales. As you read, notice what types of questions Charlotte asked and what types of student talk resulted.

1. ZACH: Who did he run into? A man or something?
2. LUCY: It's a she.
3. ROSEY: Mr. Blueberry?
4. CHARLOTTE: Who do you think Mr. Blueberry might be?
5. LUCY: A whale.
6. JORDAN: A man. Ms. Charlotte, Ms. Charlotte!
7. ROSEY: Oh, I think, wait . .
8. PD: A whale.
9. ROSEY: I think it's a blue whale.

10. LUCY: Yeah.

11. JORDAN: A blueberry.

12. LUCY: I think it's a color like a blueberry.

13. PD: No, look.

14. CHARLOTTE: Wait a minute, let Rosey finish, let Rosey finish. What do you think?

15. ROSEY: (*unclear, overlapping*) I think he wants to blueberry, Mr. Blueberry, to write something about maybe he's a whale and he knows information about whales and he's blue.

16. CHARLOTTE: So you think she's writing to a whale? What do you think?

17. LUCY: The color of blueberry.

18. ZACH: I think he want to excite, is a man that studies a whale. (*reading the text of Emily's letter to Mr. Blueberry*) "I love whales very much, and I think I saw one whale on the pond today, in the pond, in the pond today."

19. CHARLOTTE: Okay, what does it say right after that?

20. ZACH: (*reading text*) "Please send me some information on whales, as I think he must be hungry."

21. ROSEY: Might be hurt?

22. CHARLOTTE: What does she want Mr. Blueberry to do?

23. PD: (*unclear, overlapping*) Maybe Mr. Blueberry is a doctor, so he can tell his write in the paper and send it back to Emily so she can write him back.

24. LUCY: She can write her back.

In this discussion about *Dear Mr. Blueberry*, the students made most of the utterances (19 of the 24 turns of talk). Charlotte made only five utterances, and each included a question (turns 4, 14, 16, 19, and 22). These students clearly felt comfortable speaking freely without relying on Charlotte to mediate. Lucy and Rosey responded to Zach's initial question (turns 1, 2, and 3), and Charlotte's first utterance (turn 4) was a contingent, textual, authentic question: "Who do you think Mr. Blueberry might be?" These students then immediately explored who Mr. Blueberry might be (turns 5–13), until Charlotte weighed in to clear the floor for Rosey to complete her thinking out loud (turn 14). Rosey then produced the first of three student critical turns: "I think he wants to blueberry, Mr. Blueberry, to write something about maybe he's a whale and he knows information about whales and he's blue" (turn 15). In fact, Rosey was incorrect in her assumptions, but Charlotte deliberately did not explicitly evaluate them. Instead, she summarized Rosey's conclusions by phrasing them as a question—"So you think she's writing to a whale?"—and then opened the floor up to the other students with "What do you think?" (turn 16). Lucy's comment, "The color of blueberry" (turn 17), was left hanging as Zach grappled with language in proposing that the Mr. Blueberry to whom Emily is writing is an expert on whales; he then read the text to support his reasoning (turn 18): "I think he want to excite, is a man that studies a whale. (*Reading the text of Emily's letter to Mr. Blueberry*) 'I love whales very much and I think I saw one whale on the pond today, in the pond, in the pond today.' Charlotte did not correct his language, but instead specifically directed Zach's attention to where he might find information to help him identify Mr. Blueberry, with her display question: "Okay, what does it say right after that?"(turn 19). Zach read where directed (turn 20), but this point did not bear fruit, as Rosey then weighed in with a suggestion that somehow the whale might be hurt (turn 21). Charlotte attempted to clarify with another display question: "What does she want Mr. Blueberry to do?" (turn 22). Instead of closing down student talk, this flow of display questioning produced a third exploratory student critical turn, this time from PD (turn 23): "Maybe Mr. Blueberry is a doctor, so he can tell his write in the paper and send it back to Emily so she can write back to him" (turn 23). Each of the three student critical turns nominated incorrect identities for Mr. Blueberry. He is in fact Emily's teacher, and the students eventually arrived at that answer, long after the excerpt shown. As in the "Put your babe upon your back" discussion excerpted in Chapter 3, Charlotte used display questions to support her students as they explored their way to understanding. Her use of display questions reflected a classroom safe for exploration and conjecture.

By not providing her students with the identity of Mr. Blueberry, Charlotte set up a context in which the students had to figure it out— and they were not afraid to explore publicly who he might be. Charlotte's role was to listen and let them explore. When she spoke, it was to direct students to further articulation; her phrasing reminded the students that they could think out loud. She prompted them—"Who do you think . . . ?" and "What do you think?" (turns 4, 14, 16)—and let them speak without being corrected or reproved by her, although the students were comfortable adding and editing each other. Student language was peppered with markers of exploratory talk and reasoning words, such as "I think," and "maybe." All of Charlotte's utterances were contingent, and all included a question. What's more, these contingent teacher questions emphasized the role of student contributions in making meaning in this classroom. They positioned these students as having response-ability for interpretive authority and being primary knowers (Berry, 1981). Thus, although most of these questions were display questions, their contingency—their relation to the student talk that had immediately preceded them—made them effective questions as well. The contingency of the question was more important than the type of question in shaping an effective discussion.

Through questions, a teacher can choose to control the scope of the discourse and limit talk to areas that are teacher-determined and where the teacher is the primary knower, relegating students to the status of secondary knowers. On the other hand, through questioning, a teacher can open the talk to student experiences, student-suggested books, and student interpretations; attend to what is offered; and follow up on student nominations and suggestions, thus elevating the students to the status of primary knowers. Furthermore, an examination of the overall patterns of teacher questioning and the subsequent follow-up moves can reveal whether the questions are perfunctory or actual questions requiring thoughtful student input. In other words, does a teacher question initiate a treasure hunt where students strive to uncover an interpretation the teacher has predetermined, or are students granted interpretive authority and expected to explore and reason? When we understand the role a question plays within the stream of discourse, we see its potential to deepen inquiry or to shift focus.

As Charlotte's questioning has illustrated, there are hidden depths and established currents in discourse patterns. As teachers, we must be mindful of the intention behind our questions. Do we intend to invite student input? To assess student knowledge? To scaffold student inquiry? Certainly these intentions need not be mutually exclusive.

Charlotte's patterns of instructional talk were such that both across and within lessons, she spoke less than most teachers, and she posed a question half the time that she spoke. As noted earlier, 90% of her questions were contingent on previous utterances; in other words, her contingent questions were in the service of what had already been introduced. These questions could not be scripted. Rather, they emerged from Charlotte's willingness to listen, and then to risk "leading from behind" and thinking alongside her students; to share authority, time, and semiotic space; to provide opportunities for students to publicly explore and rehearse emerging understandings; and to co-construct knowledge. Charlotte's role was first to provide a classroom culture where students felt safe and engaged, and then to nudge them forward with her questioning. Over her more than 15 years of teaching, she had figured out that listening to her students and motivating their involvement in the process by harnessing their interests, skills, and contributions promoted student talk and thinking. Charlotte's consistent practice of contingent questioning created a pattern of, and time for, real talk.

THE THIRD TURN AS OPPORTUNITY TO SCAFFOLD STUDENT RESPONSE-ABILITY

More than a quarter of a century ago, a foundational critique on teacher questioning (Dillon, 1984) explicated how teacher questioning tends to pursue a teacher's agenda and does not scaffold students' inquiry. In some ways, popular endorsement of authentic, open questions is an oversimplified response to this tendency, for we must consider how even questions that seem open and authentic can easily position students in treasure hunts, as they strive to provide what the teacher wants (in terms of scope and interpretation) rather than to explore their own thinking. Established classroom discourse patterns predispose students to respond to teacher questions in particular ways. Students can tell from a teacher's third turn—how the teacher follows up their response—what the teacher's intent is. "In short, the feedback move is an act indelibly tied to teacher intent and teachers' conceptualization of the role of talk as a tool for learning" (Smith & Higgins, 2006, p. 492). To consider questioning as a scaffold for student inquiry, we must address tensions between teacher and student intentions (Dyson, 1990) and consider "who gets to build the scaffold?" (Aukerman, 2007, p. 63). In scaffolding her students' inquiry through contingent questions, Charlotte demonstrated how to use student input when building the scaffold.

When teachers like Charlotte choose *not* to evaluate or abbreviate an exchange in the third-move slot, but instead follow up with a contingent question or comment, there is opportunity to move beyond student talk as performance (Wells, 1993). This teacher uptake can encourage further student thinking and elaboration. When uptake is included in the teacher third move, a transformative exchange occurs: The student assumes the position of primary knower, and the teacher can "lead from behind" (Wells & Chang-Wells, 1992). By selectively building upon parts of student responses, the teacher can validate a student contribution, extend students' thinking, and direct the scope of the exchange (Bloome et al., 2008). This third move is in fact a marker of pedagogical (in) expertise (Lee, 2007): It can and often does shut down exchanges, but when wielded purposefully, as it was by Charlotte, it can serve to build coherence and scaffold student elaboration.

THINGS TO THINK ABOUT

- Teachers ask lots of questions. As you reread these ELL class discussions about *The Whales' Song* and Bob White, and *Dear Mr. Blueberry,* consider the impact of Charlotte's questions on who talked and what was said. Now stop and think about your own practice. Revisit the transcript you have made of a discussion between you and your students (see "Things to Think About" in Chapter 2). What questions did you ask, and what results did they achieve?

- The ground rules for talking in Charlotte's classroom were very loose. There was overlapping talk, and at times students ignored or talked over her! Describe what you perceive as the ground rules for class participation in this class of six. Would you change them if you were teaching a similar-sized group of ELL students? What if the group size was doubled? Explain and support your thinking.

CHAPTER 5

Reading Your Audience

Reading Aloud as Opportunity for Literate Talk

MICHAEL: As Matilda's parents say, "That reading, it's not good for you."

HUSSNI: But you tell us to read!

Picture a really hot and humid midafternoon in June. Eighteen third graders are sprawled on the floor; some of them are supine, quietly looking up and fanning themselves. Others are sitting cross-legged, hands behind them on the floor, their eyes on their teacher. Still others are sitting with their backs against the wall under the white board. These students are loosely grouped in a circle; all are immobile and palpably quiet as Michael, their teacher, performs his daily reading. On this day, the book is *Midnight for Charlie Bone* (Nimmo, 2003). Michael's half-moon glasses are perched on the edge of his nose so he can look down to read and up to address his students. He has his students completely with him; he stops in the middle of one sentence and asks a vocabulary question: "What's *hangdog*?" Two students respond, and together they conclude that it means not happy, "like a dog with its tail between its legs." In less than a minute, Michael has resumed bringing Nimmo's book to suspenseful life as the protagonist, Charlie, realizes he is being set up by his villainous aunts for big changes: He is to take a test for a new school, and he will be separated from his best friend. These are worries these students can identify with. They listen, enthralled.

The casual dress of the teacher and the relaxed positioning of the students belie their intense engagement. There is a rhythmic patterning of pauses as Michael deftly responds to questions and elicits students' insights. These brief exchanges underscore this experienced teacher's pedagogical expertise and deep knowledge of literature: He times these pauses to be short enough not to lose the thread of the story at pivotal moments, but rather to sustain and quickly identify why or how suspense is building, or what a key word means or foreshadows. Michael limits remarks to one focus and acknowledges students' input in a myriad of ways, while imposing a "hold that thought" discipline as the pleasure of the reading aloud is savored.

Michael and his students use literary terms with ease. Connections within and across texts are proposed and expanded upon in a relaxed, almost conversational manner; yet it is amply clear that the teacher is in control of the timing. Michael does not assign any follow-up work, and when he concludes reading for the day, he always closes the book at a terribly exciting part, knowing well that there will be loud student protests.

Michael had been teaching for 31 years, and he was still excited about it. He credited his lack of burnout to working with teachers and students who "bring enthusiasm . . . a lot of energy . . . and a lot of good ideas." Michael taught 18 third graders in Hillyside, an elementary school in a midsized college town. Over half of these third graders had at least one parent who was born outside the United States (Bosnia, China, England, Hungary, Ireland, South Africa, Sudan); several of them spoke more than one language, but none of them received ELL services. There was a full-time aide in the classroom to work with one special-needs student. Although there was a wide socioeconomic range in this classroom, the vast majority of these students came from families in which the parents were educated and learning was valued. There was a casual, comfortable feel to the classroom. Books were piled on desks; dozens of rockets were on a table, half painted; a large World Cup soccer schedule and results chart were posted on the whiteboard. Chapter books were lined up under the chart, and the chapter book read-aloud titles were listed on report cards every quarter. *Eragon* (Paolini, 2003), *Gregor the Overlander* (Collins, 2004), *Danny, the Champion of the World* (Dahl, 1975), *Rowan of Rin* (Rodda, 2001), and *The Sea of Trolls* (Farmer, 2004) were some of these.

In this classroom, the daily ritual of the chapter read-alouds was sacrosanct. It was not relinquished for other academic or social commitments. When necessary, the timing of the shared reading was changed, but the reading always happened. Michael was explicit and passionate in his rationale for reading aloud to his third graders:

> "I think third grade is an age where a lot of kids get the skills, their skills, together enough so that they can handle reading and decoding and so on, and they're at a place where they're ready to get really excited about reading. And I think through read-alouds you really, like, increase the possibility that they are going to get turned on to books and stories. And it's kind of a continuation of what a lot of kids do, like, when they're real little, with moms and dads and grandparents reading to them. I think kids just really like it. And we are all about reading and enjoying school, so . . . "

But it was not *just* fun. In his many years of teaching, Michael had privileged time spent reading and talking about books as a critical, irreplaceable medium for "learning all kinds of things about how authors work" and as "the instigation behind a lot you can talk about—whether it's types of characters, or how plot goes, or the vocabulary that authors use." And so Michael read; the kids listened; Michael briefly paused to draw attention to the author's craft or an insight; and there was a brief, focused exchange before he moved on. These patterns reflected accepted incipient literacy practices, but the rapt engagement we encountered in Michael's classroom cannot be formulaically replicated in any or every class. Michael had patiently cultivated what he described as "an environment where it's fairly safe and secure and it isn't a drudgery kind of thing." In Michael's classroom, the expectations for teacher and students were clear: active listening and active participation. Michael modeled what he expected in terms of both listening and participating. He explained:

> "I need to make sure that I'm listening, 'cause I think a lot of what I do is in reaction to what the kids are saying. If I'm *not* listening, I can't really react in any [way] other than just going, 'Yeah, that's good,' or 'Yeah, that's nice,' which is not terribly helpful feedback. You need to give specific feedback—what was good or what was nice about what they had done, and then they know that 'Ooh, that's a good thing to do in the future, maybe,' whether it's the individual who's getting the feedback or another person [who's] listening. So I have to really listen, and I hope the kids are really listening too. And they really are, especially when you notice that, you know, when somebody starts saying something and another kid says, "Oooh, me too!" or "I read that book!" And sometimes it's so wonderful, 'cause the enthusiasm really gets so high that, you know, you got kids being rude all over the place, because they got to get their two cents in—which is kind of a nice problem. But they have to listen and I have to listen, and if I do listen, again, it's . . . there will be, like, just, I will be inundated with teachable moments where something's happening in that story, which kids should realize that's part of the author's craft—and that's not there by accident."

So Michael was listening to his students and to the words he read out loud, and what he heard helped him decide when to stop and comment or ask a question. He was listening to his students' contributions, and asking questions that would push them further in their thinking and articulation. Michael expected his students to listen as well—he also expected them to talk.

This chapter explores how Michael socialized his students into loving books and talking effectively about books. We focus on this teacher's and students' listening and talking across two literacy events associated with chapter book read-alouds. During the first event (the selection of a chapter book to be read aloud), Michael not only listened, but he took notes as the students talked. In contrast, although the second event (the talk punctuating the read-aloud performance) was open to teacher or student initiation, Michael controlled the timing of when and how long an exchange survived. These two literacy events represent two distinct but complementary patterns of classroom talk. Multiple excerpts from each of these events illuminate the importance of purposeful, contingent, in-the-moment instructional decision making, as teacher talk shapes different types of classroom talk for different purposes. These instructional decisions also reflect the ongoing tensions between effective and efficient instruction that underpin the act of teaching.

CRITERIA FOR SELECTING BOOKS TO READ ALOUD

Reading aloud is common in elementary classrooms. Books are read not only for fun, but to illustrate targeted instructional points and to organize instructional content units. In Michael's third-grade classroom, books to be read aloud were usually chapter books read for pleasure, without any follow-up task or activity. He knew that this approach promoted active listening skills, as his students experienced sustained character and plot development and acquired new, more challenging vocabulary (Beck & McKeown, 2001; Santoro, Chard, Hoard, & Baker, 2008). Michael consciously selected books that were beyond some students' independent reading level; otherwise, "they're missing out on a lot of the books and pieces that are really going to grab them and make them really excited about reading." Michael took time selecting the "right" chapter books to "get them really excited," because he knew that consistently providing such experiences goes far in developing lifelong readers (Cunningham, 2005).

THE PROCESS OF SELECTING THE BOOKS

In most classrooms, the teacher selects the read-aloud text. The teacher can match text with student interests and with what is appropriate and engaging, and can also plan for a productive as well as pleasant use of class time. The importance of selecting the "right" text is heightened when chapter books are read aloud; they take more time to read, and there are extended learning and engagement consequences if a poor selection is made. Certainly Michael was well able to select literature that was gripping, relevant, and connected to either topical or academic content; he was very well read and could easily recommend both current and classic books across genres, authors, and topics. Notably, however, he typically did not draw solely from his own "inventory" of literature. Instead, Michael had a defined process for selecting the next book to be read aloud—a process that turned routine decision making into an engaging literacy event in itself that invigorated read-aloud time and student book talks. This process took place over 2–3 instructional days; it not only represented "a real great avenue for me to show my excitement about books," but provided authentic opportunities for "different kids sharing what they like." In this process, teacher and student book recommendations were embedded into excited and spontaneous talk about books. In fact, Michael noted that "a fair number of read-alouds come from the kids' suggestions."

Incorporating students' voices into this selection process had three important literacy outcomes for the students. First, it reinforced students' sense of themselves as readers, as they articulated what they enjoyed reading and why. Second, it invested them in, and prepared them for, the text selection; they became excited about the book and wanted to hear more. Third, this shared recommendation experience made reading, in a word, "cool." As students enthused about what they were reading, others took note. Peer recommendations are a powerful factor in students' future self-selection of text; when students recommend texts, other students are more likely to "take a chance" and pick up a new author or try a new text (Boyd & Devennie, 2009). So what did this process for selecting the next read-aloud look like?

The process of selecting the next chapter book to read aloud in Michael's classroom began only after the current book was completed. During the 2- or 3-day process, Michael selected a favorite short read, such as Scieszka's (1992) *The Stinky Cheese Man*; humor was a recurring characteristic of these short reads. Given busy schedules and pressing curricular tasks, it is important to note that although this particular selection process occurred over 2–3 days, the actual time taken totaled only about 30 minutes, as the students were very familiar with the procedure by this day in June.

There were five phases to this process. The first three phases occurred on the first day during class time; the fourth involved teacher out-of-class time; and the final phase happened during class time on the final day, when Michael presented his final selection and reasons for that selection (see Boyd & Devennie, 2009, for a full explication).

In the first phase, the teacher suggested books. As Michael put forward his nominations, he modeled the talk he expected in the second phase, while also piquing student interest. He pitched books for his audience—for example, "This would only be for the mature people that can handle it, because it's pretty scary" (when referring to *The Witches* [Dahl, 1983]). In just a few minutes (4 minutes, 14 seconds), Michael suggested four texts that would expand what his students were reading on their own, pick up on their interests, and suggest wider reading. All four of the teacher-nominated texts were published before 1990—not because Michael had not read the newer books, but because he considered his role to be to suggest other texts that were worth reading but that his students might not be familiar with. After setting up each of his suggestions, he opened the floor for comments from students who might have already read his nominated text.

The second phase, in which the teacher invited the students to make read-aloud suggestions, was by far the longest at 17 minutes. Students nominated 13 texts, four times more texts than Michael nominated, and more class time was provided to explore these student nominations. During this practice, the students were positioned as knowers and experts: They expanded on many of the book suggestions in response to Michael and other students, and/or asked clarifying and open questions as those who nominated the texts fielded the questions. In addition, Michael took notes, clearly indicating that student input was being considered. During this phase, Michael made about a third of the utterances as he adopted a directive mode of questioning to call upon student knowledge ("Okay, what is that called when animals or other things act like people?") and build upon student contributions ("And is it a series?"). Other questions skillfully led students not simply to summarize a text, but to make judgments that its appropriateness as the next chapter read-aloud ("Is it a book with lots of descriptions, or is it a fairly simple story?"). Michael combined an ability to refrain from dominating the talk with an intimate knowledge of who had read particular books independently. Many of his utterances were questions that drew students into the discussion: "Now you have been reading the Charlie ones [referring to a Roald Dahl series] . . . do you have any other specific ones you would like to nominate?" He modeled making judgments about suitability of texts for read-alouds: "I ruled that one out right away. I've read it, and it just didn't seem like it was a good listen-to story when I read it to a class before." If Michael had not yet read a student-nominated text, he asked the recommending student to bring him a copy.

As you read the following exchange between Michael and Sean, consider these questions: Who is the primary knower here? What does this exchange reveal about the literacy habits in this classroom?

1. MICHAEL: That isn't Merlin as in . . . that isn't about Merlin as a kid, is it?
2. SEAN: It's about Merlin starting out as a kid and becoming a wizard. It's a series. It's the first book.
3. MICHAEL: Is it the first one, *The Lost Years of Merlin* [Barron, 1996]?
4. JACK: How many people have read it?
5. MICHAEL: Has anybody read it besides Sean?
6. SEAN: Um, I don't think so. I'm not sure.
7. MICHAEL: Um, did you write about it in your reading log?
8. SEAN: Yeah, I wrote about the second book, but not the first.

This exchange took only about a minute and a half, but Sean got to pitch his nomination for the next read-aloud. Michael learned that possibly only Sean had read this book; that it is part of a series; and that Sean enjoyed it enough to have read the second one, since Michael remembered that it was a subject of Sean's reading log. Sean elaborated on his nomination as he fielded questions from Michael and another student, Jack.

The third phase of the process, initial polling on the next chapter book read-aloud, was very short but critical. In less than 2 minutes (1 minute, 31 seconds), class members made their choices, and Michael wrapped up the first day of the read-aloud selection process. After 17 recommendations (4 from the teacher and 13 from the students), a student suggested that it was time to take a class poll:

1. MICHAEL: *Witches*, well that's right there (*pointing to the bookcase where there was a copy*). Uh, how to decide . . . [upon which of the nominations to choose]?
2. JACK: Should we have a poll?
3. MICHAEL: We could do a poll.
4. KAZEM: What's a *poll*?
5. MICHAEL: Hannah, would you explain what a *poll* is? Hannah, would you explain the difference between a *poll* and a *vote*?
6. HANNAH: Just to check what people are thinking and, like, in a vote you make whoever gets more, gets it . . . and a poll is to see what it's like.
7. MICHAEL: Informational purposes, and the benevolent dictator gets to decide anyway. Kazem?

Most of these students were familiar with the distinction between a poll and a vote and could articulate the difference. This awareness that their input mattered, but that the teacher would make the final decision, is key to understanding this classroom culture. Michael consistently structured opportunities for student voice and choice, which served as instructional checkpoints. Because it was the teacher's responsibility to plan and implement instruction, he was the one who would determine the next chapter read-aloud.

The fourth phase involved Michael's taking time outside class to review the nominations and peruse any texts with which he was not familiar. Michael conscientiously reviewed his notes and read "a decent selection, so I am able to see if it will grab the kids' interests and mine." If he had not already done so, he read the winning nomination in its entirety, so he would be able to "do a better job knowing what's coming. It also allows me to be more aware of topics, vocabulary, literary devices, concerns, and who knows what."

The much-anticipated final phase of this literacy event occurred at the beginning of morning meeting on a subsequent day. Michael formally announced and explained his choice for the next chapter read-aloud. Michael took his time with his announcement (3 minutes, 26 seconds), and it accomplished much more than simply revealing the winning title. As you read Michael's announcement below, consider how he simultaneously increased the students' excitement and validated their contributions. What phrases accentuated the drama of the moment? In what ways did he show that his decision was governed by what he knew about his students? How many nominations did he acknowledge? In what ways did this announcement reveal the culture of reading in this classroom?

"I spent a bunch of time yesterday after school thinking about what you guys said about each of the books, and I kinda thumbed through them. I really wanted to do a Roald Dahl story, but a lot of you have heard them—and a couple people, who will remain nameless, are just no fun at all. Um, so I'm not going to do a Roald Dahl book. You, of course, can read them on your own. But it was very difficult. I ruled out *The Phantom Tollbooth* [Juster, 1961] because it really is better to read it yourself, although it's a fun story to listen to. And a couple of these others looked pretty enticing. Like *Circle of Magic* [Pierce, 1997], especially after looking at Reece's log . . . but it's too late. The decision has been made for what book we're reading next. *Dragon Rider* [Funke, 2004] and *Circle of Magic* both were very tempting. Dragons are kind of in these days, of course. Um, and *Circle of Magic*, Reece did this very cool reading log yesterday where it was written . . . 'it was a circle, kind of,' it was very fun to read that. And *The House of the Scorpion* [Farmer, 2002] I didn't have to look at. Here's something you should be aware of: Does anybody know what these are? It's a medal; they're pretty famous ones. They're called Newbery [Honor] Awards, and any book that gets a Newbery [Honor] Award probably is pretty good. It might not appeal to you, but it's probably well written and a lot of people like it. So if you see something like that, it's a good bet that it'd be worth trying. *The Sea of Trolls* [Faramer, 2004] sounded very enticing. There is going to be a little book group, I believe, that will be reading *The Sea of Trolls*. So I thought, hmm, if this group is probably going to read that, then I think I will pass on that one. Although I think it's on my list of ones I need to read myself and then share in class later. Now [*The Lost Years of Merlin*, especially having Merlin in it, had a lot of appeal. Um, but I just decided to pass on that one for no particular reason. And that left *Midnight for Charlie Bone*. I took a closer look at this, and started reading it; I didn't get all the way through the book last night. Um, it looks like you'll really like it, so we're going to give this one a shot. So it's really great to have all these wonderful suggestions. It's a testament to the great reading that you guys are doing." [Michael then makes the transition to reading log time and starts to hand back the reading logs he has read and responded to from the preceding day.]

Michael's announcement was clearly not scripted, as its content was contingent on these students' contributions. However, it was a culmination of a framework that is both structured and replicable, provided teachers are prepared to allow space for student voice and choice. Michael positioned his students as "capable of understanding and appreciating literature," and used reading aloud as a key time when he could foment student excitement. In transforming the read-aloud selection into a literacy event, Michael ensured an appropriate selection, while also fostering literate talk. Here was real talk about books—authentic exchanges where students expanded the scope of the conversation according to their interests, and where the teacher provided the language, tone, and varied roles to explore and articulate an understanding and appreciation of literature. This event allowed the students to set the pace and scope of the discourse, but not all literacy events do that. When Michael performed the chapter book read-aloud, he was very particular about protecting the aesthetic experience (Rosenblatt, 1978/1994) of the book. He determined when the group stopped for questions and comments, how long they stopped, and what the focus of each stop was.

PERFORMING READING ALOUD

Having announced the selection for the read-aloud in morning meeting, Michael started *Midnight for Charlie Bone* (Nimmo, 2003) that very afternoon. Listening to Michael read was a thrilling experience. These third graders settled on the floor in various positions and waited expectantly to be entertained. Michael did not disappoint them. He believed that reading aloud was worthy of instructional time in and of itself, and was to be enjoyed. Therefore, he did not plan formal instruction around the books he read aloud, although you will see how his spontaneous teaching provoked his students' thinking, extended their vocabulary, and heightened their awareness of literary craft. This time was a nonscripted time guided by the "in-the-moment resonance" of the shared experience, where reader response is unique to these readers, this text, and this context (Galda et al., 2010). Two interdependent guidelines supported this experience: First, the read-aloud performance time was protected; and second, pauses in the reading performances were kept brief and focused on one point at a time.

Pedagogical flexibility and expertise were necessary to enact these guidelines in ways ensuring that teachable moments were in support of the aesthetic experience, and in ways serving the ultimate goal of "getting kids excited about reading." It quickly became clear that Michael did not practice a laissez-faire approach when he paused in his reading. A close examination of these pauses reveals their almost rhythmic timing and length. Many of Michael's pauses were less than 10 seconds long; some lasted 20–30 seconds, others about a minute. He stopped more frequently at the beginning of a book than he did later in the reading. The first day's reading of *Midnight for Charlie Bone* lasted 17 minutes, and

7 pages were read; 10 of these minutes were spent reading, and the other 7 were spent talking. There were 18 pauses in the reading, 17 of them initiated by the teacher. On day 5, the reading lasted a little longer (for 23 minutes), and almost twice as many pages (13) were read, with again about two-thirds of the time spent in reading aloud and one-third in talking. The mostly teacher-initiated pauses (12 out of 15) directed attention and promoted noticing, but for the most part were short enough that they did not interfere with the momentum of the narrative.

Michael's stated objectives for reading chapter books aloud were (1) that students would learn to enjoy reading so much that they would become lifelong readers; and (2) that they would learn to look at books in particular ways and develop the skills to talk about them. In fact, Michael often joked that he wanted his students to love reading so much that it would get them past their fourth-grade year of standardized tests.

Why, then, did Michael pause during his read-aloud? As you read the excerpt below, pay particular attention to the role of Michael's talk. How did he support Arianna?

1. MICHAEL: Okay, who can tell me what a *prologue* is? (*a 6-second silence*) Arianna, what's a prologue?

2. ARIANNA: Isn't it, um, like—um, I don't know.

3. MICHAEL: Well, let me show you. (*Shows Arianna the two-page spread of the prologue at the beginning of* Midnight for Charlie Bone.)

4. ARIANNA: Okay . . . Oh, yeah! Is it the thingy? Um, in the book, and yeah!

5. MICHAEL: Okay . . .

6. ANA: The thingy in the book and yeah?

7. MICHAEL: A little more detail would be good.

8. ARIANNA: I was about to say what it was. Michael showed us . . .

9. MICHAEL: Well, what is it?

10. ARIANNA: Um, it's like, is it like about the book?

11. MICHAEL: Kind of. That's getting on the right track. Jack?

12. JACK: Is it sort of like a beginner? Or, not a beginner, but like, before . . . kind of hard to explain.

13. MICHAEL: It's kind of like before the talk.

14. SEAN: Before the story.

15. MICHAEL: Before the story. It usually gives you some good information that you need to have. It sets the book up so that you'll be ready to read.

16. JACK: Yeah, like [in] *Eragon*, you wouldn't know anything if it didn't have, like, how it said the lady . . .

17. MICHAEL: That was my next question: Where did we see a prologue before? And it was *Eragon*. Okay, the prologue for *Midnight for Charlie Bone* that was written by Jenny . . .

Michael started with a question: "Okay, who can tell me what a prologue is?" (turn 1). He waited 6 seconds, and then he asked a specific student, "Arianna, what's a prologue?" (turn 1). This student did not know, but Michael did not simply move to another student. He showed Arianna what it was in the book. He then worked to help her fully answer the question before opening it to the group. Shortly after this exchange, Michael began reading the prologue.

In just over 10 minutes, only two pages were read. These students discussed what a prologue was, and understood that it "sets the book up so that you'll be ready to read" (turn 15). But Michael accomplished more than that; he set his students up for the read-aloud event. And this indeed was his recurring practice: He began each succeeding session with a review in preparation for reading. He asked questions and expected answers, but he also helped students elaborate. Students made connections across texts even before he asked, because they knew that this was valued, and that this is what good readers do. They also continued to pause and appreciate good phrasing, and to check that they understood vocabulary.

Michael stopped most frequently for vocabulary and figurative language checking, as well as for discussing literary elements that move the plot along, heighten or foreshadow suspense, or reveal character. Many times the pauses were focused vocabulary checks. There were quick exchanges, such as that for *tureen,* when Michael asked, "What's *tureen*? Anybody got an idea?" When there was no response, he quickly supplied the answer, "Big bowl," and then reread the word in context: "The soup tureen was very heavy.'" Students often provided a quick response: When Michael asked, "What does *weasely* mean?", Hussni responded with "Sneaky." On other occasions, a longer exchange was needed to make sense of a word. The following exchange was initiated by Michael's question "What are *mothballs*?" As you read, notice how these students were willing to take the risk of exploring meaning publicly.

1. MICHAEL: What are *mothballs*?

2. JACK: Mmmm . . . balls that are made of moth?

3. MICHAEL: That's what they sound like, but no. Do you know?

4. SUSAN: Um, they're kind of like dust bunnies, a little bit?

5. MICHAEL: No, no. Good thought.

6. SUZANNA : They're these . . . they look like little cotton balls, and they keep away the moths.

7. MICHAEL: Yeah, they're usually white, round, although you can get flakes, and you put them in closets or drawers where you have woolly things, and they keep moths away so they don't lay eggs, and then their larvae don't go around eating your sweaters. (*Students laugh.*) But they have a real distinctive odor, and it's kind of stinky.

Michael was comfortable giving direct feedback. His evaluations were clearly not put-downs, but simply matter of fact ("No, no. Good thought" [turn 5], and students continued exploring. When Suzanna provided a response that was close enough to build upon (turn 6), Michael expanded on it, using words like "larvae" and "distinctive" that further enhanced attention to vocabulary (turn 7).

Vocabulary checks led into connections within and across texts. During another read-aloud session, Michael followed up the explication of *endowed* with an associated question about Bloor's Academy, a place for students who are endowed with special powers. As you read, notice how the vocabulary check flowed into a significance of the story check and a recognition that the prologue foreshadowed what was to come.

1. MICHAEL: *Endowed*—what does that mean?

2. SHING: Like you have powers.

3. MICHAEL: Yes, that you have something . . . that you've been given something. Um, Bloor's Academy—where have I heard that name? Susan?

4. SUSIE: In the prologue.

5. MICHAEL: Yeah, but I—we just heard it a minute ago.

6. TERESA: Oh! *Oh*! I know!

7. MICHAEL: Teresa?

8. TERESA:Um, wasn't it the orphanage? Yeah. That was burned down.

9. SUSIE: It was in the newspaper.

10. MICHAEL: Yeah, the kid in the newspaper . . .

11. TERESA: His name is Bloor!

12. MICHAEL: His name is Bloor! Good listening, guys.

Michael opened with a vocabulary check on *endowed,* the meaning of which has significance in the story (turn 1). He acknowledged Shing's response (turn 2) and moved to connect it to a place (turn 3) and a person (turns 11, 12) that he knew were important. His leading prompts elicited where the word was used in the text ("In the prologue" [turn 4]), what the context for its use was ("wasn't it the orphanage?" [turn 8]), and where the name was referenced ("It was in the newspaper" [turn 9]). Michael thus led his students to listen attentively and to notice connections and foreshadowing.

At other times, a vocabulary check resulted in couching the meaning in the context of community life. Such was the case with the discussion of the meaning of *vandal.* This followed a question to check understanding of the relationship between two minor characters, Uncle Paton and Miss Ingledew. Here we see Michael guiding his students through inference making.

1. MICHAEL: So, I think, just with that brief meeting—Uncle Paton kind of thinks Miss Ingledew is nice.

2. STUDENTS: (*in chorus*) Ooooooo!

3. MICHAEL: What do you think it is about Ingledew he likes?

4. MAEVE: That she likes to read.

5. MICHAEL: The books. He's very into them, and she has a bookshop. Okay.

   (*Michael reads for 7 seconds and then pauses again. He rereads "Uncle Paton, you're a vandal!" and pauses to ask:*)

6. MICHAEL: Uh-oh, what's a *vandal?*

7. JACK: *Ohh!!*

8. MICHAEL: Teresa?

9. TERESA: Um, like a bad person who kind of like steals stuff or . . .

10. MICHAEL: Might steal—what else?

11. JACK: Wreck property.

12. MICHAEL: Yeah, he might wreck things here and there, like if somebody came and broke windows in the school or damaged something around the school, they'd be a vandal. Yes. Okay, good.

In this excerpt, we see two pauses in their entirety. We get a sense not only of the "stop, notice, consider, move on" nature of these interludes, but of their overall coherence in service of the story. First Michael established that Uncle Paton and Miss Ingledew might like each other (turn 1) and why (turns 3–5). Michael then continued reading until there was an unusual use of the word *vandal*. Michael ensured that students understood the meaning (turn 6), they explored what a vandal does (turns 9–11), and Michael offered a local context for meaning (turn 12). They noticed the use of the word, but did not discuss further why Miss Ingledew would call Uncle Paton a vandal; it was sufficient that they understood its meaning (turn 11).

Other vocabulary checks extended to figurative language, such as when the author uses the phrase "drown language" and Michael asked, "How do you drown words? Hannah?" Hannah immediately responded, "Um, like, it was too loud so you couldn't hear the words, and you only hear the thunder."

These brief vocabulary check excerpts illustrate how the pauses in the read-aloud were very much in the service of making meaning, of clarifying, but also were very clearly not allowed to get in the way of enjoying the book as an aesthetic experience. Michael's pauses also drew attention to the craft of the author as she builds suspense.

1. MICHAEL: Ooo . . . he's in the dark.
2. HERBERT: Nooo . . .
3. MICHAEL: Scary basement . . .
4. MAEVE: With that box . . .

Note how these utterances took on the character of an intimate shorthand. This exchange could be considered short and choppy, but in fact Michael and the students were engaging in a form of *coded speech—* incomplete sentences that nonetheless communicated effectively and built upon the previous utterances (Vygotsky, 1986). They signified an ease and rapport that could only be developed over time. These staccato beats conveyed and emphasized the suspense; then the teacher and students returned to the action. However, during other suspenseful moments, Michael slowed the pace down, drawing out the anticipation. Notice the exploratory "could" language in the next excerpt.

1. MICHAEL: If she'd been right outside the door, then they know we could go out the back—but she's not there. So where is she?
2. SAM: She could be in the back?
3. MICHAEL: She could be.
4. SUSAN: She could be hiding.

5. HERBERT: She could be . . .

6. MICHAEL: She could be anywhere.

In this excerpt, we see the possibilities as students responded to the openness and suspense of Nimmo's writing and Michael's reading. Michael drew attention to what they did not know (turn 1) and invited conjecture. Sam's " . . . in the back?" (turn 2) was a possibility, as was Susan's suggestion that "She could be hiding" (turn 4). Michael talked over Herbert's suggestion and concluded, "She could be anywhere" (turn 6). The students had noticed that the author withholds information.

Associations with vocabulary and their clues to contexts in the reading were also explored. Often, as in the example below, students had to pull from their background knowledge to make sense of Michael's question.

1. MICHAEL: So he's going to stay there all week and will call home just on weekends. Wouldn't that be kind of hard to do?

2. ANA: That's like boarding school, except you don't even come home on the weekends.

Michael's recognition of Ana's response was his return to reading aloud. These students wanted to listen; they did not want to stop. This was apparent in the following excerpt, occurring right at the end of the school day, when most students want to get out as fast as possible. In this class, they wanted one of their peers, Maeve, to take up the reading when Michael announced he was going to stop. Michael firmly, and with humor, ended the reading and the school day.

1. HERBERT: Uh-oh!

2. STUDENTS: *Nooo!*

3. MICHAEL: I have to stop!

4. MAEVE: No, you don't. No, you don't. No, you don't.

5. MICHAEL: Yes, I do.

6. MAEVE: We don't care if we stay after school! We don't care!

7. NICK: Aw, Maeve, why don't you just read it?

8. ANA: Maeve, don't say anything.

9. HERBERT: Keep reading!

10. MICHAEL: It . . . there was a note right in the book that said, "Stop here!"

It is apparent that these students were engaged in active listening. In this excerpt, we also see the banter that marked this classroom environment.

In this part of their day, students' public responses were delimited by Michael's tight control of the floor. Michael decided when to stop, what to focus on during a stop, whose contribution counted, and when he would continue reading. He mediated the flow and interruptions of the read-aloud as a form of on-the-fly assessment—spot checks, as it were, of the students' vocabulary, comprehension, enjoyment, and engagement. His "Did you notice this?" or "What did that mean?" focused the students' attention on the purposefulness of the author's craft, and provided the language that they needed to describe it. This was largely accomplished in brief, teacher-controlled exchanges with a single focus. This contrasted with the openness of the talk surrounding the selection of the next book to read aloud. There were times to listen and times to talk. Michael and his students experienced a range of literacy events throughout the day. The two types explored here were part of the overall literacy event of reading aloud.

READING ALOUD, STANDARDS, AND REAL TALK

Expert teachers practice pedagogical flexibility. Michael did not preplan the scope and timing of his "stops" during reading. These breaks from reading aloud were not predetermined, but born of an experienced and attuned intent to enhance the read-aloud event. We witness this again in Michael's responses during the selection of the next read-aloud text. Student input provided two kinds of feedback: what they enjoyed reading about and how well they could articulate their ideas. As the teacher, Michael could respond to this feedback, considering interest, proficiency, and curricular objectives in his instructional decision making. Furthermore, this whole process explicitly and authentically addressed learning standards (whether they be the state learning standards that were in place while these data were collected or the Common Core State Standards adopted in 2010).

Michael was very familiar with standards because he valued and understood them as sought-after behaviors in the elementary classroom. These sought-after behaviors included "comprehending and critiquing imaginative texts ... drawing on personal experiences and knowledge to understand the text and recognizing the social, historical and cultural features of the text" (NYS Learning Standard 2) or "reading closely to determine what text says explicitly and making inferences from it" (CCSS Reading 3.1). Across both measures, understanding literary elements such as setting, character, plot, theme, and evaluating literary merit were sought after behaviors. Michael did not script a lesson to teach for these behaviors; rather, they were an organic part of productive talk about books in his classroom, one where collaborative reasoning (Chinn et al., 2001) was invited. This classroom's embedded practices of language for critical analysis and evaluation were anticipated outcomes documented in both state standards and the new Common Core Standards. In his classroom, Michael both modeled and highlighted the language that literate people use as they listen and read to "analyze and evaluate experiences, ideas, information and issues." His students were supported as they developed critical discernment; they were expected to "make decisions about the quality and dependability of texts and experiences." In fact, learning standards align so well with Michael's objectives for reading aloud that he could have written them as lesson objectives. He did not teach to a test, nor did he consciously think, "I want to teach standard three today." He taught what made sense in each instance, sense in terms of exploring the book itself, and in terms of the students' ideas. This in-the-moment decision making resulted in opportunities for Michael's students to engage in ways of experiencing books, ways to listen, and ways to talk about books as he first modeled and then invited student participation in literate talk.

THINGS TO THINK ABOUT

- What is the purpose for assigning students book talks to present in class? In what ways does Michael's informal practice of eliciting student talk about books differ from traditional book talks? Compare and contrast the student learning benefits of these two experiences.

- List ways you think a teacher's pedagogical content knowledge (in Michael's case, his knowledge of children's literature) influences a teacher's ability, comfort level, and willingness to be flexible. What do you consider to be your areas of deep knowledge? How can you exploit them in your classroom?

CHAPTER 6

Learning Felicity

Morning Meeting, Reading Logs, and Talking about Books

I'm going to stop here at the exciting part—because you always do that in <u>Eragon</u> and other books. I know you will be anxious to know what happens next. Ha! Ha! Ha!—**Sean** (closing comment in one of his reading log entries)

Eight-year-old Sean pulls his reading log from his backpack, finds his pencil, and squirms around a bit to get comfortable at the kitchen table. With some automaticity, he writes the date and "Dear Michael"; then he stops. He chews on his pencil as he reads the preceding entry. He has been reading the second book in Suzanne Collins's *Underland Chronicles* series. Last week he wrote, "Like everybody, Gregor [the main character] can be nice and he can be mad and so on." He chuckles as he rereads Michael's comment that the author gives Gregor "bad qualities once in a while."

He gets up to sharpen his pencil, then sits down again to write. He begins, "As you know, I am reading *Gregor and the Prophecy of Bane* by Suzanne Collins" [Collins, 2005]. He ponders for a short while, then drops his head and begins to write in earnest.

Gregor is a lot like Harry Potter and Merlin because they all have powers that they didn't know about. Like when Merlin shouted, "Look there's a seagull" and ran away from the village bully. Then a real seagull appeared. Thats sort of like when Gregor turned into rager mode and killed the squids. This is also like when Harry Potter ran from Dudley's gang and then Harry ended up on top of the school by magic.

Sean gets up, pours himself a drink of water, and looks at the time: soccer practice in 30 minutes. He sits again and quickly writes,

> I really like the fact that Gregor is the warrior of the prophecys in that series. He was talked into being a warrior by the underlanders. I think that is pretty wierd. Your friend, Sean.

Sean was a member of Michael's third-grade classroom community—a literate community where particular ways of thinking, talking, and writing about books were modeled and privileged in safe and recursive ways. Members of this community were provided with structured and pleasurable contexts where reading and writing were expected, where they had choices about what they read, and where the teacher's talk continually modeled embedded use of literate language. For example, Michael, their teacher, used the terms for elements of fiction (e.g., *plot, character, climax*) when he asked questions and built upon the students' talk as they shared their reading logs. With frequent use of humor and of specific examples from student readings, he encouraged these third graders not just to summarize a book but to notice the language that denoted excitement or climax, to understand the characters, and to connect readings to other texts. He encouraged them to articulate what they thought as they responded to the text (Rosenblatt, 1978/1994), pushing them a little farther to support their responses, and providing the language and guidance to do so. He was teaching them how to select books, how not to give away the ending when talking about a book, and how to read books in various ways. Michael's language and expectations shaped how his students thought and expressed their responses to the books they were reading; he made literate language relevant to his students by applying it to their readings; and he explicitly encouraged them to appropriate literate phrasing and thinking, and praised them when they did.

These 8- and 9-year-olds were developing literate language and ways of talking (Pellegrini & Galda, 1998). In more scholarly terms, they were rehearsing an *elaborated code* (Bernstein, 1971) where they could understand and begin to use specialized *decontextualized language* (Olson, 1977) that aligned with successful schooling. Michael recognized that this kind of literate language did not just happen. There needed to be, as he put it,

> "just this constant talking about books and literature and relating it to other things that they do. I think that if you talk about it a lot, it becomes more of a natural thing, an easier thing.

They are going to have a lot more felicity in the whole thing. It's a learned ability; I don't think kids can just come along and talk about books. They need to have those ways of looking at books to be able to do that."

Teacher and student talk in this classroom allowed students to learn to use literate talk and to develop their membership in this classroom community. The *morning meeting*—the traditional practice of gathering the entire class in a community circle for activities and sharing (Kreite & Bechtel, 2002)—was a central means through which these third graders practiced, and heard consistently modeled, literate ways to talk about books. Michael exploited and expanded the full value of the morning meeting ritual through the well-developed sharing of *reading logs*.

In this chapter, we explore the routines and strategies that Michael put in place to support his students to become literate thinkers, speakers, and writers (Boyd & Devennie, 2009; Galda et al., 2010; Morrow, 2009). Classroom talk reveals how Michael enacted routines and strategies, as well as whether (and, if so, when and how) he deviated from them in the 2 weeks of morning meetings that are the focus of this chapter.

BUILDING A LITERATE THIRD-GRADE COMMUNITY

About half of these students had been decoders when they entered third grade; that is, they were just "sounding out" words when they read. The other students' reading had ranged from fairly fluent to fluent. By June, almost the end of the academic year, these 8- and 9-year-olds had benefited from the structures and routines that Michael had maintained all year long to support literate behaviors. Michael's first priority was to create and nurture a learning community where students *wanted* to read. So he embedded purposeful reading, writing, and talking about books into structured routines that "tend more to the more enjoyable and the fun end of things." Like all the teachers at Hillyside Elementary, Michael had daily English language arts (ELA) time, but here we focus on another daily routine where literate behaviors were learned and practiced: the morning meeting, and specifically the role reading logs played during the morning meeting.

Morning Meetings

As the third graders in Michael's class arrived, they hung their backpacks on the hooks in the hall outside the classroom and put things into or took them out of their "cubbies" as they prepared for the day.

It was an unstructured, relaxed social time that preceded gathering in the circle for morning meeting. On one morning, Michael was sitting at his computer, browsing pictures; a parent from a previous class had sent photos of Michael moving a beehive (Michael's brother was a beekeeper, and there was an annual field trip to visit him). Sean joined him and spent several minutes looking at the photos with Michael, and discussing the logistics of splitting hives, before wandering off. Then Susie happened by, looked at the photos, and called Teresa over to "come see, all bees . . . this big."

Another morning, Michael informally shared a poem he had just retrieved from his mailbox. It was from one of Michael's former students, now in fifth grade, who had read a poem called "Turtle Thoughts" and "thought we might like it because we [this classroom community] have a turtle, and the poem goes like this . . . " Michael then read the poem to the students in the circle, ending with the comment, "Doesn't he [the turtle in the classroom] look like he's up there thinking a lot of the time?" Michael asked Sam to go stick the poem onto the turtle tank, as "I thought he might like to read it . . . well . . . maybe not."

These two anecdotes illustrate how the sense of community fostered by Michael extended well beyond the immediate third-grade class, and how reading, sharing, and learning were parts of everything this class did, not simply of the formal curricula. We see the relaxed, inclusive, and warm way Michael directed his students; there was humor, there was sharing, and there was space to explore and share learning.

By the time the Pledge of Allegiance had been read over the intercom, the students had all usually made their way to the circle, and Michael was taking care of attendance, notes from home, and other necessary housekeeping. Although morning meeting traditionally includes a sharing time where students bring artifacts from home and share about happenings, the framework for morning meeting in this class was the scheduled sharing of, and talking about, reading logs.

Reading Logs

The use of reading logs was a consistent and well-defined literacy event in this classroom. At the beginning of the academic year, Michael had assigned every student a day of the week for sharing his or her reading log. Michael had also provided a letter-style reading log model (see Figure 6.1), which each student had taped to the inside of an exercise book used exclusively for reading log entries. There were 18 students in this class, so typically 3 or 4 students read their logs on a designated day. In Sean's case, his reading log was due every Thursday.

The guidelines for reading logs were simple. Students could write about any book they were reading independently. Each student read his or her weekly log aloud in class as part of the morning meeting, and other students responded with questions or comments. After this sharing, Michael collected each reading log, read it carefully, wrote specific dialogic comments, and faithfully returned it at the beginning of the next day's morning meeting. Michael articulated the reading–writing connection captured in reading logs:

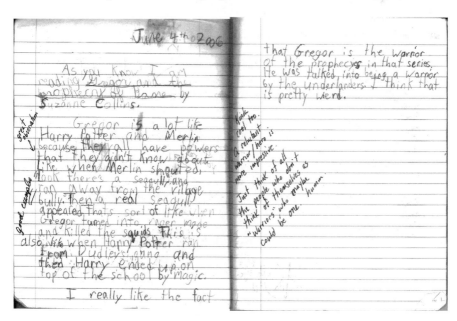

The following is an example of what a letter should/could look like:

September 11, YEAR

Dear Michael,

    I have been reading <u>The Twits</u>, by Roald Dahl. I chose this story on the suggestion of my dad. I have really liked the story so far because it is very funny. The characters that I have read about so far are Mr. and Mrs. Twit. He is kind of gross because he has food stuck in his beard. Both of them are mean to each other. Once Mrs. Twit put worms in Mr. Twit's spaghetti! I can't wait to find out what happens next. I think it has something to do with monkeys, because I saw an illustration with some monkeys in it.
       Sincerely,
       Guinness

Notice:

- The capitals in the date, greeting, title of the book, author, names, and the closing.
- The commas in the date, after the teacher's name, and after the closing.
- It's indented right after the greeting.
- The title of the book is underlined.

Here are some ideas as to what you could write about in your log (you probably wouldn't use all of them at one time):

- Tell who the author is.
- Who are the characters? Tell about them. Do you have a favorite? If so, why?
- Talk about the plot or what happens in the story. Tell about the action or events. Are there problems that the characters have? Is there a solution?
- Where and when does the story take place (setting)?
- Talk about the illustrations or pictures. Who is the illustrator? Do the illustrations make the story better?
- How do you feel about the story? Are there some really good parts, funny sections, exciting happenings, and scary scenes? Why do you like or dislike the story?
- If you were the author, would you change anything?
- Do you think others would want to read the book? Why or why not?
- If you are not finished with the book, making predictions would be interesting.
- If you're done, you might write about what will happen after the story ends.

FIGURE 6.1. The reading log information given by Michael to his students.

"By having them read, pushing a half hour every night, I think that that's real good time spent, if they're really on task and they're really reading. And by giving them a purpose of writing a letter to me and their classmates about what they've been reading, they have to kind of pay attention to what they've read. 'Cause a lot of kids will sit with a book in front of their face, and they may read all of the words and turn all the pages—but if they haven't been thinking about it as they go along, you know, they're . . . they really don't get too much out of it. And so, the purpose of the log, I think, it . . . it takes care of that somewhat. The other thing with the log: It gives kids a chance to reflect on the story, both in just . . . in terms of what happened and what the plot was; but, as the year goes along, what I like to see them doing is give their own personal thoughts about the book, to compare it to other books that the same author has written. So that there are a lot of different things that they can go with other than just retell the story. And the kids are really getting the idea and so on, and start to do that— sometimes with a little help from here or from parents, or if they take the time to read the sample letter and suggestions in the front of the book. Those things start to happen more and more as the year goes along, and I think that that's what makes reading so much more fun is the . . . not just retelling the story, but thinking about it. So the reading logs help to get us going in that direction."

And so reading, thinking, and writing were nurtured in the preparation of reading log entries. Through sharing and talking about reading logs in morning meeting, Michael accomplished two additional important literacy-learning objectives. First, Michael pushed *in-the-moment* thinking, or "shaping at the point of utterance" (Britton, 1993); second, he used reading logs as springboards for feedback and modeling of literate language and literate behaviors.

In-the-moment thinking was evident as students responded to teacher questions such as the following:

"Yeah, now, why did he let himself have that happen to him?" [*The Lion, the Witch and the Wardrobe* (Lewis, 1950)]

"Do you remember why he wants to do that?" [*Eragon* (Paolini, 2003)]

"What do you mean by *gripping*?" [*Kirsten Saves the Day* (Shaw, 1988)]

"Is the Bard gonna be able to get everything straightened out? Solve all the problems, do you think?" [*The Sea of Trolls* (Farmer, 2004)]

During discussion of reading logs, Michael posed many questions. Sometimes these teacher questions, though inspired by a particular reading log, were posed to the group as a whole—for example, "Why would that . . . why do all these authors have their characters be orphans?" But for the most part they were specific and addressed to the writer of the reading log, with the purpose of positioning that student as knower (Berry, 1981); he or she knew what information was needed to answer the question and could make judgments accordingly. As you read the excerpt below, notice how Maeve answered Michael's question about Mullet Fingers, a character in *Hoot* (Hiaasen, 2002). As you read, consider the ways she displayed interpretive authority. Maeve had just read a long entry in which she explained how the name Mullet Fingers was given.

1. MICHAEL: Oh, well, what's the name, Mullet Fingers? Would you like that name?
2. MAEVE: Well, it's a nickname, because he doesn't really want a name and he doesn't need one. And, um . . .
3. MICHAEL: How could you not need a name?
4. MAEVE: Well, he lives in the woods.
5. MICHAEL: Oh, I see.
6. MAEVE: And, um, he's very cool. He can catch alligators and poisonous snakes. And, um, the dog bite, the swelling went down a little bit, and on his other arm is a big bruise because he had to take the—there's like a tube in the hospital on his arm, that he had to take it out . . .
7. MICHAEL: Now, did you say you've seen the movie yet?
8. MAEVE: No, I'm reading the book before, and Suzanna told me that she finished the book in 2 days.
9. MICHAEL: Uh-huh, cool.

Note that the longest utterance in this exchange was made by Maeve, the student (turn 6). Michael's initial question was a general one, because (presumably) he had not read this text. Maeve's response was specific, and so Michael's next question, "How could you not need a name?" (turn 3), was contingent on Maeve's response. Maeve then volunteered a longer explanation, which displayed her understanding of the text. Michael's evaluative "Uh-huh, cool" (turn 9) terminated the exchange.

As the Mullet Fingers exchange illustrated, Michael did a lot of the questioning. In many ways, Michael and the reading log sharer "performed" individual conversations, while other students listened and learned. For the most part, the other students were likely just to comment, but occasionally they asked questions such as "How did he have a sword in his hand?" or "How thick was Jack's book?" On one occasion, shown below, this led to a gentle reinforcement of the value of student questioning. Michael made a generalized statement and then quickly moved on, immediately returning authority to his students:

1. ARIANNA: I have a question for Jack.
2. MICHAEL: Go ahead.
3. ARIANNA: Um, why does he kill . . . (*inaudible*)?
4. JACK: Wait, you mean, why did he kill the lady?
5. ARIANNA: Yeah.
6. JACK: 'Cause she was trying to, like, kill him. She turned into, like, this flying monster, like [I described] in my reading log. And she's trying to, like, eat him or something, so he sliced her in half.
7. ARIANNA: Yeah, but why'd he kill his mom too?
8. JACK: No, he didn't. The Minotaur did.
9. ARIANNA: Oh, and he killed the Minotaur.
10. JACK: Yeah.
11. ARIANNA: Oh.
12. MICHAEL: Always good to ask questions.
13. JACK: And he has the Minotaur's horn as a souvenir.
14. MICHAEL: I wonder if there are any special powers by having the Minotaur's horn?

This exchange began with Arianna's bidding for the floor because she had a question for Jack, the student whose reading log was the focus at this time. Her question and follow-up question (turns 3, 7) were handled by Jack, who first made sure that he understood the question— "Wait, you mean, why did he kill the lady?" (turn 4)—and then provided an elaborated response (turn 6) and a clarification (turn 8). Michael's evaluative contribution ("Always good to ask questions" [turn 12]) did not shut Jack down as he added one more detail ("And he has the Minotaur's horn as a souvenir" [turn 13]). Michael's wondering aloud about the possible special powers of such a horn validated and extended thinking about Jack's reading log. Here we see how the design of the reading log sharing was such that the students were the authorities: They had selected and read the books; they were positioned to make judgments about characters and plots, as well as comparisons across books. It also encouraged other students to ask questions, as they actively listened.

Sharing and talking about reading logs facilitated a second literacy-learning objective: It provided authentic and immediate opportunities for embedding another level and type of feedback and modeling. Michael's questioning and comments immediately recast student sharing in terms of literate language and literate behaviors. For example, we see the sophisticated critical literacy skill of making connections across texts. As you read the following exchange, notice the student-proposed connections across characters from different books.

1. MICHAEL: Does anybody know a character from another story that when, uh, he or she is being given a really hard time and made mad, like, special powers help save the day for him? . . . Does your character *know* that they're special powers?

2. SUZANNA: Um, well, Harry Potter is sort of like that.

3. MICHAEL: That's the one that came to my mind. Okay . . .

4. SUZANNA: It's not exactly when he's mad, but, like, um, he wasn't really mad when the snake . . .

5. MICHAEL: Um, correct. But the kids at school . . . I think there are other books that are like that too—where kids find, like, resources, like, hidden resources within themselves that help them deal with problems.

6. SEAN: Oh, Gregor!

7. JACK: Oh, yeah, Gregor!

8. HANNAH: Gregor and Matilda [the title character in Dahl's (1988) *Matilda*].

9. MICHAEL: Like Gregor in his "ragey" thing, and Matilda and, you know, with her, like, er . . .

10. SHING: TV. When she's watching TV.

11. MICHAEL: Yes, okay . . .

12. KAZEM: And the TV turns on.

13. SUSAN: Well, in *Eragon*, when Eragon said (*inaudible*) during that sort of . . .

14. MICHAEL: Yeah, he didn't know he could do that. But just, like, the necessity or the real big trouble he was in brought that on. Excellent examples, guys. Okay . . . one of the things that is fun to read when I'm reading your reading logs is when you make connections like that. When you have something happen in one story and you go, "Oh, I remember that thing happening in another story!" and like that there—that's always pretty good. Jack?

Michael initiated this discussion of characters that have special powers to help save the day (turn 1). Seven students responded, offering four different characters. Suzanna proposed Harry Potter (turn 2). Michael explicitly affirmed Suzanna's nomination with "That's the one that came to my mind. Okay . . . " (turn 3), but his students had more to add. Suzanna further supported her choice (turn 4), and then Sean and Jack put forward Gregor (turns 6 and 7). Hannah repeated Gregor and added Matilda (turn 8); Shing and Kazem built on Hannah's suggestion of Matilda (turns 10 and 11); and Susan nominated Eragon (turn 13). Michael's contributions affirmed all his students' nominations (turns 5, 9, and 14). He explicitly praised this way of communicating in talk and in writing.

Now think of the intertextual connections 8-year-old Sean made in his reading log in the opening vignette. Perhaps, as he was writing, Sean was remembering the conversation during the morning meeting that took place earlier that day, part of which you have just read. When he read this log entry aloud the next day, Michael responded, "Okay, excellent, excellent! I love it when people relate what's happening in one story with what they've heard in other stories. I think that's a really interesting thing to do. Excellent! So you're really enjoying that, right?" Sean beamed.

Michael recognized that students required explicit support in making these kinds of connections, and he explicated the greater strategy:

> "Well, the reading logs start out with almost all of the kids just being a retelling of what they've read. And then what I try to do is ask them to elaborate. And when kids do a little bit of elaborating initially, then we jump on that. And I make sure that those kids share in some form or other what they've done and what they've said, because modeling is one of the strongest teaching tools—and especially coming from the kids, not me. And so when Sean came in and started talking about how some story he was reading reminded him of another one, then you

really, like, just, like, fawn all over that. And then the other kids get the idea 'cause they all want that feedback."

In the process of talking about what they had written and shared, Michael provided language useful for discussing books—literary language such as *plot, character,* and *series books.* When Michael asked Susie, "How did you decide to read that book [*Talking to Dragons* (Wrede, 1993)]?" and Susie responded, "Because it was in the series of the last book that I read," Michael pushed her a bit further: "Series are always a good way to go. It's kind of fun. Now, do they have the same characters, some of the same characters?" His question wove in another use of the word *series* and reminded the students that this was one way to make choices about what to read next. These third graders understood and sometimes used words such as *protagonist, antagonist, synopsis,* and *flashback.* When Herbert was sharing his reading log about *Charlie and the Chocolate Factory* (Dahl, 1964), he defined *flashback* and then wittily appropriated it: "It's like a memory . . . and . . . sorry, I was just having a little flashback."

So how do we place value on these necessarily unscripted instructional practices? In this time of accountability, standardized tests, and mandated curriculum, what value do we place on building a literate community in a third-grade classroom? The lessons (both literal and metaphorical) from Michael's 31 years of teaching experience enabled him to take a long-term perspective:

> "If I can get it so kids are readers—and by that I mean that they are confident, that they have the skills to read the words, to decode, to comprehend, to understand—but most importantly that *it is something that they will do.* That they will spend *time* doing. And that comes through enjoyment. Otherwise, they can have all the skills in the world, but if you don't use them, it isn't going to do them a whole lot of good."

In this third-grade classroom community, reading, writing, sharing, and talking about reading logs constituted a daily routine that not only provided the practice these students needed in reading and writing, but socialized them into literate ways of thinking and talking. To be effective, such routines do not have to take a lot of time, but they do have to be consistently honored and followed. Michael devoted a consistent chunk of time to reading logs and morning meeting; he followed guidelines that were relatively fixed, yet allowed for digressions in some instances. This is evident in the patterns of classroom talk surrounding the reading log literacy event.

EFFECTIVE VERSUS EFFICIENT TEACHING: DISCUSSING READING LOGS

Reading logs were implemented at the beginning of the school year, and so by June these third graders were practicing some of the writing and speaking behaviors Michael expected. For the most part, despite Michael's explicit encouragement to "skip details and tell me more about your reaction to the story and what you think is going to happen and that sort of thing," students mostly still told the story in their reading logs. Patiently and consistently, Michael's questions during sharing reading log time built on student contributions to elicit more commentary.

For example, when Jack was reading his entry on *The Lightning Thief* (Riordan, 2005)—"And then he figures out that he has, like, some power. 'Cause he's . . . "—Michael interrupted to ask, "Do you know what kind of power?" Jack's response offered more interpretation:

> "No, it's kind of weird 'cause he's in his bathroom getting, like, bullied by this other big girl, and then he's about to be dunked in the toilet when he—and all of a sudden he uses something and the toilet water splashes up and hits the lady . . . and the bathroom is, like, flooded, except he doesn't have one drop of water."

Michael's persistence was rewarded when Jack embedded judgment and an awareness not to give away the end: "The most exciting and weird part was that—that doesn't give anything away—is when Percy gets in trouble with Ms. Doss." In another example, when Teresa wrote in her log, "I wouldn't have guessed some of the things that have happened so far in *Eragon*. Well, this is how it goes. Eragon woke up in as much pain as a blue whale eats," Michael immediately praised Teresa's simile: "Well, that's a cool comparison there. Because blue whales eat a lot!" But these examples illustrate the importance of the teacher's actively listening and building on student contributions to make teaching points relevant and recursive. Michael's goals for reading logs were long-term literate practices, not checked-off decontextualized skill practice boxes.

The total time spent on these daily reading log sharings during morning meetings varied according to the number of reading logs read. With one exception, three or four reading logs were shared each day, and the daily time spent in sharing logs varied from 5 minutes to 37 minutes. The one exception during the 2-week observation period occurred when the class missed morning meeting due to a whole-school assembly. Thus, on June 1st, Michael ended up with nine reading logs (2 days' worth, plus a log from a student who had been absent and wanted to present her entry), and committed just over a half hour to this activity. The decision to include all nine of these reading logs showcased their importance. Time spent on individual sharings ranged from 30 seconds to approximately 4 minutes, with the average sharing lasting between 1 and 2 minutes. Because these tended to be conversations between Michael and the log reader, plus one or two other students, Michael considered it critical that each student had his or her "moment of sharing." As you read the long excerpt below, notice how many students out of this class of 18 were participating. What might the students who were not participating be learning? Notice, as well, the several examples of literate talk. In this excerpt, Hussni had just shared about Eoin Colfer's *Artemis Fowl* series, and Michael began the discussion of his reading log.

1. JACK: I have a question for Hussni, except I haven't read any of the books.

2. MICHAEL: Oh, I thought you had. Go ahead.

3. JACK: Um, what happened to the troll?

4. HUSSNI: Oh, yeah, the troll.

5. JACK: Did he just run off?

6. HUSSNI: No, the troll is still there. Yeah.

7. MICHAEL: Now, usually in stories trolls are usually—would they fall under the protagonist end of things or the antagonist?

8. HUSSNI: Antagonist.

9. MICHAEL: Yeah, but in this story is he totally, like, a bad guy?

10. HUSSNI: Yeah.

11. MICHAEL: Hmm, I don't know . . .

12. HUSSNI: Yeah, he is.

13. MICHAEL: Who is he . . . who is he . . . isn't he helping in some way?

14. HUSSNI: No, he's trying . . . well, he's helping the guys trying to kill someone. The dude, yeah. So if the troll dies, then they bomb the place. (*Students laugh.*)

15. MICHAEL: But the good guys, the fairies—you'd say the fairies are the good guys in the story, as opposed to Artemis?

16. HUSSNI: Yeah.

17. MICHAEL: Well, if the good guys are using a bad guy to help them?

18. HUSSNI: Right. But they did, like, a mind-wipe thingy. So they controlled him.

19. MICHAEL: And can you explain the acorn dealy?

20. HUSSNI: Oh, yeah! Okay, so if a fairy puts, like, an acorn in the earth, then they say some words and then blue sparks come out of it, and they get healed with magic and then they are full with magic.

(Hussni and Michael continue discussing the plot, and Michael asks whether Hussni would recommend the book. Hussni notes that this book and others in the series contain some "swear words.")

21. MICHAEL: Have what you might call "swear words" in them. If . . . why are the swear words there?

22. HUSSNI: Because they're mad and they want to use them.

23. MICHAEL: Do you think they're there so that somebody—a third-grade kid reading it—will go "Cool!"?

24. HUSSNI: No, because it's a young adult book or something.

25. MICHAEL: Do they seem to fit the characters and what's happening and everything?

26. HUSSNI: Yeah.

27. MICHAEL: I think when they're used like that, it's kinda okay. Of course, if you're writing an exciting story in third grade, like for your writing sample *(students laugh)*, swear words, I would suggest you leave them out *(students laugh again)*. Well, thanks, Hussni. So we're all set with reading logs from yesterday. Hannah?

In this long exchange (3 minutes, 22 seconds), Michael and Jack asked Hussni many questions. Jack asked two questions about the troll (turns 3 and 5), and then Michael wove use of literate vocabulary into the exchange with his question about the antagonist–protagonist continuum (turn 7). In the extended conversation-like questioning of Hussni in this excerpt, we can see that Michael's contingent questions (turns 9, 15, 17, 23, 25) "raised the ante" as they built on Hussni's response and positioned him to think and elaborate in the moment. Both Michael's pedagogical expertise and the established safety of the classroom community are evident in this excerpt. Michael's questions required Hussni to make judgments, and then to support his thinking: "He's helping the guys trying to kill someone" (turn 14). Michael then pursued this good–bad dichotomy with "But the good guys, the fairies—you'd say the fairies are the good guys in this story, as opposed to Artemis?" (turn 15). When Hussni responded, "Yeah"(turn 16), Michael persisted: "Well, if the good guys are using a bad guy to help them.?"(turn 17). But Hussni refuted Michael's subtle distinction and offered his plot support of the "mind-wipe thingy" (turn 18), which Michael followed with the "acorn dealy" (turn 19) question. By this point, Michael's persistence had paid off, and we see Hussni thinking on the spot and elaborating. When Hussni brought up the presence of swear words, we see Michael extending the exchange to teach about the very sophisticated literacy skill of appropriate language and context. Michael positioned Hussni to explain that swear words are used "because they're [the characters are] mad" (turn 22), and Michael made it clear that even in an exciting creative story, he "would suggest that you [these third graders] leave them out" (turn 27). It is easy to forget that these students *were* third graders!

Through this classroom talk, these students listened to, and Michael directed them into practicing, particular ways of talking and writing about books. Michael reminded his students that many characters are complex mixtures of traits; they heard the terms *protagonist* and *antagonist* in use; and they learned that language expresses emotion and should fit the character. As Michael commented, there needed to be "this constant talking about books and literature and relating it to other things they do" for all this to happen.

As we have discussed, Michael's classroom was distinguished by two literacy routines that other teachers might consider "extra" but that Michael considered essential to his classroom learning community: the chapter book read-aloud (the focus of Chapter 5) and the morning meeting with the sharing of reading logs as its organizing framework. When reading logs were handed in, how they were read, and what was written in them revealed more about the importance of reading logs in this classroom.

OTHER ASPECTS OF USING READING LOGS

When and How Reading Logs Were Handed In

In this classroom, making time for all students to read and share their reading logs ensured that all students had times when their reading was given center stage, in addition to times listening to others talk about their reading. And as Sean's reading log suggests in the opening vignette, these experiences informed each other. Michael's reading log routine also provided immediate written feedback to his students' comments about the books the students were reading ("Sounds like we are coming to the climax, the calm before the storm"), their writing style ("Good editing!"), and their illustrations ("Great drawing! He doesn't look nice, that's for sure!"). These comments let students know that Michael had taken the time to read and consider what they had written, that he valued their ideas. Every morning meeting, Michael's first action was handing back the previous day's reading logs with his dialogic comments.

However, while Michael was consistent about making time for everyone to share each week and about providing timely written feedback, he made gentle accommodations for students when "life" got in the way. As long as there was a plan in place for students to do their reading logs, Michael would readily postpone due dates because "yesterday was my showcase for gymnastics," or because there was a note from a parent indicating that "the past few days have been hectic with traveling and all things related." When Maeve explained that her log was late, Michael offered no rebuke, but gently moved responsibility for the solution to her: "So what are *we* [our emphasis] going to do about it?" He then accepted her plan to "write it tonight," but sought assurance from her "so you can really make it happen tonight."

Sometimes Michael made even greater accommodations so that students could be successful. For example, Sam had been having problems finding time to read and do his reading log because of demanding athletics commitments. Michael did not insist that Sam miss lunch; instead, Sam wrote his log entries on his assigned day when he got to school, even though this writing sometimes extended into morning meeting time. Michael was understanding and flexible, but he did not relieve Sam of his responsibility to read and to write in his reading log.

1. MICHAEL: Too busy with baseball every evening?

2. SAM: Yeah, *every* evening.

3. MICHAEL: You gotta get that done. I would think you would be dying to get that [book] finished.

4. SAM: No.

5. MICHAEL: Oh?

6. SAM: I just let my mom read the rest and tell me what happens, so that I can start reading *Gregor*.

7. HERBERT: You bad child!

8. MICHAEL: I gotta call your mom up and tell her to not just tell you the rest. You've gotten most . . . you're done with most of the book. Get her to read the rest to you. Okay, let's hear your letter, Sam.

Here we see that Sam, who was a struggling reader, wanted to start reading *Gregor and the Prophecy of Bane* (Collins, 2005) (turn 6). He was excited by the class conversations about this book. Such viral curiosity was a regular feature of this classroom. One student would read a book and talk about it, and then other students would take it up; soon half the class would have read a particular title. Michael wanted to support Sam's interest, and he understood Sam's impatience, but he also reaffirmed his expectation that Sam would complete the other book by whatever means were necessary (turn 8).

This notion of a reading log as a physical artifact of value—a profile of where and who each student was as a reader—was not explicitly spoken, but was enacted by Michael's practice of accepting reading log installments written on loose-leaf paper but declining to return them until they could be affixed to the reading log proper:

1. MICHAEL: Did you bring your reading log so we can put this in it?

2. SAM: No.

3. MICHAEL: Then I'll keep it, 'cause you'll lose it.

How Reading Logs Were Shared

There was also some variability in how the reading logs were read. For the most part, students read their own logs aloud to the class. Sometimes this entailed a bit of persuading. For instance, when Jack asked Michael to read his out loud for him, Michael remarked, "Why don't you read it? You have such cool print and everything"; when Herbert asked the same thing, Michael responded encouragingly, "You do such a good job of reading." Another example was when Reena handed in her reading log, saying, "Not allowed to read it out loud." Michael responded knowingly, "Oh, I know, I'm supposed to read this later. That's what it is. I can't wait." He knew that Reena had prepared a very special reading log entry about *Circle of Magic,* written into a circle on her page.

Occasionally Michael focused on the mechanics of writing:

1. MICHAEL: Tell me something, Susan, about writing the title of the book.

2. SUSAN: You have to underline it.

3. MICHAEL: Underlining it is a good idea.

4. SUSAN: Capitalized.

5. MICHAEL: And what?

6. SUSAN: Capitalize.

7. MICHAEL: Okay, what do you capitalize?

8. SUSAN: The, um, the title.

9. MICHAEL: Okay, how about if it says—let's just say you were reading the book, such as, like, *Kirsten Saves the Day*—what words would you capitalize? All of them?

10. SUSAN: Uh, no . . . *Kirsten, Saves,* and maybe *Day*?

11. MICHAEL: Exactly. Looks good.

In this exchange, Michael and Susan quickly and publicly reviewed underlining the title of a book (turns 1–3) and then, on Susan's suggestion (turn 4), the use of capitals in a title (turns 5–11). This was not a separate lesson, but nestled within the reading log context.

What Was Written in the Reading Logs

When Herbert prefaced his reading by telling the class that his dad wanted him to write more than a page, Michael's response was "Well, quantity isn't always, you know, the goal here. But when you do write a bunch, sometimes you say more too. Let's hear it!" Michael was interested in thoughtful written responses, not necessarily lengthy ones. He also appreciated creative drawings. Many of the students ended their reading logs with hand-drawn illustrations or with riddles or questions. Michael responded to these expressive modes as well.

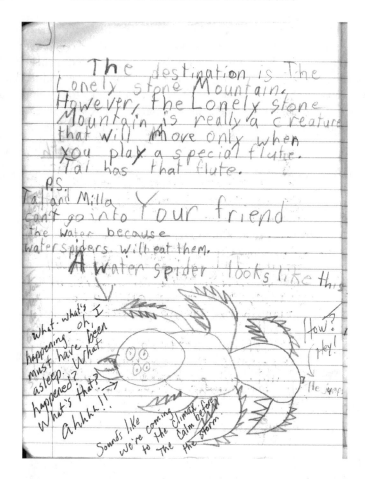

What constituted good writing in Michael's class was clearly not prescribed. The following example sharply bent the "rules" for reading logs: Arianna submitted a piece of original writing. Michael recognized that the purpose of the reading log had nonetheless been met. When Arianna declared, "I'm not gonna read it [aloud] and neither are you!" Michael recognized her self-consciousness, scanned it silently, and asked to read one particular sentence aloud. Note how he deftly lowered Arianna's resistance, drawing her into a rich exchange:

1. MICHAEL: Just one. Um, she [Arianna] made up a story. And one line is "I woke up dazzled for a moment by the sun flooding through my open window, the sky was a milky blue." This . . . you didn't, like, steal this from some famous author, did you?

2. ARIANNA: No.

3. MICHAEL: That's great. That's a wonderful line.

4. MAEVE: Yeah, keep reading.

5. MICHAEL: I'm seeing if there are any . . . it's all good. I was wondering if there were any more like that.

6. ARIANNA: What about the one that has my name in it?

7. MICHAEL: Oh . . . "I passed through the town where cars and buses were, the train whistle blew, and the smell of gas lingered in the air." (*Whistles like a train.*) Very, very . . . " . . . moonlight played across the water and fireflies danced . . . " That's very cool. You sure you don't want me to read the story? I like it. Were you inspired by any reading that you've done to come up with those lines? 'Cause those . . .

8. ARIANNA: It's something I've been listening to . . .

9. MICHAEL: What have you been listening to?

10. ARIANNA: [A] *Harry Potter* [book] on the tape.

11. MICHAEL: Uh-huh. But you haven't actually heard those lines, but they're making you think of your own?

12. ARIANNA: Yeah.

13. MICHAEL: Okay, that's very, *very* cool. One of the ways to get to be a good author is by listening to—or reading other authors and seeing how they work and how they describe things.

14. JACK: Reading other authors? How can you read other authors?

15. MICHAEL: Well, if you're an author, and you read somebody else's book, then you're reading another author.

In this exchange, Michael first complimented Arianna on her writing skills (turns 1 and 3); another student then directed him to keep reading, presumably so he could share more of Arianna's writing (turn 4). Arianna had been loath to share her writing, but it was she who suggested the next excerpt to be read (turn 6), and she explained that listening to a book in the *Harry Potter* series on tape had inspired her to write (turns 8 and 10). Michael built on this experience to remind students how they could learn from "listening to—or reading other authors"(turns 11 and 13). The students had been listening attentively, and when Jack asked, "How can you read other authors?" (turn 14), Michael had another opportunity to position his students as authors and to connect reading and writing (turn 15).

These students took risks with their reading logs—whether these were Arianna's creative writing; Sean's illustrations; or, as in the following exchange, Ana's admission that "I haven't read anything, but I was so eager to know what happened that I asked my sister." As the students laughed at this, Michael teasingly responded, "Cheater!" Any sanction was negated both by the laughter and by Michael's then sharing another "naughty" reading behavior that his wife indulged in when she was excited to know what happened:

> "Maybe we better not hear it. But, um, you cheated and asked your sister what was going to happen? Uh, bad girl! Okay, did any of you . . . my wife does this sometimes. She goes and looks at the end of a book before she gets to the end. Any of you ever do that?"

In this classroom community, as the teacher and students shared how to read books, there was the underlying message that everyone read and that there were many ways to do this. These students listened to books on tape, were read to by their parents and Michael, read independently, and talked to family members about what they read. In this context, it was permissible (if not encouraged) for Ana to ask her sister about the book and share that as her reading log for this week.

Michael articulated how he viewed the opportunities that reading logs offered to support student thinking and embed his learning objectives in relevant and engaging ways:

> "I think most learning starts with the learners and goes from there. And so to start with their reading logs, or what they are talking about, and try to expand on that and to bring other things into that . . . when they say something, it might be the perfect opportunity to slide something in. Like, in the book about Rowan we were talking about yesterday, and . . . and they are going to climb a mountain, and so we were talking about climaxes and things . . . and *the kids* brought up that it's going to, like, lead to some real exciting point or something like that. And so it's pretty easy to then start talking about similes or metaphors—or even if you don't use the terms, which it's fun to use once in a while—I think it makes the kids [excited] to know that the bad guys—the antagonists—I think they feel like they are pretty smart using that word. Maeve is always going, "And it's a really great antagonist in this story!" So I think it makes it kind of exciting—it gives them the sense that they are pretty smart, literate people. Umm . . . and they really are."

As you read the excerpt below, think about how literate talk was used in this classroom—and note how exciting the process was.

Teresa asked Michael to read her reading log to the class, and he agreed. As he read, he commented. So in the exchange below, we see two voices in each of Michael's turns of talk: Teresa's voice as Michael reads her log (this is presented in *italics*), and then Michael's own voice as he commented (this is presented in regular type).

1. MICHAEL: *So I will just tell about the book a little. I am really, really enjoying this book and think it is the best out of the whole series.* Oh! Well, that's really good to know. 'Cause a lot of times books start out like—the first book is really good—sometimes the sequels just aren't as good. Not always. *There is action, tragedy, excitement and a lot more.* What's tragedy? Teresa, what's tragedy?

2. TERESA: It's like something that—something really bad.

3. MICHAEL: Bad, sad. *I am thinking that you and Sean are going to think the same of it. Now for some questions.* Oooo. *When Gregor saw The Marks of Secret, that means that they're all going to die. But the main characters cant die, I mean, what will the next Gregor book be like if there isn't any Gregor?! Well, I'll find out in the next thirty pages.* So you have 30 pages to go? You know, that is one of the things about books, is that the hero—the protagonist, the main person—almost always things work out right for them. Maybe not totally. But usually, you know, things are . . .

Note Teresa's use of literate language: *"There is action, tragedy, excitement and a lot more"* (turn 1). She asked questions—*"What will the next Gregor book be like if there isn't any Gregor?"* (turn 3), and she builds suspense and excitement for other readers. No wonder Sam wanted to finish his book to get started on *Gregor*!

TALKING ABOUT READING LOGS: THE PERFECT OPPORTUNITY TO "SLIDE SOMETHING IN"

As this chapter makes clear, these third graders were part of a literate community where they thought, read, talked, and wrote about books. Morning meeting, including sharing reading logs, started the day off with conversations about books they had selected and were excited to share. This sharing rarely took more than half an hour. But of course, half an hour every day for 40 weeks makes for many hours of rich literate talk.

For those who may still be nervous about committing time each day to share reading logs or engage in another such literacy routine, it is important to note that reading logs embody the intent of learning standards (whether the individualized state standards or the recently adopted Common Core State Standards). Students are expected to speak and write for literary response as they present interpretations, analyses, and reaction to the content and language of a text. As students create imaginative texts, they use language and text structures that are inventive and often multilayered. As they present personal responses to literature, they make reference to the plot, characters, vocabulary, and text structure and observe the conventions of grammar and usage, spelling and punctuation. Michael's students do this every day. Moreover, they were doing it in a meaningful way, having fun learning, and setting in place reading practices that would serve them well as students and throughout life.

We recently talked with Sean, who was now 12 years old. When we handed him his third-grade journal, it was like reintroducing him to an old friend. We directed him to the journal entries that are featured in this chapter. He remembered reading *Gregor*, writing that particular entry, and drawing that picture. *And* he remembered Michael's responses. He told us, "I didn't actually want to write my entries, but once I sat down and started to write, I started to enjoy it. I liked reading, and Michael allowed me to express my thoughts." The reading log literacy event helped set the context for what were deemed important in Michael's classroom: thoughtful, creative insights.

THINGS TO THINK ABOUT

- Preschool and early childhood programs traditionally begin with a ritual, often called *circle time*. During circle time, the teacher takes attendance, and the children gather for a song, practice counting, and share. Morning meeting evolved from this practice, building on children's needs for social guidance, structure, and interaction. How did Michael's practice of morning meeting replicate or extend these daily routines? How might you implement morning meetings in your classroom?

- Making connections across literature was a practice Michael explicitly promoted in this classroom community. List the structures and practices he had in place to encourage and support his students. Consider each of these in light of time spent, routinization, benefits and drawbacks. Then reflect on your own practice. Which of these practices is [or will become] a regular event in your classroom?

CHAPTER 7

Talking through Weaving and Weaving through Talking

Crocheting a Classroom Community

"I love it. It's fun. We're making a afghan out of it.
It's my 2ed best hobbie. I LOVE crocheting."

Sarah holds the hand-crocheted afghan close to her chest. She looks again at each of the single crocheted squares, touching the stitches and remembering how many crocheting hooks, how much concentrated effort, and what joy and sheer good will have gone into the making of this afghan. She is proud of her second graders; they have woven their stories into this afghan, and together they've learned so much. She folds the afghan carefully and sets it on the chair she has placed at the front of her classroom. Mrs. March will arrive after lunch, and the class will present her with the afghan.

The academic year is ending, and the passing on of this afghan to a community member seems like appropriate closure, a fitting capstone for the "crazy about crocheting" class. This afghan also signifies Sarah's growing understanding of literacy as a social practice. Her students will soon move up to third grade, but Sarah feels confident that what they have learned together about social responsibility and student cooperation, creativity, and empowerment will endure. For Sarah, this second year of teaching has been transformative. Crocheting—which started out as an end-of-the-day classroom management activity, something to help develop fine motor skills and improve handwriting—has taken on a life of its own and transformed itself into a literacy event. It has inspired student engagement and provided authentic purpose for classroom literacy activities. Sarah has learned to follow her students' lead, and together they have woven meaningful literacy practices emanating from crocheting into their classroom.

After lunch, the second graders sit quietly listening to Mrs. March's brief but heartfelt thank-you speech, and Sarah is struck by this quiet moment associated with crocheting. Somehow, right from the start, engaged talk has gone hand in hand with crocheting. The types of student talk associated with crocheting have marked the ways in which crocheting has patterned its way into this classroom community.

Sarah taught second grade in a rural community not far from where she had grown up in central New York State. There were fewer than 500 students in this school (one of two elementary schools in town), and the average class had about 20 students. Most of the students were white, most came from lower-middle-class backgrounds, and 32% received free or reduced-price lunches. Typically there was some movement over the school year; in Sarah's class this year, 3 students left and 1 joined; for most of the year, there were 20 students. This was Sarah's second year of teaching second grade; as it happens, it was also her second year in a master's-degree literacy program. Sarah was a reflective and creative teacher, eager to apply what she was learning in the classroom, and warmly receptive to student input.

At the end of her first year of teaching, Sarah identified two concrete things she felt she could improve on: developing the students' handwriting, and classroom management at the end of the day, when the students had to spend over 20 minutes waiting for buses.

> "Initially I hoped that I would be able to build fine motor development in my students. I also wanted an activity that my students would be able to complete during their bus dismissal time. I figured, this is a generation of multitaskers, so why not give them an activity to build fine motor [skills] while listening to a read-aloud at the end of the day?"

Sarah had just read *Starting from Scratch,* an autobiographical ethnography of Levy's (1996) classroom, in which he described teaching his fourth graders to knit as one of his most rewarding and fruitful classroom activities. She thought that teaching her second graders to crochet would provide a fun, ongoing activity that could be picked up at the end of the day, and that would at the same time help develop the fine motor skills needed for good handwriting. Like Levy, Sarah soon discovered that a "real-life" activity that students enjoy and practice daily can not only inspire and present coherent and relevant learning opportunities, but also connect school reading and writing to what people *do* with literacy, and show students how their literacy practices can have an impact on their community and their place within it (Boyd & Kneller, 2009; Finn, 1999; Kneller & Boyd, 2008; McLaughlin & DeVoogd, 2004).

In this chapter, we describe classroom talk practices associated with crocheting across the academic year in this second-grade classroom. We discuss how these talk practices indexed and contributed to the growing impact crocheting had on these second graders' thinking over the school year, and how opportunities for this talk shaped this classroom community. We tell the story of how talk about crocheting framed and then informed, rehearsed, and prepared the context for these students to engage in appropriate literate practices. We invite you to substitute for crocheting whatever pastime or passion you pursue that can conceivably be connected to literacy. The critical element here was not crocheting per se, but the enthusiasm Sarah brought to it; the interest students displayed in crocheting; the relationships that developed between literacy and crocheting; and Sarah's willingness to provide curricular time and physical space and support in response to students' growing interest, and to explore relevant applications.

FOSTERING A COMMUNITY WITH YARN AND HOOKS

A community is not just its participants; rather, it is made up of the social relationships among these participants (Halliday, 1978). In Sarah's classroom, as in all classrooms, social relations were framed by what was said, when it was said, and how it was said (Heath, 1983; Hymes, 1971). In this second-grade classroom, there were multiple and varied opportunities for both the cognitive and social functions of talk: expressing and reflecting on ideas, and managing relationships. Increasingly across the year, student talk centered around crocheting ideas and was framed in social and ideational relations—relations to each other, to home, and to the greater community; across reading, writing, and speaking; across disciplines; and between school-imposed literacy practices and empowerment.

In this classroom, students routinely talked in pairs and trios and increasingly contributed to and shaped the scope of class discussions. They talked as they crocheted, they talked about crocheting, and they even talked to make sure they could continue crocheting. Over time, as they developed their school voices, they talked to learn about each other, to share ideas, and to figure out how their literacy practices could make a difference to their world. Classroom talk helped make literacy, and to some degree numeracy, an embedded social practice (Bloome et al., 2008; Maybin, 1994)—in large part because Sarah quickly learned that when a teacher listens and responds to student cues, applications for learning across the curriculum present themselves, as students read the world and not just the word (Freire, 1993).

An important factor that enabled Sarah to add crocheting to daily activities was that it did not involve a huge investment of money (a serious consideration in activity planning for all teachers). Her principal gave her some funds at the beginning of the year to buy yarn and hooks; ultimately, the lack of available financial resources inspired these students to learn to distinguish wants from needs, and to find inventive ways to procure what they needed. The reality of limited funds created an authentic context for these students to experience literacy as an embedded, relevant social practice.

> "Once my kids showed a strong interested in crocheting, I knew it would be a good 'snag' for instruction. We were able to use the lack of supplies as a springboard for writing business letters, which then led to writing a class book from the letters. We also created shopping lists, [and] the students wrote entries in their daily journals about crocheting experiences. The students also wrote thank-you notes during center time any time an adult came into our room to help or someone donated supplies."

Sarah's pedagogical risks were responsive and cumulative. She started small—trying to make better use of time at the end of the day, and expecting simply to improve fine motor skills and classroom management. It was only when crocheting evoked such a positive response in her students that it evolved first into the focus for an optional learning center, and later into a unifying reference for math, social studies, and language arts. The adoption of crocheting as a class activity created an extraordinary by-product: a class identity.

> "Initially, my only focus for the project was the end of the day. When the students took hold of it, I guess I moved the project to fit their enthusiasm. The projects developed from whatever was happening with crocheting."

Not only isolated "projects" developed from crocheting at the end of the day. Sarah and her students used these projects to create a literacy event that had ramifications across the curriculum, the community, and the school year.

WEAVING CROCHETING INTO A LITERARY EVENT

Talking to Figure Out "How to" and to Get Acquainted: September

When Sarah talked to her principal about money for crocheting supplies, the school secretary overheard their discussion and volunteered to help Sarah teach crocheting at the end of the day. Accordingly, the two of them began showing the second graders how to crochet at the very beginning of the school year. The routine during the last 30 minutes of school was as follows: First the students prepared their schoolbags for home and got their jackets. Then they settled with their belongings on the carpet and learned to crochet while waiting for their buses to be called. Right from the get-go they chatted, as Sarah and the secretary taught them how to use a crochet hook and to chain stitches.

News quickly spread that this class was learning to crochet, and community members, mostly neighboring grandmothers, volunteered to help also. As they learned, the students figured out "how to," and the talk was explicit as the volunteers assisted and demonstrated. But the talk was also personal, as these second graders built relationships with one another, with the volunteers, and with Sarah. At the end of the instructional day, crocheting time was relaxed and intimate, and the talk reflected this. Over the course of the year 11 community members got involved, and each eventually received a handwritten thank-you letter from one of these second graders as part of the "Thank you Thursday" letter-writing class routine.

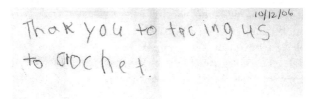

Talking to Build the Crocheting Community: October

A month later, some students were still chaining stitches; others were beginning to make a second row; and a few students were already making single crochet squares. Sarah reduced the time for crocheting at the end of the day to 15 minutes as students waited for buses. However, her students were so clearly enjoying crocheting that Sarah decided to add a crocheting center as an optional learning center during center time.

> "The students constantly talked about crocheting; they brought in projects they had created at home. They were always asking if they could take out their crocheting. They looked forward to pulling out their bags at the end of the day. Parents would also tell me about their students looking for ideas at home or crocheting at home."

Meanwhile, Sarah read about the Warm Up America! project (*www. craftyarncouncil.com/warmup.html*) and presented to the class the idea of making patches for an afghan. These second graders were excited at the prospect of making an afghan, and Sarah planned future read-alouds such as *Show Way* (Woodson, 2005) and *The Patchwork Quilt* (Flournoy, 1985) "themed around the impact their work making a class afghan could have."

Students chatted and helped each other as they crocheted. They talked about themselves, their families, what they liked to do, their favorite TV shows, and the read-aloud Sarah had already begun (*The Lion, the Witch and the Wardrobe*; Lewis, 1950). Student enthusiasm for crocheting was apparent in the popularity of the new center (by the end of the month, Sarah made it an "after you have done other work" center), and in the students' excitement about sharing what they had made with each other and with Sarah. Crocheted hairbands and bracelets were being worn in class, and crocheted bookmarks were being used. Students' families had also contributed spare yarn from home.

Talking to Share Ideas: November

As winter approached, these second graders were becoming proficient and enthusiastic crocheters. The end-of-the-day and optional center crocheting times both continued, and students now freely referred to crocheting throughout the day. Crocheting featured prominently in the "free writing" of student daily journals: "As soon as I lerend I thought it might be relacxing. I was right."

Sarah consulted with the school librarian, and together they put together a bin of "how-to-crochet" reference books. Now, while students still chatted about everyday matters, as they crocheted, conversations also included references to the crocheting books and to different stitches and items that they hoped to create. These conversations continued in the students' daily journal entries to Sarah. These entries kept Sarah apprised of what her students were creating ("I am making a blankit owt of crochet It is very big so is my ball of yarn") and of how they felt about crocheting. As Charlie put it in his daily journal, "I talk about crocheting when I crochet because I like to crochet."

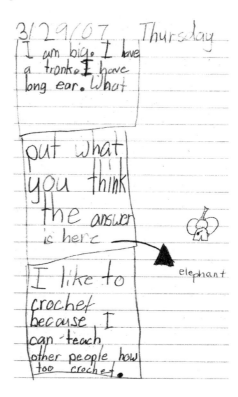

As these second graders continued practicing making rows that were even and uniform, Sarah deftly began to weave in math connections. Talk about crocheting had become a common, shared reference for many activities. When Sarah was making up math problems, she embedded her students' names in crocheting scenarios. For example, "Charlie went to the store to buy four balls of yarn. He had $10.00. Each ball of yarn cost $1.50. How much money was left out of Charlie's $10.00?" On one occasion, the students took it upon themselves to solve crocheting problems that were real-world math; for example, how many rows were needed for a square measuring 7 by 9 inches? Sarah reported, "During indoor recess, I found two students huddled together trying to figure out how many rows were in one of their 7-by-9 squares. They were measuring each row with a ruler." And in fact, this became the practice; each student measured his or her square to ensure that it was 7 by 9 inches.

1/26/07

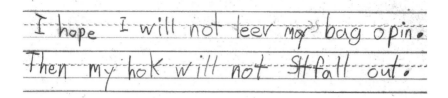

During circle time, Sarah also explained the notion of resources and responsibility in terms of crocheting. Some hooks had been broken in small accidents; others had been lost. Sarah explained that the students must be very careful with the limited supplies they had, and then introduced the notion of "hook responsibility letters." When students needed a new hook, they had to write a note explaining what had happened and how they would address the problem. This specifically crocheting-related literate practice made sense to these second graders. They composed letters such as "I am going to take good care of it I won't lose it I won't brake it or I won't drob it" and immediately got a new crochet hook.

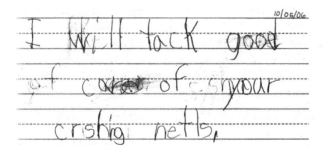

Talking to Generate Ideas: December

As the holidays neared, the status of crocheting to Sarah's class was made plain. "All I Want for Christmas Is Crocheting Stuff" (sung to the tune of "All I Want for Christmas Is My Two Front Teeth") was frequently heard. Journals included revelations like "At nite if I can't go to slep I crochet the hole nite!" But despite their best efforts at conservation of resources, the class was quickly running out of crocheting supplies. Sarah reported that they "were running out of yarn and our crocheting hooks were broken." In this rural community, although many family members crocheted, students and their families had already contributed all the extra supplies they could afford.

Sarah carefully considered the problem and saw yet another literacy opportunity. She decided to make this crocheting supply problem an issue for public discourse at circle time. Sarah selected two picturebook read-alouds with the purpose of planting some ideas. *The Jolly Christmas Postman* (Ahlberg, 1991) and *I Wanna Iguana* (Kaufman Orloff, 2004) both demonstrated the power of letter writing, and Sarah hoped that the suggestion would percolate into the class discussion as a way to generate either supplies or money so they could keep crocheting. Her gentle nudge succeeded: In addition to offering to sell their toys, the class members resolved to write letters to local businesses. Together, Sarah and her students discussed the elements of a letter (salutation, body, and closing), what they would write in the body (including use of "please"), and to which businesses they would send letters. These letters included the name of their school and teacher and various iterations similar to the following, by Aidan:

> We are makeing afghans for people in need. We please need yarn and hooks for our crocheting because we are accidentally breaking hooks and we lost some others. We appreciat your help. Love, Aidan

As a class, they decided to make a photocopy of each letter before the original was sent to the local business; the photocopy was published in their own class letter book, in the interactive style of *The Jolly Christmas Postman*. This class publication of letters asking for crocheting supplies became a popular book for students to check out, read, and talk about with their kindergarten "reading buddies."

Talking to Share Experience and Expertise: January

When students returned from the winter holidays, it was clear from their chatter that crocheting had not lost any popularity. Many holiday gifts had been crocheted, and parents related to Sarah that many hours had been spent chatting as families crocheted together. Sarah observed that "it far exceeded my expectations how much the students and their families embraced the idea and made it something that defined our classroom."

As the students recorded in their journals, crocheting was not always easy ("it was hard not to make knots"), and not everyone at home joined in ("I'd teach my sister to crochet but she'd rather play on the competer or wath tv"). But students continued to chat together as they worked on crocheting personal projects. Boys and girls helped each other: Maggie told how "Bobby taught me to make necklaces, bracelets and rings. Bobby changed my mind [about crocheting]." In January a student invented a new stitch, "the 42nd crochet," which became wildly popular with classmates. Students now talked about different stitches, and the crochet reference book bin continued to be well browsed.

Talking to Prioritize: February

Several weeks after the students had sent out their letters to local businesses, Sarah received a phone call telling her that one business was going to contribute $50.00 for supplies.

> "And when I told [the students], they were ecstatic. They wanted to buy every color imaginable and gold hooks. We immediately created a shopping list of all the supplies we would buy. Every student was able to say a color."

Deciding how to prioritize needs and wants became the focus of much private and public classroom talk.

> "We agreed as a class that our first investment would be metal hooks; we had learned that plastic [ones] break. After that we needed yarn. All students were able to provide their input. I had a student write everyone's ideas on chart paper, and I copied it down on a Post-it so I could take it shopping."

The list these students generated as a class was the result of much consideration and discussion. Literacy and numeracy were experienced as pragmatic and empowering practices—and talk mediated the whole process. These second graders were the experts: They were crocheters; they had experience and confidence in what they needed and wanted; and Sarah made sure that they had classroom time and space to articulate and elaborate on their wishes. Sarah went shopping with her Post-it list.

A "share the pen" thank-you card was sent, and the new supplies were enthusiastically put to use.

Talking as Engaged Classroom Citizens: March

As the long winter showed signs of ending, the sense of community in this classroom continued and deepened into something even richer. Sarah's students had come to feel an ownership stake in this community they had built, and with it had developed a feeling of classroom citizenship— a responsibility to preserve and maintain the classroom, to "leave things right." Some students started chatting about how they might solve the problem of the messy yarn basket (students had not been careful as they returned balls of yarn, and so students who went to get new yarn had to spend a long time untangling the balls). Others joined in this discussion, and soon a student-identified problem became the focus of a circle time discussion, with Sarah recording student ideas. The agreed-upon solution, putting elastic bands on the balls of yarn, was practiced until the end of the year. This was a time of prolific crocheting: In addition to making squares for the class afghan, the students continued to be both creative and busy. Anna reported in her journal:

> I have crocheted 2 blankets, a mit. 4 purses, 7 patches, 1 stripe that I didn't finish a tunnel that you can look through, a little stripe that I made for fun. a mit for in the kitchen. a flower that I'm working on.

Talking to Share with Others: April

Crocheting was firmly a part of the fabric of this second-grade classroom by now, and as spring arrived, the class was humming with crocheting talk, shared writing, read-alouds, classroom chatter, and examples in math. Crocheting was even used for understanding the social studies curriculum on community (Boyd & Kneller, 2009). In addition, when a speaker came to the class carrying a crocheted bag, these students were excited to ask her how long it had taken her to make it and which stitches she had used. And for Grandparents' Day, the students invited their grandparents in to crochet with the class (some grandmothers were already serving as crocheting volunteers, of course). These students were "crazy about crocheting," and not just at school. Mike explained in a journal entry:

> Yes, I do crochet at home, watching tv or in the car. I talk about what I'm making and who it's for. Dad is making an upstairs, and Mom is crocheting a blue-greenish blanket for me (with grany paches).

Talking, Writing, Making Decisions: May

These second graders continued to be productive and creative. They saw no limit to what could be crocheted ("Do you think this is big enough for an infant?"), and they generously gave away what they created. However, not enough squares had been crocheted to meet the Warm Up America! afghan deadline, so the students brainstormed the best new purpose for the class afghan. After much discussion, making of lists, and revisiting, they decided that the recipient would be Mrs. March, a parent member of their school community who was receiving chemotherapy.

Talking about Identity: June

As noted in the vignette at the beginning of this chapter, the class presented the completed afghan to Mrs. March. She received it with these simple but powerful words: "Thank you for sharing your very special blanket with me. Your care and concern are as warm as the blanket."

A few days later, it was Field Day, an anticipated end-of-year tradition at this rural school. One of Sarah's students, Tom, carried a two-tone green granny-square flag that he had crocheted. The other second graders, wearing green t-shirts with crocheted accessories, followed behind as they walked to each event. Laughter and pride were evident as they ensured that their flag was standing before they competed. Sarah explained:

> "So each class is given a color, and we're the green team. We had discussed how we could crochet headbands, bracelets, and necklaces. Many of the students had been working on these

accessories during their crocheting time. One student worked at home and crocheted a granny-square flag. It was a project he did independently. I only provided the pole to hang the flag."

Sarah's very literal provision of a flagpole is an apt metaphor for what her introduction of crocheting provided for this class: It served as the axis and support for the community created by her students.

WEAVING RELATIONSHIPS

The story of these second graders' relationship with crocheting is a compelling one. We are drawn to the image of these children chatting as they crocheted. The relaxed, social component of chatting during this shared activity reminds us of sewing circles, and offers an antidote to images of classrooms doggedly pacing through a curriculum, obsessively preparing for standardized tests, and enervated by the resultant stress to be efficient. Crocheting evokes a sociocultural/historic resonance too: This activity clearly aligns with family practices and values in this and many communities. But while we as teachers enjoy the connections across school and home, and recognize the power of coherent, relevant, and authentic learning opportunities to address both literacy and social studies state standards, the process of learning is too often sacrificed for the more easily achieved completed skill check. This is why Sarah's example is important. Here is her summary of what she and her students learned from her classroom crocheting experience:

> "I think it showed me that you need to take risks as a teacher. I didn't know if the idea was going to amount to anything, and if it failed, well, there is something to learn from that too. I would hope that my kids learned that their actions make an impact. They didn't have to spend any money, yet they were able to create something beautiful and from the heart to show they cared."

Sarah was in only her second year of teaching. She did not preplan a huge unit that would unfold throughout the year. She introduced an activity and gave it appropriate time, space, and support. If her students had not embraced crocheting as wholeheartedly, it would have remained a productive and fun end-of-day activity, and handwriting would presumably have improved as these second graders practiced their fine motor skills by crocheting. A critical factor in crocheting's "taking hold" was the classroom culture into which crocheting was introduced, and the role that classroom talk played in shaping and being shaped by that learning culture. Classroom cultures are constructed by what gets to count—what knowledge is valued and what is considered cultural capital. Ideas and thinking are not just expressed in language; they are framed, shaped, and constructed through language (Vygotsky, 1986), through the opportunities and types of classroom talk. Furthermore, the patterns of talk that are privileged and responded to in the classroom shape students' predispositions to talk in particular ways (Bakhtin, 1981; Boyd, 2010b; Smith & Higgins, 2006). The recursive cycle of learning in and through talk continues.

Sarah provided time and space for the two basic functions of language: to manage relationships, and to explain, share, and reflect. Relationships were privileged through crocheting practices. It would be very hard to sit and crochet with people and not get to know them. The *phatic communion* (Malinowski, 1923/1994) of "Hello" and "What are you doing?" was established from the first week of school. Both Sarah and the volunteers modeled it, and it was a practice that was authentic in the "learning to crochet at the end of the day" daily experience. There was lots of talk even when Sarah was not directly involved. Concurrent practices like learning center time and kindergarten reading-buddy time strengthened these second-grade school voices.

Crocheting also helped with the other function of talk: to explain subject matter, share ideas, and reflect. Crocheting organized the talk; it imposed coherence across the many little conversations and prepared students, in terms of both content and confidence, for large-group discussions. Daily journal writing paralleled and reinforced knowing and willingness to share. As students became more adept at crocheting, they gradually gained expert status and could talk from experience. These opportunities to talk and write produced a groundswell of engagement to which Sarah responded with curricular literacy applications. Connections among crocheting, reading, writing, listening, and speaking emerged from the context. Carrying out these literacy tasks was not imposed work, but community practice, and these second graders showed energy and enthusiasm as they discussed and undertook these meaningful tasks. Literacy practices were thus framed as pragmatic, caring, and empowering, and as expected of all members of the classroom community.

It is through dialogue and relationships that individuals become a group, a community. We see this in the dialogue (Alexander, 2006; Boyd & Rubin, 2006; Nystrand, 1997) of Sarah's classroom. Sarah reflected:

> "I truly feel that it helped created a classroom community that
> was based on stronger friendships, for the simple reason they

were given opportunities to get to know each other; they were able to *talk* to each other. So often our students are shushed throughout the day, and we wonder why our students feel disconnected or don't feel comfortable sharing their ideas. Midway through the year I noticed that when we had a class discussion, even my more reserved students were sharing their ideas and providing their input."

These second graders learned and addressed things together in a relaxed and safe environment; they listened and then built on each other's contributions; and Sarah had clear educational goals in mind. Sarah encouraged her students to explore both the cognitive and social dimensions of language as they figured crocheting out together.

THINGS TO THINK ABOUT

- As you read about the positive effects crocheting had on literacy practices in this classroom, think about your own practice. How do you make the reading and writing activities in your classroom relevant and empowering? Do you have special interests or expertise that you can integrate into meaningful literacy practice? Make a list of ways you can connect the real world to the written and spoken words in your classroom.

- This was Sarah's second year of teaching, and crocheting showed her that "you need to take risks as a teacher." Reflect on those risks. How could you justify them in terms of student learning and classroom structures? In your own classroom community, do you take risks? Why or why not?

CHAPTER 8

Constancy and Variety

Multiple Opportunities for Literacy Learning through Real Talk

Reflecting back on the year, I learned to trust myself, the literature, and, most of all, the students. Putting students at the center of my teaching and giving students the gift of time was the key for me, although . . . this change was not always comfortable for me. However, the gift of time allowed the students to learn how to discuss and think about the texts they were reading. The daily repetition of the experience of talking about books was vital in their development as critical readers. I was given the opportunity to get to know these fabulous students as human beings, and over time, we developed deeper understandings of ourselves and others.—LISA

[My students] are eager to share their newly acquired knowledge with the group and to be the "teachers" or providers of the information, thus taking on the role of teacher.—CHARLOTTE

[I give them] an avenue to then talk about the books, and I think that is where, you know, the real excitement can come along because it's the books—and it's a way of communicating, it's a way of sharing—and to then continue that sharing from author to the reader to the other kids is just a really exciting thing.—MICHAEL

[Crocheting] provided learning opportunities that were important to the kids and showed how concepts we were learning were used in life outside the classroom. However, I feel the learning was something far beyond academics. We learned about working together to give back, and at the risk of sounding hokey . . . that they could make a difference.—SARAH

These comments, from the four teachers you have gotten to know through the pages of this book, offer insights into some of the benefits that accompany the use of real talk to teach in a planful and responsive fashion. They acknowledge that teachers must trust themselves, and learn to follow their instincts, the books, and the students (Lisa); let the students share what they know (Charlotte); let them talk about books (Michael); and let learning extend beyond traditional academics (Sarah).

In Chapter 1 of this book, we discuss oral language in general and present arguments for talk in classrooms, specifically talk about literacy events. These literacy events are often (but not always) related to books, and are usually shaped by understandings about the nature of reading and literary response. Chapters 2 through 7 present four teachers who use talk for many purposes—some of which are shared across their classrooms, and others that are particular to each individual classroom. Whether their purposes are shared or not, the principles evident in the ways these teachers use talk are remarkably similar, as are their overarching beliefs about how talk can function to help students learn. Lisa, Charlotte, Michael, and Sarah all build on the social nature of talk, using talk as a way to share the cognitive load of the tasks at hand as they and their students work together to create new knowledge—in these cases, knowledge about literacy. These teachers and their students use talk to generate, shape, develop, and validate ideas that are frequently fresh, in-the-moment discoveries about books or life or learning.

Observing these four effective teachers makes apparent four interrelated and foundational conditions common to their practices. First, these teachers understand the importance of a classroom community based on shared trust and respect as a necessary climate for learning. Second, they know that there must be engaging material to think about, and most often these materials are children's books. Third, all four understand that learning occurs more easily when there is joy in the process; such joy comes naturally when students are pursuing their interests in ways that support them as they stretch toward growth. Fourth, they understand that there are multiple paths to learning—many ways to attain their goals and those of their students—and they plan and respond accordingly. They recognize the tension between effective and efficient practice, but understand that no practice is efficient if it is not also effective.

Together, these four interrelated components are the pillars that create and constitute real talk—conversations that reflect committed inquiry and communal responsibility. Furthermore, these four teachers realize that supporting this kind of talk is both planned for and contingent, requiring teacher knowledge, organization, flexibility, and attention. We take each of these components in turn, describing how they were present in each classroom and how they relate to and expand how we think about classroom talk, particularly talk centering around literacy events.

COMMUNITY

The idea of the importance of developing a safe and supportive classroom community has permeated the research literature on literacy for many years (Alexander, 2006; Nystrand, 1997; Wells & Chang-Wells, 1992). Learning is hard work. It requires learners to take on tasks that they do not already know how to do, and when anyone is trying something new, the possibility of failure is very real. Children who thrive have a person or people in their lives who support them as they are developing. One example is the reciprocal scaffolding of early reading, documented by researchers such as Wood, Bruner, and Ross (1976), Snow (1989), and others. When children enter elementary school, those who support them in their lives outside school are still present, of course, and are important contributors to their success in school. However, support from the adult they are with during the school day—their teacher—is crucial to their progress. Both practicing newly acquired skills and sharing tentatively formed ideas require a teacher-atmosphere of trust and respect. Every teacher featured in this book has created such a classroom community.

As Dyson (1990) and Aukerman (2007) remind us, guided participation, or effective scaffolding, is as early researchers described it: reciprocal. Both experts and novices contribute to the construction of a strong scaffold beginning with where learners are, what they are capable of, and what their interests are, as well as a consideration of curricular demands. It requires incorporating students' ideas in order to make the scaffolded task more interesting, engaging, and relevant. It also requires that teachers tap their own expertise about curricula and state standards, about the strengths and weaknesses of their students, and about the tasks at hand. For example, the teachers described in this book knew how talk can function effectively and how children's books can provide an important foundation for language arts instruction. They summoned their expertise to support their students' learning in both short- and long-term ways, while also basing that support on the demonstrated circumstances, funds of knowledge, wishes, predispositions, needs, ideas, and interests of their students.

The curricular area of literacy offers some particular challenges to both students and teachers because of its content. The English language arts include learning the skills of reading, writing, listening, and speaking, but also consist of the *ideas* that students talk, read, and write about. These ideas range from entertaining to challenging, from knowledge about the world to deeply held feelings, and these ideas are what spur many students' willing engagement in literacy tasks. Yet talking about these things can be a daunting activity if that talk is in the classroom. Sharing tentative ideas through exploratory talk (Barnes et al., 1990; Mercer & Hodgkinson, 2008; Rubin, 1990) is safe only when those listening accept these ideas seriously, treat them respectfully, and add them to the shared knowledge of the classroom community.

Community in Lisa's Classroom

As we have seen repeatedly in Chapter 2, Lisa both explicitly or implicitly confirmed and validated the ideas expressed by her students, even those that seemed tangential. When one of her students offered an idea that was leading him or her astray (increasing rather than resolving confusion), Lisa would ask that student to reconsider or rethink the comment, rather than telling the student that his or her idea was "wrong." This was one way she made the discussion group a safe place for her students. She also validated and confirmed ideas that they offered, by restating, asking for clarification, echoing, or explicitly evaluating with phrases such as "That's interesting." Although evaluative comments such as this are often thought to shut down conversation, in many cases Lisa used her evaluations as an invitation for more; when her students heard her say, "That's interesting," they eagerly shaped their own contributions to echo the one that she had singled out. As she did this daily across the course of the school year, she created the safe space that allowed students to think about the books they were reading in terms of their own lives and share their ideas with others, bringing their lives into a discussion in order to help them understand a book. Remember the final transcript in Chapter 2, where the students talked about love in families, what they themselves needed to thrive, and how single-parent families can provide that kind of love—all things that they shared because they knew they were safe.

Lisa also supported her students through her demonstrations of how she thought about texts. She brought her own life into the classroom to help the students understand the books that they were reading and discussing. She also shared her life with her students so that they could share theirs; in other words, she demonstrated how they could do that. Moreover, she supported them through her intense listening and questioning as she helped them not only communicate what they were thinking, but, in many cases, understand what they were trying to say.

Think of Hao and his comment about liking strawberries. Lisa helped him articulate that thought in a way that others could understand. In addition, the time spent on evaluating their own performance during discussion after winter vacation was intense scaffolding as she guided her students to observe, identify, and articulate productive and nonproductive discussion behaviors. The scaffolding created by her demonstrations, direct instruction, and commentary supported all of her students as they developed as readers and thinkers.

Lisa's classroom community was a safe and supportive place because she trusted her students to do their best, trusted herself to know what her students needed, and respected both her own knowledge and skill as a teacher and the funds of knowledge (Moll, 1992) that her students brought to the discussion group.

Community in Charlotte's Classroom

"I want to provide an atmosphere of respect and one in which my students are willing to take risks." Charlotte's words are brought to life in Chapters 3 and 4. Here we have seen that Charlotte's classroom was a place where these ELLs wanted to be and where they spent a lot of time talking. As they practiced English, these students learned about themselves, about whales, and about books. Remember that Charlotte shared her classroom with the reading specialist; the physical space was tiny, but the space for student ideas and student talk was expansive. The daily routines in this classroom, the presentation and discussion of content, the activities students engaged in—all these not only helped build a sense of a shared English language classroom community, but also established relationships among that community, the students' homes, their mainstream classrooms, and life in the United States. Talk about whales provided the practice in the target language these ELL students needed to participate fully in the social and academic communities of their lives in the United States, and it gave them important and immediate social capital as they studied whales with their mainstream peers. Talk about whales was a vehicle for learning how to find and discern information, and how to tease out and make explicit the relationships between the natural world and human society. This focus on community in content paralleled practices that supported this classroom community.

Talk in this classroom served a dual purpose with regard to building community: It promoted both social and school-related ways to talk. The communal function of greetings and chit-chat as these students trickled into class built confidence and encouraged practice in communicative competence in an authentic, relaxed, and safe context. As they shared about their day or the books they were browsing, or asked about an activity, these students were initiating, maintaining, repairing, and ending conversations. During the small-group discussions that constituted their class time, they were learning and rehearsing school ways to talk and engage with ideas. They learned about the different types of whales and could discuss their differences. In this classroom, students contributed an extraordinary two-thirds of the utterances consistently across the 6-week unit, even when they were struggling with comprehending a text. Such confident exploration was possible in this safe community because what they had to say was valued, space was made, and support was provided for them to figure out meanings and connections. The "Put your babe upon your back" conversation was an extended, even circuitous search for meaning. PD's calling out and initiating a discussion of the border art and secondary narrative in *Kayuktuk: An Arctic Quest* (Heinz, 1996) demonstrated how comfortable he felt doing so. Respect was present as these students acknowledged and built on each other's contributions, expressed agreement, and actively listened. In tandem with overlapping talk and excited outbursts, this classroom community privileged respect for ideas and for one another, and this was continuously practiced through dialogue and dialogic instruction.

Charlotte kept the talk flowing by asking supportive questions that were tightly contingent on student contributions. When she asked open questions inviting connections to the students' homes or experiences or to the text, there would often be a flurry of sharing. When Charlotte asked whether her students believed that the whales had called Lilly's name in *The Whales' Song* (Sheldon, 1991), these students connected and shared all kinds of home experiences when either they or family members were not believed. These students were comfortable sharing what they knew and forging connections as they did so. And Charlotte was active in her support of this, because through their talk they were developing linguistic and academic proficiency. It was not surprising, then, to note that in this atmosphere of acceptance and deep respect, students felt comfortable grappling with language and making meaning, and felt free to make errors on their way to understanding.

Community in Michael's Classroom

Exploring connections among books through both talking and writing about them were core practices in Michael's classroom community, as presented in Chapters 5 and 6. The classroom culture that he and his students established was explicitly that of a reading and talking community, and in some ways it was difficult to separate content from community.

In Michael's third-grade classroom, reading was "cool," and talk among students about reading was exciting conversation. There was always time for reading: independent reading, read-alouds, sharing reading logs, and even bonus picturebook read-alouds that Michael slid in because they fit with a social studies or science focus. And there was time to talk about books. At morning meeting, each person had time to shine when his or her reading and reading log were the focus, and everyone got to know one another a little better. Reading was "almost never just a fun thing," and its practice made evident the norms and values of this classroom community. There was time to hear from constituents; there were well-established procedures, but room for variety; there were expectations for active and respectful participation; there was lots of humor; and there was an ease with which it all came together.

During morning meeting, students shared about what was important to them and updated the class about what they were reading. During this talk, we didn't learn only about what students were reading, but also about reading habits and how reading fits into life. We learned that Michael's wife liked to jump to the end of a book; we discovered that Ana and her sister read the same books and talked about what was going to happen, and that this was okay (even if Michael teasingly called it "cheating"). In this community, reading log time was protected: It faithfully happened every week and with every child.

We heard student voices as the class and Michael negotiated what the next chapter read-aloud would be. As they nominated various books, students talked about these books and their content with ease and growing felicity. They were assured, knowledgeable, and confident that their opinions counted. It was a student who suggested they do a poll so a decision could be made, and it was the students who volunteered to obtain copies of nominated books. Students were vested in the process and committed to the classroom culture.

Finally, membership in Michael's literate community did not end in June, as the turtle poem sent to Michael by a fifth grader demonstrates. Michael's response illustrated what counted. In the less than a minute that it took to share the poem and direct Sam to tape it on the turtle tank, these students saw that Michael's community was valued and privileged, and that this community continued beyond the year spent in his classroom.

Community in Sarah's Classroom

In Chapter 7, we have seen that introducing home community practices into the classroom can have unexpected benefits. Over the course of a year, Sarah's inclusion of a practical and simple activity—crocheting at the end of the day—"helped create a classroom community that was based on stronger friendships, for the simple reason they were given opportunities to get to know each other." As these second graders crocheted, they chatted. As they chatted, they talked about what was important: their families, their pets, the things they were making. When they ran low on crocheting supplies, they solved this problem together. The hook responsibility letters reminded these second graders that they had limited supplies and that they had to share these. As a community they discussed needs and wants, and as a community they shared and helped each other. Many members of this class brought in yarn from home to share with the class. Crocheting also brought community volunteers into the classroom and inspired these second graders to reach out to community businesses. Crocheting bridged school and home, and created an authentic context for reading and writing practice and purposeful communication: thank-you letters to people who had helped in their classroom, letters to businesses asking for supplies, and lists to help them decide what supplies they would buy with the money given to them *because* of their letter writing.

The sense of group identity these students felt as the "crazy about crocheting" class grew while they chatted and crocheted. The excited interest in crocheting pulled students in, with boys and girls choosing to crochet at home rather than "play on the competer or wath tv," as one student wrote. And they taught each other, expanding the circle of community, as demonstrated by Maggie's explanation that "Bobby taught me to make necklaces, bracelets and rings. Bobby changed my mind [about crocheting]."

This common interest, and the students' shared concern to protect and maintain it, brought them together as a community to raise money for supplies, to decide what to spend the community money on, and to work together to make all the granny squares needed to make an afghan. Remember how they organized the yarn balls, and how they measured their granny squares to make them all the same? These second graders understood the notion of rules and responsibilities. They were functioning as a caring community.

This happened because their teacher was willing to take a risk. Sarah gave crocheting a try: "I didn't know if the idea was going to amount to anything, and if it failed, well, there is something to learn from that too." As Sarah found, her intended but limited goals in introducing crocheting were wildly exceeded: As activity fostered talk about common subjects, this engendered mutuality, which in turn built relationships, which organically coalesced into community and finally (though not finitely) into an identity.

ENGAGING MATERIAL

Children are voracious learners, having practiced learning about their worlds since birth. Just as "What's that?" is a question uttered almost constantly by toddlers, "How does this work?", "What does this mean?", "How do I think about this?", and "How does this relate to me?" are questions that children ask themselves every day at school. Smart teachers give their students plenty to think about, and the four teachers described in this book all chose children's literature as one of their main classroom resources. Children's literature offers the ideas of others—ideas that children are not necessarily exposed to in the course of their lives in and out of school. Books offer young readers a vast array of information about virtually every topic they might be curious about. In addition to narratives, poetry, and picturebooks, there are informational and reference books, many with colorful illustrations to support understanding and imagination. Books also offer young readers experiences that go far beyond their own experiential realm, as they read about people, places, and ideas across time, space, and circumstances in fictional narratives or nonfiction texts created by gifted writers. Moreover, these texts offer young readers examples of interesting language used in interesting ways—language that is crafted to express the very ideas that engage young readers.

Children's literature is different from textbooks for children in many ways, one of which is that it spans a wide range of reading levels. It also is much more varied, with an abundance of books providing a range of information and ideas that cannot be captured between the pages of a single textbook or basal reader, no matter how good it is. Children's books also offer children the opportunity to find themselves, or a glimpse of themselves, in a book—the opportunity to know that others have the same feelings and desires as they. Reading children's books also provides opportunities to discover that people are different in how they look or live or think or believe, and that this is okay. Nothing is better than children's books for offering opportunities to think about life and learn about the world (Galda et al., 2010). In English language arts instruction, children's books are effective ways to provide the ideas that make learning skills worthwhile, that promote good discussions, but most of all that children want to think and talk about.

Lisa's Materials

Lisa's classroom was filled to overflowing with books. She had always loved children's books and had purchased hundreds over the years, but this year she was using a new basal reader that was organized around six themes. So she sorted her books, bought new ones, and raided the school library for stories, poetry, and nonfiction related to the themes they were required to cover. Several things about her classroom library stand out. First, there was a wide range in reading levels both among her students (second grade through fifth grade) and in her library. Her library contained picturebooks, easy readers, transitional chapter books, and novels—a rich mix of narrative fiction, nonfiction, blended genres, and poetry. This mix reflected the needs and preferences of her students as well, with Cong gravitating toward the nonfiction, Susan sometimes needing to relax with a picturebook, and Charlie forging ahead, devouring novel after novel.

Lisa also combined the literature in her shelves and bins with the literature presented in the basal reader, moving easily with her students from their "reading books" to her "children's books." Across all of the material, she planned experiences that included reading aloud, reading in pairs, reading silently and individually in the classroom, and reading at home with family members. Her students read entire texts both individually and together, and they took books of their choice home and brought them back to share during discussion, as we have seen in Chapter 2's description of the initial days of the school year. These individual choices reflected the full range of books in Lisa's classroom, with students moving freely from picturebooks to novels and back again. Lisa also sampled the range of books available for reading aloud, as she read from the basal text, from picturebooks (both fiction and nonfiction), and from chapter books. The first chapter book that students listened to, *Arthur, for the Very First Time* (MacLachlan, 1980), became foundational in their subsequent growth as readers.

The opportunities for experience and understanding that Lisa offered her students through the books she had in her classroom were invaluable. The books were the key to what happened across the course of the year, as they gave students meaningful things to discuss: the ideas found in books that engaged their interest.

Charlotte's Materials

Charlotte, too, filled her classroom with books that supported her students' learning. During the whale unit, for example, there were over 100 reference and picturebooks on whales, and her ELL students were encouraged to browse through them in class, to take them home, and to share interesting findings. There was also a 6-foot annotated poster of a northern right whale on the classroom wall. These students became very knowledgeable about the characteristics of particular whales—so much so that when Charlotte added a clip art graphic to her handout of the

"Killer Whales" poem (Yolen, 1996), they were affronted that it was the wrong type of whale.

Charlotte was explicit in her conviction that just because these students were ELLs, this did not mean that they were unable to engage with fourth- and fifth-grade content. Using carefully selected literature, she planned lessons in instructional units so that there would be overlapping vocabulary and concepts and a sense of growing expertise as her students engaged with ideas. She also focused on how to gather information, what to look for, and how material related to their essential questions. Addressing "What sources of information can be used to find out about whales and other topics?" and "What are the interactions between whales and mankind?" (two of the three essential questions for the whale unit), Charlotte helped students build needed academic skills that extended far beyond content knowledge alone; she placed these skills in a context that was relevant, empowering, and connected to what they already knew. Both within and across lessons, Charlotte started with what the students knew, using strategies such as the KWL chart. Then they talked about it. Not only did Charlotte want to remind students of what they knew; she also wanted them to articulate what they wanted to know. At the end of the unit, these ELL students shared with others in the school community what they had learned from the materials they had thought about.

Michael's Materials

"Well, books are a real big part of the classroom," Michael explained. Then he began to list all of the daily opportunities to read books in his classroom and corrected himself: "Books," he said, "are *huge*." It was expected practice that students always had a trade book to read, and it was common practice that books "did the rounds." At times there was a waiting list for certain titles, and students were cajoled by other students during morning meeting to read faster because they wanted to borrow the book. Students were aware of what other students were reading and took heed of feedback and recommendations. *The Sea of Trolls* (Farmer, 2004) and *The Lightning Thief* (Riordan, 2005) were particular favorites, as were the *American Girl* and *Rowan of Rin* series. There was even a birthday party where, rather than presents, students brought three favorite books to swap for three others.

Michael had a deep knowledge of and great love for children's literature. He had read most of the books his students had, and if he had not, he joined the line to borrow those books. For example, when students were talking about *The Sea of Trolls*, a book he had not yet read, he noted that "it's on my list of ones I need to read myself and then share in class later." There were dozens of books in his class library, and the class made frequent visits to the school library; all members of this classroom community knew the librarian well. Michael was purposeful in his recommendations. The reading log class routine kept him current in his knowledge of what individuals were reading independently, and Michael strategically recommended books that aligned with the genres, interests and reading abilities of his various students, but that they might not be likely to find on their own.

These books were full of ideas to think about. In Michael's class, talk about books encouraged and generated connections among known ideas and new ideas. Characters in books were talked about like old friends. Matilda, the two Charlies (Bone and Bucket), Throgil (*The Sea of Trolls*), Harry (Potter), Kirsten (an American Girl), Gregor (the Overlander), Mullet Fingers (*Hoot*), Eragon, and Rowan (of Rin) were characters these classmates referred to with ease and insight, and their circumstances, trials, and successes were related to the everyday happenings, concerns, and ruminations of these students.

Sarah's Materials

Suggestions embedded in Sarah's book selections played an important supportive role in generating ideas to think about in her second-grade classroom. When Sarah wanted to reinforce the idea that writing letters is a powerful literacy practice, she selected two picturebooks to make her case: *The Jolly Christmas Postman* (Ahlberg, 1991) and *I Wanna Iguana* (Kaufman Orloff, 2004). When she realized how crocheting activities had knitted their community together, she selected picturebooks in which hand-made artifacts tell their stories to read aloud. When students were trying to make stitches, they referred to "how-to-crochet" books. Books in Sarah's class pointed to possibilities of what could be done, and sometimes they also pointed toward how to do these things.

In this classroom, materials to think about went beyond books and traditional literary modes to include the art and mechanics of crocheting, the discussions that crocheting fostered, and the physical artifacts produced by their labors (their hand-crafted creations). Acquiring and organizing the raw materials needed for these creations, and making decisions about whom to give their products to and what they represented, provided additional fodder for much conversation and thought. In Sarah's classroom, crocheting—which some might consider an idle pastime, suitable primarily for whiling away the hours—was catalytic, providing rich material for powerful and relevant literacy applications.

JOY

Learning new things may be difficult, but as Michael has reminded us, it shouldn't be "a drudgery kind of thing." Children come to school having learned a tremendous amount in their first years of life. It is true (if too often stated) that young children are sponges, soaking up knowledge and new ideas, and they do this with visible joy in the process. Why, then, shouldn't pleasure in learning occur in schools? Enjoyment in learning has much to do with motivation: Children learn best when they want to learn something, when they have choices about what to learn, and when what they learn is meaningful to them. Interest, both personal and situational, is a significant intrinsic motivator (Guthrie & Anderson, 1999; Guthrie & Knowles, 2001; Wigfield & Tonks, 2004). Effective teachers seek to know and capture students' personal interests and design an environment, a classroom situation, that fosters and stimulates interest—just as Lisa, Charlotte, Michael, and Sarah did.

Joyful learning not only springs from motivation, but is the result of classrooms that are safe and supportive, are filled with interesting material, and offer engaging literacy practices. This combination of safety, interesting material, and engaging practices creates a structure that supports itself: Students' enjoyment in pursuing their interests within the broad parameters of the curriculum (as in the cases here) feeds literacy practices that are engaging and lead to more enjoyment, which leads to more literacy practices—a lovely cycle.

Joy in Lisa's Classroom

This circular process was certainly evident in Lisa's classroom. Lisa loved books, and her love of books was contagious. Her students were representative of most classes in the fall: Some already loved to read, and some did not; some had many experiences with children's books, and some did not. Lisa, however, had made engaging with books a long-term goal for the year, as she knew that engaged readers are likely to become lifelong readers. Wisely, she began with her students and their choices, as we have seen in the talk from the first day of book discussion. Students were free to choose from a wide array of books, and their initial sharing consisted of their own likes and dislikes. This was a simple, reinforcing, and positive way to begin a year-long focus on their responses to literature.

As her students grew increasingly adept at talking about the books they read, Lisa kept them engaged by selecting books that she hoped would be interesting for the whole class to share. For example, when she saw that *Arthur, for the Very First Time* had been so popular with her students that they asked to listen to it again, she not only figured out how to do so (during lunch hour), but also built on their pleasure in Patricia MacLachlan's writing with an author study using many of her other books. When she saw how engaged they were with *The Whipping Boy* (Fleischman, 1986), she slowed down the reading process a bit, allowing her students time to read, savor, and discuss thoroughly the experience they were having as they read. Lisa's dual focus on comprehension and aesthetic response across the year nurtured both her students' growth in reading ability and their development of literary understanding anchored in powerful aesthetic responses to the texts they were reading. This joy (and pride) was evident when they all agreed that they were indeed "some kids."

Joy in Charlotte's Classroom

Charlotte's students exhibited their joy in many ways, one of which was to come early and stay late. During class, their enthusiastic, overlapping sharings marked their growing linguistic competence and their engagement and delight in participating in class. Their interests and enthusiasm helped Charlotte determine the order for shared oral reading, and the focus and scope of the talk as they discussed those books. These students relished the art in picturebooks, taking time to note the border art in *Kayuktuk: An Arctic Quest* and the painted representations in *The Whales* (Rylant, 1996). Charlotte actively stoked student enthusiasm by adding sticky notes to pages in books (often reference books) that she thought would pique interest, and leaving them on the table for students to see when they arrived for class. In turn, students responded by sharing their favorites. These students displayed their joy in the process by spending large amounts of time at home creating artifacts to support this study of whales, such as Rosey's coloring book, in which she outlined the shapes of different types of whales. Had resources and time allowed, Rosey and Lucy would have been out selling t-shirts and bookmarks to raise funds to "save the whales!"

By organizing material through instructional units, and presenting it through literature, Charlotte strove to maintain the integrity of the "whole picture" and the connectivity of learning. For these students, making rich connections across languages, content, experience, and ideas preserved their pleasure in the process. Like the rest of us, these students entered school wanting to learn; in Charlotte's class, the social nature of the process, the constant talking, and the support of beautiful illustrations accentuated the joyful nature of learning, even though it was in a second language and was very hard work.

Joy in Michael's Classroom

Sometimes the hard work of learning can be swept away by the delight of engaged learning. Michael's read-aloud of *Midnight for Charlie Bone* (Nimmo, 2003) confirmed the joy of listening to an exuberant, polished reading. Combining an animated performance with a considered decision not to assign a follow-up task, Michael made reading aloud an experience to be savored. It was quite possible that these third graders understood somewhere in the backs of their minds that they were in fact learning as they listened to and talked about books, but Michael's classroom culture provided such a vibrant context that it was hard to separate "learning" from the excitement about and anticipation for what would happen next. There were ample demonstrations of this: when Maeve's classmates wanted her to read in Michael's stead so they could keep going; when excited students submitted nominations for the next chapter book to be read aloud; and when Suzanna's reading log sparked a discussion of how Charlie Bone, Harry Potter, Gregor, Matilda, and Eragon all have special powers. Reading fluently aloud, giving a book talk, making connections across texts—these things were practiced in Michael's class, and they were fun.

Even writing reading log entries was not drudgery, as they were framed as letters to Michael, housed in a journal that was a record of a student's readings for the year, and called for students' personal thoughts about each book they had selected. To make logs even more engaging, once a month parents or friends were allowed to be "secretaries," giving students the opportunity to focus on ideas without concern for mechanics. Creativity was praised, and students felt empowered to play with fonts, or add illustrations and messages to Michael—and he responded! Each week, the first thing students did upon the return of their reading logs was to read Michael's comments and then write back again. Sean's reading log entry quoted at the start of Chapter 6 closed with "I'm going to stop here at this exciting part—because you always do that in *Eragon* and other books. I know you will be anxious to know what happens next. Ha! Ha! Ha!" Michael's response was "You STINKER!" This special, playful dialogic interplay is redolent of the pleasures of the epistolary relationship; it is delightful to receive a message meant for oneself alone. Michael understood this, and used the reading log process as yet another way to inspire joy.

Joy in Sarah's Classroom

In Sarah's classroom, joy was evident in the pride her students took in accomplishment, in generosity, and in empowerment to make a difference in the community. This joy was the outcome of hard work. These second graders crocheted gifts for their families and friends; one of them even invented a new stitch, which other students learned and used; and together they experienced the satisfaction of working together on something special, a beautiful class afghan, which they gave away with immense pride.

When these students heard that their letters to local businesses had resulted in a donation for crocheting supplies, they experienced the impact of powerful, meaningful literacy. Sarah described them as "ecstatic." Their joy in their crocheting projects was apparent in other ways, as when two second graders huddled together during recess to figure out how many rows they needed to make their granny square the right size for the afghan, and thus experienced the joy of accomplishment. Finally, in donating the class afghan to Mrs. March—a community member undergoing chemotherapy and in need of emotional support—they experienced the joy of generosity.

MULTIPLE PATHS TO LEARNING

There are many routes to a goal. Some are circuitous and some direct, some are fast and some slow, but good practices can all lead to the same ends. Effective teachers know this, understand the principle of equifinality, and select the paths that seem to be most effective; they judge effectiveness by the responses of their students and follow the students' lead. Lisa, Charlotte, Michael, and Sarah were quite planful. Their knowledge allowed them to work on both long- and short-term goals, as they constantly evaluated their students' progress and assessed their engagement in tasks. While day-to-day successes and failures mattered to them, and they reflected on them, they always held their long-term goals in mind as they made instructional decisions. At the same time, their instructional decisions were very much influenced by the responses of their students.

As these teachers carried out the decision-making process, they were aware of the growing abilities of their novice students, and the need to provide experiences that would safely yet thoroughly prepare them for success in school and life. Knowing what paths were available allowed each teacher a multiplicity of responses, and thereby facilitated responsiveness—contingency—during the act of teaching. There were recursiveness and overlapping in the material presented and the strategies employed. The content and the learning processes were adjusted during and at the end of each lesson, as Lisa, Charlotte, Michael, and

Sarah considered "what worked" and what needed to be realigned or discarded. These teachers shared an understanding that the fastest route might not provide sufficient experience for independence. Consequently, they would often circle around and back into a topic, phrasing, or practice. In these four classrooms, effective practice included time in the daily routine, time to explore during the act of learning, and a clear understanding of how short-term objectives must support long-term learning goals.

Goals and Paths for Lisa

Lisa's goals included moving her students toward becoming *critical readers*—readers who "think about what we read." Another goal was to help her students become *engaged readers*—those who would probably continue to read across their lives. A third goal was to improve her students' reading ability, as measured by the mandated tests given in the spring. To work toward those goals, she chose the vehicle of reading and responding to children's books through discussion, because she knew that talking with others could be a way to attain all three. It was not necessarily efficient; it took a great deal of time and energy to teach and learn this way, but it held the potential to be one effective path. Lisa listened carefully as she closely monitored what was occurring in the class discussion group. She knew who was participating and who was silent; she saw the differences between students' written responses and their oral responses; she structured and supported their participation in many ways; and she stopped and refocused just after winter break, when she realized that this was necessary. She also planned for each discussion while seizing the opportunities for new paths that student talk provided. She recognized that her plans were but one way to accomplish her goals, and that the directions opened by students' interests and conversation held the potential of being as, or more, effective. It would have been much easier for her to assign workbook exercises, ask students to do book reports, have them work primarily in the basal reader, and assign them books for homework assignments. She did not do this because she believed that these seemingly efficient assignments would not be effective, and she had seen how her students had already blossomed in the discussion group in the fall, so she continued to put forth the effort necessary to support them in their growth as readers. Because Lisa was concerned with engagement and aesthetic response, she knew that she had to both guide and follow her students as they read and talked. She could not "tell" her students what their responses were; rather, she had to help them recognize, utter, and build upon their ideas and questions. She took the "long view" of what it meant to be a reader: developing skills, engaging critcally with text, learning how literature works, and learning about life. Her students gave her the courage to pursue these goals through book discussions by their many demonstrations of developing fluency, engagement, critical thinking, and literary understanding.

Goals and Paths for Charlotte

Like Lisa, Charlotte took the "long view" for her ELL students. She understood that the experience of grappling with language and the process of making meaning served her long-term goals more effectively than providing her students with ready answers would. This was apparent in the number of turns of talk it took to figure out what "Put your babe upon your back" meant in the "Killer Whales" poem. At least three times, students left the phrase, moved on, then circled back into it. After the lesson, Charlotte indicated that "the last thing I wanted to do was go through that poem line by line," but the conversation made it plain that this was what the students needed to do. During most other lessons, they "got" meaning quickly and discussed the ideas; in the "Killer Whales" lesson, her plan (to compare the perspective of the whales as hunters and the whales as nurturers) was quickly set aside. Charlotte made a similar decision, but for a different reason, in the first lesson of the whale unit, when she had planned to read *Dear Mr. Blueberry* (James, 1991) and use this text as a springboard for her KWL chart on how and where to get information about whales. But her students were avid to know more about an author they liked, Ed Young, so the planned content was set aside and the objectives and process shifted to student-selected material.

Charlotte was able to make such shifts effectively, in part because she was able to draw quickly on her resources and expertise. She had a deep knowledge of literature, her students, and educationally effective pedagogical practice. She knew how to "lead from behind" and to make explicit the connections between student contributions and her lesson objectives. Just as important, though, was Charlotte's awareness that this was an ELL class and that talk in the target language was always productive. Talking together and building on each other's ideas built both communicative and academic competence, and for most of her students, her classroom was the classroom where they enthusiastically chose to participate. Often Charlotte sanctioned digressions in pursuit of that noisy chatter—those exploratory exchanges and elaborated utterances. To paraphrase Rosey when she talked about Ed Young's (1992) *Seven Blind Mice*, the right path was "when you go all over the place."

Goals and Paths for Michael

In Michael's classroom, there were times for "going all over the place" and times when he wanted just one or two points to be made, but in both cases the specific path was not predetermined. Michael was explicit in his long-term goal of nurturing a community of readers. In the shorter term, he wanted them to leave third grade enjoying reading so much that they would survive fourth grade in New York State, when there is a sudden and constant emphasis on assessment. He reasoned that if he got them completely besotted with books, they would continue as readers, and his planning reflected this.

Two key elements were predetermined and consistently adhered to: the routines of literacy events and the careful selection of literature. When daily routines were disrupted on occasion, time for reading aloud and for sharing reading logs was not sacrificed. While there were established norms for participation within particular literacy events, there was no script. Michael actively listened and contingently responded to students' reading logs as he heard them for the first time; he collected them for review after the students shared them. There were thus multiple paths for his response, many stimuli worthy of response, many ways to frame each response, and many potentially fruitful digressions. In these discussions, Michael's experience and expertise came to the fore as he exercised deft pedagogical flexibility. His in-the-moment instructional decisions were made in the service of his long-term goals. Michael was artful in his attention to students' contributions and in his responses to elicit student elaboration, clarification, and eventual appropriation of literate language. His felicity with language, his wit, and his insightful knowledge of his students culminated in his ability to introduce the appropriate frame, concept, or character trait and immediately apply it to what students contributed. In these moments, he enacted the bottom-up, experience-driven concepts of students while also meeting the organizing frames and language of schooling. This practice embodied Vygotsky's (1986) notion of spontaneous and scientific concept formation. During morning meeting, Michael allowed time and space to wander; during reading aloud, however, he maintained a tight rein, pausing briefly for a comprehension check here and a prediction there before continuing.

The selection of appropriately engaging trade books was as critical to the success of literacy events in Michael's classroom as the routines were. Michael had a planned routine for selecting chapter books to read aloud, and this plan too was structured but unscripted. He took book selection seriously, and his students offered thoughtful nominations in response. Rich discussions of literature followed, opening multiple paths of exploration and reflection.

Goals and Paths for Sarah

In Sarah's classroom, we have seen a new teacher take small steps; reflect on where she was; and then, based on what she observed, take another few steps and repeat the process. The goals she began with were narrow—improving the students' manual dexterity for handwriting, and filling the time before the buses arrived—but broadened into larger literacy goals as her students offered her opportunities to help them pursue meaningful literacy outcomes. The paths she forged involved courage and an attitude of "let's find out." Sarah's incremental, carefully considered steps, inspired by her students' responses to crocheting time, opened multiple paths to literacy. As Sarah started down the path of authentic practice, she observed more and more indicators that this was the right path for her students. As students wrote thank-you letters to volunteers in their classroom, or "hook responsibility letters," or letters to businesses requesting donations, the importance of careful writing and good spelling to clear communication was evident, and her students responded with diligence and motivation. As they moved from individual squares to working together to create a larger piece, Sarah also helped them move toward using their crocheting, and their developing literacy skills, to have a positive impact on their community.

REAL TALK: PLANNED AND CONTINGENT

All of the teachers described in this book chose as their main instructional practice the vehicle of talk—real talk as inquiry, exploration, conversation. During the real talk that occurred in their classrooms, these teachers were not often controlling the discussions, but rather were responsive to student input. Their instructional goals were planned and present, but supported rather than controlled the conversations they had with their students. The better these teachers' plans were, the better able they were to attend to the in-the-moment event of conversation. Their understanding that detours very often lead to a destination allowed them to travel down new paths of inquiry and exploration with their students.

The talk examined in Chapters 2–7 is lived discourse; in Charlotte's words, it is "real language in real situations to accomplish real goals." When we look closely at this real talk, we see what is actually taught, in all its messy, dialogic, exploratory, embedded, unfolding, and unpredictable glory. The lived language of the classroom has the potential to be relevant, empowering, and varied, but only insofar as the local potential is exploited to bridge home and school literacy practices, to link what is known with what is being presented, and to connect what is being talked about to effective learning practices. To mine this potential, these teachers provided opportunities for spontaneous responses, and prompted students in "shaping at the point of utterance" (Britton, 1993). These teachers then listened attentively to what the students offered, gently challenged them to delve deeper, and then moved aside to allow the students to get on with the hard work of real talk. Effective teachers like Lisa, Charlotte, Michael, and Sarah wield the dominant instructional tool of the question to assist, not assess, as they facilitate student thinking and articulation. Each of these four teachers practiced contingent questioning, using such questions to scaffold students as they moved toward elaborated talk, with elaborated thought behind it. Successful teachers know their students well and anchor their scaffolding questions in student contributions; they know the material well enough to manipulate it with some ease and fluency; and their deep reservoir of instructional strategies allows them to tailor their instruction to suit student input.

As we have discussed in Chapter 1, an utterance both responds to and anticipates other utterances, and the process of composing it increases awareness of linguistic and communicative fluency. Good teachers create opportunities for dialogue in the classroom to build students' facility with language. They encourage students to experience *oracy* (the verbalization of experience and the experience of verbalization). They plan contexts, activities, and opportunities, and then they prompt, encourage, and even supportively challenge students to participate. These teachers also practice *uptake*; they build on what students offer. They become adept at restating student comments fluently and accurately. They also learn how to employ contingent questions that arise from the moment and facilitate real talk for both first- and second-language students and across the curriculum. The four teachers described in this book exemplify this kind of skillful teaching through talk.

Real talk is also communicative. Even talk that could be construed as merely idle conversation has a greater social purpose, as it creates an attitude of sociability that builds relationships and trust. It, too, is evident in the conversations described in this book. However, real talk looks different in every class, as it responds to and anticipates of local context, content, and participants. The teacher is a major factor in shaping opportunities and expectations for real talk.

During Lisa's second-grade language arts time, real talk served to develop her students' literary understanding as she created a book discussion group that grappled with issues important to the students. She effectively shaped the discourse through the structures she put in place, the questions she asked, the examples of response she offered, and her obvious interest in what her students were saying. With her fourth- and fifth-grade ELLs, Charlotte deftly positioned contingent questioning to share the cognitive load by building a responsive scaffold to support and extend the students' communicative and academic competence through dialogic and ever-more elaborated utterances. Real talk looked different again in Michael's third-grade mainstream classroom: The literacy events of morning meeting and reading aloud highlighted and encouraged variations of literate talk, as Michael made modeling and eliciting such talk an entertaining and interactive classroom practice.

Lisa, Charlotte, and Michael were all experienced teachers who were increasingly adept at promoting real conversations about important things. There was a certain ease with which they elicited student responses. There are patterns and principles of practice evident in the talk in their classrooms, but the key catalysts were their ability and willingness to think and respond flexibly in the moment. This contingency required real effort, attentive listening, and the ability to learn from and leave behind floundering digressions. Sarah was not as experienced as these three teachers but in her second-grade classroom, she made space for real conversations—a brave move on her part. As Sarah supported her students in their growth through crocheting talk, she came to an important realization: Sometimes it was simply a matter of getting out of their way.

Talking to Develop Literary Understanding in Lisa's Classroom

Lisa's focus on helping her students become engaged, thoughtful readers necessarily included attention to fostering their aesthetic experiences with appropriate texts. She did this by carefully considering the novels they read together, the questions she asked them, and the example she set. Furthermore, she paid very close attention to the class conversations, always looking for the opportunity to build on a student response, confusion, question, or seemingly tangential idea. Elements of Lisa's expertise included her knowledge of literature and how it works; her understanding of the importance of aesthetic engagement with narrative fiction; her facility with comprehension strategy instruction; and her knowledge of her students' lives both inside and outside school. She also understood the dual nature of response to literature: It is both intensely personal and highly social. These understandings allowed her to help her students develop facility with the language of literary talk as they learned to understand and articulate their responses to the books they read.

This multifaceted expertise was evident in every discussion Lisa and her students had during the school year. To complement her expertise, she brought with her an openness to students' ideas and interests; a willingness to listen closely to what they were saying (and trying to say); and a determination to let their ideas and responses structure the discussions they had together, even as she was alert to those perfect "teachable moments" that sometimes occurred during discussions. She resisted the urge to take over the conversations to teach something, and instead waited for the moment a student comment offered that same opportunity. Then she did not hesitate to seize such an idea and pursue it. Learning the language of literature, discussing connections between text and life, and making many connections across various texts helped ensure that her students would develop a more sophisticated understanding of how literature works, as well as how they thought about it as they read. This learning originated in the real talk that surrounded reading and responding.

Lisa used contingent questioning in another way to help her students clarify their own ideas. She was adept (increasingly so across the school year) at understanding that her students might not know how to express their ideas in a way that others could comprehend, and so she frequently either restated them and asked for confirmation of her restatement's validity, or asked questions that would allow her and others to understand. In this way, she gave her students—when they demonstrated a need for them—the words with which to express themselves.

Real talk about literature is full of opportunities for exploring ideas that are important to readers. The teacher's task is to offer ideas or to clarify student-offered ideas; to assess the students' interest in and uptake of those ideas; and then to put aside those that students do not take up and to pursue those they do. There are many ways to understand literature or to respond to any given text, and the talk that follows engaged aesthetic reading, when effective, is necessarily spontaneous. Even the best teacher-generated ideas are not effective if students are not ready for them.

Both students heard *Arthur, for the Very First Time* read aloud, and they were asked what it meant to "look through the faraway end." This was a good question to think about, as it got at one of the themes of the book. For these students at these times, however, it was not an effective question, because they were not yet capable of—or perhaps not interested in—thinking about it, much less discussing it. Imagine Lisa's surprise when Abeo walked into the classroom in April, fully 3 months after the second reading of the book, and announced that she knew what it meant to "look through the faraway end." Ever ready to follow promising student leads, Lisa used Abeo's new insight as a springboard for discussion. She and her students talked about perspective, about how authors often have a central metaphor in stories, and about remembering important books. Lisa remarked, "Some books do that," and Charlie, a gifted reader, expanded on her idea:

> "Possibly some books are better than others and some books you read more deeply. Like we read. We really get deeply into a story. We read about what happened, and think about why it happened. We read more deeply than people I know. They'd say, 'That's cool that happened.'" We think, '*Why* did that happen?', 'Who made it happen?', and all that other stuff."

Lisa followed Charlie's comment with a question about what reading is, eliciting several answers, one of which came again from Charlie: "I think it depends on what kind of book. If you read a book like *Arthur, for the Very First Time*, you kind of understand life better." This 8-year-old understood the results of an aesthetic engagement with text, as well he should. The conversations that he, his peers, and his teacher had been having across the year shaped his ability to read and talk about books in a manner that allowed him to understand life—and literature—better. This conversation also confirmed for Lisa that she had indeed met her goal of helping her students become more fluent, engaged, thoughtful readers.

Using the Contingent Question to Support ELLs in Charlotte's Classroom

To develop language and literacy capabilities, language learners must practice them. This practice is scripted in some classrooms, and students learn effective ways to respond to particular contexts in principled, structured sequences. In other language-learning classrooms, any kind of talk is encouraged—so much so that Pennycook (1994, p. 311) described some communicative language teaching as "empty babble." In Charlotte's classroom, language learning was communicative, substantive, and a little messy as students explored ideas, verbalized experience, and learned content through the context of shared children's literature and individual research from the host of reference materials provided in their classroom. As we have seen in Chapters 3 and 4, these six ELL students had been learning English for over a year and were able to express developmentally appropriate thoughts and ideas in English, the target language. In Charlotte's classroom, they were expected to use real language in varied situations to accomplish relevant goals, so they could not only participate in ELL class but join in the chatter and engage in discussions when they were with their mainstream peers.

In the service of these goals, real talk opportunities were planned and embedded into daily routines. This was a "pull-out" ELL classroom, and the students arrived in Charlotte's room before Charlotte did and at slightly different times, as they came from several different mainstream classrooms. Typically, there were things for the students to do upon arrival—activities that permitted settling-in time and encouraged phatic communion. This was not Pennycook's (1994) "empty babble," but rather spontaneous response to and elaboration of ideas they formed as they browsed reference books, made connections, and shared experiences. Most days, there were Charlotte's sticky notes on books drawing attention to striking illustrations or interesting comparisons. These "things to do" scaffolded the initial interaction as students arrived; they also encouraged a joint "doing," since there was usually only one copy of the book and note to look at. Typically, when Charlotte arrived, her students eagerly shared whatever readings or illustrations they found most interesting. She would almost always prompt them to connect and compare these with other references. Enactment of this informal daily routine afforded the students regular opportunities to practice communicative competence, and simultaneously to make progress toward the academic competence they needed to talk about content and books and to succeed in school. Furthermore, this routine sometimes resulted in Charlotte's realigning formal class lessons to build on the ideas generated in informal talk.

Charlotte supported the students' exploratory talk not only by facilitating interaction, but by facilitating interpretation as she consistently prompted with questions that were tightly contingent on what had been said and directed the students to "tell me more." She patiently supported and nudged her students toward exploration and elaboration. The ease with which these students discussed the texts they read, and the many elaborated connections they offered in response to those texts, had been learned, meaningfully practiced, and supported all year. Charlotte was consistent in how little she spoke (one-third of the time), when she spoke (usually her utterances launched student elaborations), and what she said (generally contingent questions). She did not distinguish between questions eliciting one or more possible answers (closed or open questions) or questions to which she did or did not know the answer (display or authentic questions). Her intention was to promote real talk leading to language-learning proficiency, so she consistently gave students back their own language and prodded them forward, offering embedded scaffolds in her contingent questions for her students to take up if they were so inclined.

This was the case even when the making of meaning was difficult. Charlotte was there, listening, contingently responding, and not simply providing "the answer," although it might have been easier for all concerned. Charlotte's verbal "nudging" did not shut her students down; on the contrary, her consistent contingent questioning, putting the onus for thinking back on her students, made it clear that they had interpretive authority and that she expected them to exercise it. This was the case whether there was a simpler answer, such as the meaning of "five and fifty," or a more complex one, such as the identity of Mr. Blueberry. Since these students had been consistently positioned as "knowers," they were willing to explore possibilities and to risk being wrong, because that was safe in Charlotte's classroom environment.

Charlotte continued her discursive practices of uptake through contingent questioning. She provided specific, individualized, and effective scaffolding for her students to collaboratively construct meaning, elaborate, and think. Notably, she did not ask questions without having interest in the answer. When she asked, "What do you think about this story?", she was open to real exploration; it was not a treasure hunt where the acceptable or correct answer was already decided. She also consistently refrained from that terminal act of evaluation; she understood that for students to grapple toward meaning, they had to feel safe and engaged in the process. In place of the evaluative third turn, Charlotte wielded the contingent question; this practice not only showcased her pedagogical expertise (Lee, 2007), but contextualized her students' efforts. As she listened attentively and then anchored her questions in what her students provided, she built upon, extended, challenged, revoiced, and raised the ante to push her students forward. This questioning was formulated in the moment, working within the individual and dynamic learning space Vygotsky (1986) has called the *zone of proximal development*. With her help, students were able to do more than they could do alone. Her use of contingent questions was dialogic, as these questions both responded and expected response (Bakhtin, 1981). They nudged students to shape at the point of utterance (Britton, 1993), to explore (Barnes et al., 1990), and to reason (Mercer et al., 1999).

Variations of Literate Talk in Michael's Classroom

By the end of the school year, Michael's classroom community overflowed with talk: Students had learned ways to talk about books, ways to talk about reading books, and ways to select books. This was *literate talk*—elaborated language through which students engage constructively and critically with each others' and their teacher's ideas, and develop principled, deep understandings of the particular concepts and skills taught (Kramer-Dahl, Teo, & Chia, 2007, p. 169). We have seen many examples of how to talk about books in Chapters 5 and 6. Michael's students rehearsed and developed notions of intertextuality, such as when they discussed characters with "endowed powers." There was also running commentary on how to read books—by, for example, noticing implications (such as in the discussion of family time and having to stay in a boarding school over the weekend) or analyzing an author's craft in writing (such as the deliberate selection of characters' names). Michael also explicitly directed how to select books, as in his long and exciting announcement of his decision about the next read-aloud. Embedded in this was not just a reference to almost every book that had been nominated, but also an explicit and detailed raising of awareness for the Newbery Honor Awards: ". . . any book that gets a Newbery [Honor] Award probably is pretty good. It might not appeal to you, but it's probably well written and a lot of people like it. So if you see something like that, it's a good bet that it'd be worth trying." Such talk shapes and is shaped by literate thinking; it is the bridge to literacy (Rubin, 1990) and informs ways of reading and writing (Wells, 1999). We have seen this, for example, in Arianna's creative writing, modeled on J. K. Rowling's style in the *Harry Potter* series.

Literate talk in Michael's classroom was tightly connected to exploratory talk (Barnes et al., 1990; Mercer et al., 1999; Soter et al., 2008) and talking-to-learn (Boyd, 2009; Britton, 1993), where students explore ideas out loud and partners engage with them. As students tried out ideas, Michael's role was to be the discourse guide—to label and make explicit what was being described, to raise awareness of a particular frame or term, and then to focus the talk for a moment or two on that awareness. Michael did not belabor points with these third graders, but there was constant talking about these things. He deftly modeled by building on what was offered and showing how literate terms and concepts applied to their thinking and talk about books. Particular ways of saying things were part of the everyday classroom talk for these third graders. There was a constant drawing of attention to how an author crafted a sentence, or to ways a student connected ideas. Michael understood that literate talk is "a learned ability. I don't think that kids can just come along and talk about books. They need to have those tools and those ways of looking at books to do that."

Michael was explicit in his fostering of a literate identity: He modeled, he directed, and he reinforced. This was a safe and supportive, but also demanding, classroom culture. Michael was both explicit and supportive in his expectations when he asked, as he began reading *Midnight for Charlie Bone* aloud, "Okay, who can tell me what a *prologue* is?" He reinforced student understanding by pointing it out in the actual book, in the same manner as he shared illustrations in picturebooks. When Arianna explained it in terms of a "thingy," Michael gently directed, "A little more detail would be good." Similarly, during a reading log discussion during morning meeting, when Susan responded with one-word answers, Michael restated the question and explicitly prompted, "This is where you elaborate." Michael was again explicit when he praised Sean's making connections across texts: "Okay, excellent, excellent! I love it when people relate what's happening in one story with what they've heard in other stories."

In these ways, this classroom talk was not just social, in-and-of-the-moment conversation; it reflected an explicit, planned, ongoing cognitive goal. As Michael privileged his students' growing expertise, he responded to what they offered and provided them with literate frames that gently challenged and extended their thinking and language. There were both planful and contingent dimensions to this classroom talk. The literacy event of embedded reading logs in morning meeting was a planned and protected routine. Reading logs positioned these third graders as experts, since they selected the texts for independent reading; as each student read what he or she had previously written and thought about, Michael and other students directed the talk to the expert, asking questions and clarifying ideas. This in the moment talk worked toward Michael's long-term goal of having students do more than just retell the story, but "really relate it [a book] to yourself and to other things you have done and seen, and it just brings a whole other dimension or life to the books." Thus, in Michael's classroom, literate talk extended and provided creative practice in concept formation (Vygotsky, 1986): Michael started with a student's verbalization of experience or understanding of text, and made that idea or purposeful language choice the object of scrutiny, offering ways of saying (and, by extension, ways of thinking) to his students. This was done in the moment. The context was planned—time for the routines of the literacy event was safeguarded, and it built on an established learning environment—but it was enacted in the moment. These contingent practices made framing literate talk in the specialized language of schooling more relevant, specific, and engaging. Doing this takes repeated, explicit, and engaging modeling and attentive listening. Michael's felicity with language, his facility with language, his enjoyment of language, and his continuous use of it in particular ways apprenticed these third graders into the elaborated code (Bernstein, 1971) of literate talk.

Talking to Make Changes in Sarah's Classroom

Like literate talk, being intentional and fluent in planful, contingent instructional practices is learned through repeated practice in a safe yet demanding environment. Good teachers recognize and build on opportunities that engage their students. Sarah, a second-year teacher, wanted to offer something to fill time at the end of the day when her second graders were waiting for their buses. That, in combination with her belief that fine motor practice would help her students to improve their handwriting, resulted in her plan to teach crocheting and to practice it at the end of the day. She started this at the very beginning of the school year. There was no formal educational purpose for this "chatter while you crochet," but it became part of the daily routine. Students helped each other crochet and talked about their day, their pets, and their favorite television shows; in many ways, it was talk for its own sake. The students got to know each other well, and they enjoyed their time crocheting. Tammy put it this way in her daily journal: "As soon as I lerend I thought it might be relacxing. I was right."

This relaxed social practice shaped Sarah's classroom community. Strong friendships and a deep sense of community emerged. Charlie and Martha talked as they huddled together at recess to measure their granny square. Taisha explained what the letters they wrote were for and what they accomplished before reading aloud one of the letters from the class book "Our Crochet Letters" to her kindergarten buddy. Sarah was not part of most of these conversations, but she overheard many of them. When reflecting on all the powerful literacy practices connected to crocheting that had occurred during this year, she said, "The greatest literacy [practice] that transpired through crocheting was the discussions students had while crocheting." In this classroom, talk while students crocheted and talk about crochet-related practices created a discourse and attitude of possibilities. This talk took children from the world of doing reading and writing as school tasks, to "understanding how reading and writing are embedded into the power structures of our society" (Boyd & Kneller, 2009, p. 436; see also Freire, 1993). As crocheting influenced their world and their words, they understood the possibilities and power of literate practices to shape their role in the community and to give back to the community around them.

CONCLUSION: A CASE FOR REAL TALK

Teaching in the way Lisa, Charlotte, Michael, and Sarah taught is not easy, but it is effective. What they did themselves as well as asked their students to do was difficult, and they were aware of that. As Michael noted, "If it's too hard, a task can sometimes lose its appeal, [but on the other hand] I would hope not to give anyone the idea that it's not necessary to put forth some real effort in order to get good results (kids or teachers)." It was difficult for precisely the same reasons that it was effective. It is difficult to create a safe and supportive classroom community; yet it is impossible to teach effectively when students do not feel safe and supported. It is difficult to find materials to supplement the basics that are provided; yet going beyond the basics is the only way to provide enough food for thought for students to thrive and grow. It is difficult to learn, tap, and build on student interests while also working within a curricular frame; yet it is this that fosters motivated and engaged learners. Knowing and pursuing multiple paths toward goals is difficult, and often makes us vulnerable to failure; yet students' abilities, needs, and interests are so varied that it would be impossible to reach all of them without doing so.

Lisa, Charlotte, Michael, and Sarah were all committed to the monumental task of teaching—so committed that they used real talk as a way to build community, create joy, and engage all of their students. They did this by having real conversations in collaborative situations for purposes that were relevant to their students. They and their students were willing to put in the real effort that is required for learning.

Today, a new movement toward scripted education is occurring. As policy makers and administrators take an increasingly "teacher-proof" attitude toward instruction in an effort to improve "delivery" of curriculum, research-based practice such as that displayed by Lisa, Charlotte, Michael, and Sarah is of more importance than ever. As Wells (2001) reminds us, a "universal blueprint" is contrary to effective instruction. In this view, *scripted education* becomes an oxymoron, if *education* is defined as learning.

These four teachers understood that "it is on *knowing in action undertaken jointly with others* that the emphasis needs to be placed, and on opportunities for reflecting on what has been learned in the process" (Wells, 2001, p. 180; italics in original). Accordingly, they created opportunities for their students to do just that. This kind of learning—"situated knowing, involving both action and reflection"—allows students to "make personal sense" of the "knowledge of more expert others," and Wells (2001, p. 180) contends, to incorporate this knowledge "into one's own personal model of the world."

Research such as that discussed in Chapter 1 makes it clear that facilitating dialogic, exploratory talk in a safe, collaborative classroom environment for relevant purposes is a robust approach that results in academic growth. Lisa, Charlotte, Michael, and Sarah have demonstrated four sets of "situated" practices that built on student expertise and supported student learning. These are but four teachers, working within their four classrooms. Their students ranged from ELLs to fluent speakers, from struggling readers to fluent readers, and from students born in the United States to new immigrants; their backgrounds spanned a wide ethnic and socioeconomic range. These four teachers worked under the constraints of mandated curricula, state standards, and high-stakes tests. Yet they all chose to use the vehicle of talk to help their students learn. All students deserve the opportunities that they gave to theirs.

Glossary

accountable talk: Talk that sustains learning by supporting the norms of the learning community, and meeting the need for accurate and appropriate knowledge and rigorous thinking (Michaels et al., 2008).

aesthetic stance: The intention, or *stance*, of the reader influences the dialogue between text and reader. Stance varies along a continuum from *efferent* to *aesthetic* (Rosenblatt, 1978/1994). From a primarily aesthetic stance, a reader focuses on participating in the possibilities for the "virtual" experience that a text has to offer. A more aesthetic stance is effective for reading stories and poems that present visions of the possibilities of life.

agentive flow: The freedom, space, time, and willingness to plan lessons and then make flexible, in-the-moment decisions about pacing, materials, foci, and process.

authentic question: A question for which the questioner does not know, and wants to know, the answer; also called an *open question*. An authentic question (Nystrand & Gamoran, 1991) allows a range of responses and invites students to contribute something new to the class interaction, thus holding the potential to shape the scope of the discourse.

classroom talk: The teacher and student talk that occurs in the context of the classroom (Cazden, 2001). Each utterance is called a *turn* of talk, and the pattern of teacher question, student response, and teacher follow-up often predominates (see **IRE/IRF**).

cognitive load: The thinking necessary to make sense and make meaning. When conversants think and make sense together through talk, they share the cognitive load.

coherence: The imposed patterns of understanding needed to make sense of a text. The notion of coherence is connected to a reader's *schemas* (the ways the reader makes sense of how the world in general and a text in particular are organized). Coherence is also imposed by the reader, not exclusively located in the text (Carrell, 1982).

communalizing function of language: The use of language to define relationships between participants. Such talk varies from intimate to formally articulate (Rubin, 1990).

communicative competence: Appropriateness in terms of word choice and communication strategies (grammatical, sociolinguistic, strategic, and discourse competence).

contingent questions: Questions that explicitly build on contributions made within the preceding three utterances. Their form can be open or closed, authentic or display—but they function to facilitate students' thinking and exploration, as they offer coherent bridges across ideas and contributions. They increase the scope and depth of inquiry (Boyd & Rubin, 2006).

conversant: A person who participates in a conversation by listening and speaking.

critical-analytic stance: A stance that encourages various opinions and perspectives about texts and promotes reasoning and comprehension (Chinn et al., 2001).

dialogic classroom community: A community in which teacher and students listen and respond as they build on each other's contributions and explore ideas that support thinking, not just recall. The classroom environment is one where conjecture is welcome, where students articulate ideas without being afraid to make mistakes, and where the teacher plans with particular educational goals in view (Alexander, 2006; Nystrand, 1997; Wells, 2001).

discussion: Classroom talk in which conversants share ideas generated with others, confirm and extend those ideas, and learn from the ideas of others. Conversants adopt varied roles, and there is purposefulness to the talk.

display question: A question to which the questioner knows a particular predetermined answer and is asking the respondent to display knowledge of that answer. Also called a *closed question*.

efferent stance: The intention, or *stance*, of the reader varies along a continuum from *efferent* to *aesthetic* (Rosenblatt, 1978/1994; see **aesthetic stance**). From a primarily efferent stance, a reader focuses on gaining knowledge to use in the real world. A more efferent stance is effective in reading various types of nonfiction for information.

elaborated utterance: An extended turn of talk.

epistemic function of language: The use of language that varies from reproducing to transforming knowledge. Reproducing and transforming are at either end of a cognitive continuum; in our talk, we move freely along this continuum as we make sense of our new experiences by relating them to what we already know (and can reproduce) (Rubin, 1990).

exploratory talk: Classroom talk that is "working on understanding"; it is incomplete and hesitant as learners reason out loud. It is talk that can only occur when learners feel relatively at ease (Barnes et al., 1990).

extended student exchange: Several student–student utterances sustaining a stream of thought. The teacher may contribute, but in a supportive as opposed to a directive role (perhaps with back-channeling, like "ah-hah," or asking a question that may or may not be answered).

gradual release of responsibility: Pearson and Gallagher (1983) coined the phrase "gradual release of responsibility" to describe instruction that progressed from explicit modeling and instruction to guided practice and then to activities that positioned students into becoming independent learners.

heuristic function of language: The use of language to gain knowledge about the world.

imaginative function of language: The use of language for pretend play and other imaginative endeavors.

informative (or representational) function of language: The use of language to display knowledge to others.

instructional stance: A teacher's way of teaching, which is evident in the teacher's talk. This stance encompasses a coherence and resonance across patterns of interactions; it embodies a teacher's orientation and purpose and what a teacher counts as knowledge, teaching, and learning. It is manifested in the amount of time students have to talk, the type of talk required (e.g., exploration, presentation, discussion), the subject of talk, turn-taking norms, who determines the scope of the talk, and who has interpretive authority. The patterns of interaction associated with an instructional stance influence how comfortable students are with inquiring, sharing, or taking risks.

interactional function of language: The use of language to develop relationships with others.

inter-thinking: Thinking in which students publicly and often collaboratively explore knowledge and test new ideas (Mercer, 2002).

instrumental function of language: The use of language to communicate needs to others.

IRE/IRF: The common acronyms for the prevailing discourse pattern in traditional classrooms. That is, the teacher Initiates through a question, a student Responds, and the teacher either Evaluates that response (IRE; Mehan, 1979) or Follows up on the student response (IRF; Wells, 1993) with, for example, an evaluation or another question. The default IRE/IRF discourse pattern has been closely associated with display questions and student recitation. Wells, however, has documented the potential of the third turn in the IRF pattern for actually expanding student dicourse.

language socialization: The process through which we acquire the knowledge, orientations, and practices that enable us to build relationships and participate effectively and appropriately as members in "communities of practice" (Lave & Wenger, 1991; Ochs & Schiefflin, 1982).

linguistic competence: A speaker's knowledge of the rules of a language.

literate talk: Particular ways to talk about books and literary ideas, including noticing the writer's craft, identifying elements of fiction, and making connections within and across texts.

mathetic function of language: Linguist Michael Halliday's (1978) term for the "learning" function of language.

pedagogical content knowledge (PCK): The ability to transform content-specific representations through instruction that honors both the content and the students at hand, in order to enhance student learning (Shulman, 1986).

personal function of language: The use of language to express feelings, opinions, or oneself in general.

phatic communion: The term for a view of seemingly meaningless small talk (e.g., "How are you?") as important cultural practices that help meet the needs of individuals, communities, and society (Malinowski, 1923/1994).

pragmatic function of language: The "doing" function of language (Halliday, 1978).

quality talk: An overarching term for student talk that positions authentic teacher questions as pivotal, since they can lead to more elaborated student utterances and thus provide opportunities for more student reasoning (Wilkinson & Son, 2011).

question event: A question embedded within the relevant sequence and flow of classroom discourse. Its aspects include authenticity, uptake, level of evaluation, cognitive level, and question source (Nystrand et al., 2003).

real talk: Dialogue in the classroom. It cannot be scripted since it is talk-in-use that unfolds as what one conversant says influences what other conversants think and say. It looks different at different times, in varied situations, and for differing purposes; its properties vary according to local context. Real talk is often messy, hesitant, recursive, incomplete, and choppy, as speakers grapple with word choice and idea exploration in their striving for meaningful, exploratory, and engaged communication. The property of contingency—of woven dialogue—is recurrent, as speakers adopt varied participant roles to connect, communicate, think, and do.

recitation: The dominant pattern of classroom talk associated with traditional classrooms. Students are expected to "fill in the blank" in a teacher–student–teacher turn-taking sequence by recalling information that is already known.

recursive talk: Talk that returns to what was said before. It involves circularity and repetitiveness as conversants build on what they and others have previously said, to explore the idea further and reexamine it, recast it, or move it forward together.

regulatory function of language: The use of language to command others.

scripted education: A formula for teaching that provides the questions that teachers should ask—and the answers they should expect. Also known as *scripted teaching.*

student critical turn: A student utterance that is linguistically extended, structurally coherent, and socially engaged. To be an SCT, the utterance must meet the following criteria: The turn of talk must be elaborated (more than 10 seconds), coherent (building on the preceding three utterances), and engaged (evidence of uptake). Such turns of talk are evidence of students' communicative competence and markers of cognitive activity (Boyd & Rubin, 2002).

talking-to-learn: Using language to explore meaning publicly. (Britton, 1993).

teacher-proof curriculum: A curriculum designed by specialized experts who determine the goals, materials, methods, order, and pacing of instruction for generic classrooms.

third turn: The teacher's utterance after the student's response to a teacher question. It is the E (evaluative) or F (follow-up) slot of the IRE or IRF. This turn can open up a conversation by being contingent on the student's response and inviting further elaboration, or can close down the exchange with a positive or negative evaluative comment.

transactional theory: A theory developed by Louise Rosenblatt (1978/1994), which describes how readers' experiences, abilities, predispositions, preferences, knowledge, and attitudes influence the meaning that they create when reading. *Transaction* implies mutual contributions of reader and text: Readers use text to create meaning by infusing the words on the page with meaning. In other words, meaning is shaped not only by the words on the page (put there deliberately by the author), but by the reader of those words.

uptake: What occurs when one conversant, perhaps the teacher, builds on or asks a question about something another person has said previously (Collins, 1982).

utterance: A turn of talk in a conversation.

References

Alexander, R. (2006). *Towards dialogic teaching: Rethinking classroom talk* (3rd ed.). Cambridge, UK: Dialogos.

Applebee, A. N., Langer, J. A., Nystrand, M., & Gamoran, A. (2003). Discussion-based approaches to developing understanding: Classroom instruction and student performance in middle and high school English. *American Educational Research Journal, 40*(3), 685–730.

Au, K. H., & Carroll, J. H. (1997). Improving literacy achievement through a constructivist approach: The KEEP demonstration classroom project. *Elementary School Journal, 97*(3), 203–222.

Aukerman, M. (2007). When reading it wrong is getting it right: Shared evaluation pedagogy among struggling fifth grader readers. *Research in the Teaching of English, 42*(1), 56–103.

Bailey, K. (1996). The best laid plans: Teachers' in-class decisions to depart from their lesson plans. In K. Bailey & D. Nunan (Eds.), *Voices from the language classroom* (pp. 15–41). Cambridge, UK: Cambridge University Press.

Bakhtin, M. M. (1981). *The dialogic imagination: Four essays by M. M. Bakhtin* (M. Holquist, Ed., C. Emerson & M. Holquist, Trans.). Austin: University of Texas Press.

Barnes, D. (2008). Exploratory talk for learning. In N. Mercer & S. Hodgkinson (Eds.), *Exploring talk in schools* (pp. 1–11). Thousand Oakes, CA: Sage.

Barnes, D., Britton, J., & Torbe, M. (1970). *Language, the learner and the school*. Portsmouth, NH: Boynton/Cook.

Barnes, D., Britton, J., & Torbe, M. (1990). *Language, the learner and the school* (4th ed.). Portsmouth, NH: Boynton/Cook.

Beck, I. L. & McKeown, M. G. (2001). Text talk: Capturing the benefits of read-aloud experiences for young children. *The Reading Teacher, 55*(1), 10–20.

Bernstein, B. (1971). *Class, codes and control* (Vol. 1). London: Routledge & Kegan Paul.

Berry, M. (1981). Systemic linguistics and discourse analysis: A multi-layered approach to exchange structure. In M. Coulthard & M. Montgomery (Eds.), *Studies in discourse analysis* (pp. 120–145). London: Routledge & Kegan Paul.

Bloome, D., & Egan-Robertson, A. (1993). The social construction of intertextuality in classroom reading and writing lessons. *Reading Research Quarterly, 28*(4), 305–333.

Bloome, D., Power Carter, S., Morton Christian, B., Madrid, S., Otto, S., Shuart-Faris, N., et al. (2008). *Discourse analysis in classrooms: Approaches to language and literacy research.* New York: Teachers College Press.

Boyd, M. (2009). Writing-to-learn: Different ways of writing in the process of researching. In K. Bromley (Ed.). *Writing for educators: Personal essays and practical advice.* (pp. 21–23). Charlotte, NC: Information Age.

Boyd, M. (2010). *Intentions, questions, and pedagogical flexibility: Shifting classroom discourse in response to student needs.* Manuscript submitted for publication.

Boyd, M., & Devennie, M. K. (2009). Student voices and teacher choices: Supporting chapter book read-alouds. *Childhood Education, 85*(3), 148–153.

Boyd, M., & Kneller, S. (2009). The 42nd crochet: Getting students hooked into a literacy community. *The Reading Teacher, 62*(5), 434–441.

Boyd, M., & Maloof, V. M. (2000). How teachers can build on student-proposed intertextual links to facilitate student talk in the ESL classroom. In J. Hall & L. Verplaetse (Eds.), *Second and foreign language learning through classroom interaction* (pp. 163–182). Mahwah, NJ: Erlbaum.

Boyd, M., & Rubin, D. L. (2002). Elaborated student talk in an elementary ESol classroom. *Research in the Teaching of English, 36*(4), 495–530.

Boyd, M., & Rubin, D. L. (2006). How contingent questioning promotes extended student talk: A function of display questions. *Journal of Literacy Research, 38*(2), 141–169.

Britton, J. (1993). *Language and learning* (2nd ed.). Portsmouth, NH: Boynton/ Cook.

Bruner, J. (1986). *Actual minds, possible worlds.* Cambridge, MA: Harvard University Press.

Carrell, P. (1982). Cohension is not coherence. *TESOL Quarterly, 16*(4), 479–488.

Cazden, C. B. (2001). *Classroom discourse: The language of teaching and learning* (2nd ed.). Portsmouth, NH: Heinemann.

Chinn, C. A., Anderson, R. C., & Waggoner, M. A. (2001). Patterns of discourse in two kinds of literature discussion. *Reading Research Quarterly, 36*(4), 378–411.

Christoph, J. N., & Nystrand, M. (2001). Taking risks, negotiating relationships: One teacher's transition towards a dialogic classroom. CELA research report. *Research in the Teaching of English, 36*(2), 249–286.

Cochran-Smith, M. (1984). *The making of a reader.* Norwood, NJ: Ablex.

Collins, J. (1982). Discourse style, classroom interaction and differential treatment. *Journal of Reading Behavior, 14,* 429–437.

Cunningham, P. (2005). If they don't read much, how they ever gonna get good? *The Reading Teacher, 59*(1), 88–90.

Daniels, H. (1994). *Literature circles: Voices and choice in the student-centered classroom.* York, ME: Stenhouse.

Dillon, J. T. (1982). The effect of questions in education and other enterprises. *Journal of Curriculum Studies, 14*(2), 127–152.

Dillon, J. T. (1984). Research on questioning and discussion. *Educational Leadership, 42*(3), 50–56.

Dyson, A. H. (1990). Weaving possibilities: Rethinking metaphors for early literacy development. *The Reading Teacher, 44*(3), 202–213.

Early, M. (1960). Stages of growth in literary appreciation. *The English Journal, 49,* 161–167.

Echevarria, J., & Graves, A. (2007). *Sheltered content instruction: Teaching English language learners with diverse abilities.* Boston: Allyn & Bacon.

Eeds, M., & Wells, D. (1989). Grand conversations: An exploration of meaning construction in literature study groups. *Research in the Teaching of English, 23*(1), 4–29.

Finn, P. (1999). *Literacy with an attitude: Educating working-class children in their own self-interest.* Albany: State University of New York Press.

Florio-Ruane, S., & McVee, M. (2000). Ethnographic approaches to literacy education. In M. Kamil, P.B. Rosenthal, P.D. Pearson, & R. Barr (Eds.), *Handbook of reaching reseach* (Vol. 3, pp. 153–162). Mahwah, NJ: Erlbaum.

Freire, P. (1993). *Pedagogy of the oppressed* (new rev. 20th-anniversary ed.). New York: Continuum.

Galda, L. (1998). Mirrors and windows: Reading as transformation. In T. E. Raphael & K. H. Au (Eds.), *Literature-based instruction: Reshaping the curriculum* (pp. 1–12). Norwood, MA: Christopher-Gordon.

Galda, L., Cullinan, B. E., & Sipe, L. R. (2010). *Literature and the child.* (7th ed.). Belmont, CA: Wadsworth/Cengage Learning.

Galda, L., Rayburn, S., & Stanzi, L. C. (2000). *Looking through the faraway end: Creating a literature-based reading curriculum with second graders.* Newark, DE: International Reading Association.

Gambrell, L. B., & Almasi, J. F. (Eds.). (1996). *Lively discussions!: Fostering engaged reading.* Newark, DE: International Reading Association.

Garrett, P., & Baquedano-López, P. (2002). Language socialization: Reproduction and continuity, transformation and change. *Annual Review of Anthropology, 31,* 339–361.

Guthrie, J. T., & Anderson, E. (1999). Engagement in reading: Processes of motivated, strategic, knowledgeable, social readers. In J. T. Guthrie & D. Alvermann (Eds.), *Engaged reading: Processes, practices, and policy implications* (pp. 17–46). New York: Teachers College Press.

Guthrie, J. T., & Knowles, K. T. (2001). Literacy and motivation: Reading engagement in individuals and groups. In L. Verhoeven & C. Snow (Eds.), *Promoting reading motivation* (pp. 159–176). Mahwah, NJ: Erlbaum.

Gutierrez, K. D. (1994). How talk, context and script shape contexts for learning: A cross-case comparison of journal sharing. *Linguistics in Education, 5*, 335–365.

Halliday, M. A. K. (1978). *Language as social semiotic: The social interpretation of language and meaning.* London: Edward Arnold.

Halliday, M. A. K. (1982). Three aspects of children's language development: Learning language, learning through language, and learning about language. In Y. Goodman, M. Haussle, & D. Strickland (Eds.), *Oral and written language development research: Impact on the schools* (pp. 7–19). Urbana, IL: National Council of Teachers of English.

Heath, S. B. (1983). *Ways with words: Language, life, and work in communities and classrooms.* Cambridge, UK: Cambridge University Press.

Hunkins, F. P. (1970). Analysis and evaluation questions: Their effects upon critical thinking. *Educational Leadership, 27*(7), 697–705.

Hymes, D. H. (1971). *On communicative competence.* Philadelphia: University of Pennsylvania Press.

Hynds, S., & Rubin, D. (Eds.). (1990). *Perspectives on talk and learning.* Urbana, IL: National Council of Teachers of English.

Kneller, S., & Boyd, M. (2008). "We were slow; it was challenging" and "It was hard not to make knots": Crocheting as a literacy event in a second grade classroom community. *Early Childhood Education Journal, 36*(2), 135–147.

Kramer-Dahl, A., Teo, P., & Chia, A. (2007). Supporting knowledge construction and literate talk in secondary social studies. *Linguistics and Education, 18*(1), 167–199.

Kreite, R., & Bechtel, L. (2002). *The morning meeting book* (2nd ed.). Turners Falls, MA: Northeast Foundation for Children.

Langer, J. A. (1995). *Envisioning literature: Literary understanding and literature instruction.* New York: Teachers College Press.

Lave, J., & Wenger, E. (1991). *Situated learning: Legitimate peripheral participation.* Cambridge, UK: Cambridge University Press.

Lee, Y.-A. (2006). Respecifying display questions: Interactional resources for language teaching. *TESOL Quarterly, 40*(4), 691–713.

Lee, Y.-A. (2007). Third turn position in teacher talk: Contingency and the work of teaching. *Journal of Pragmatics, 39*, 180–206.

Levy, S. (1996). *Starting from scratch.* Portsmouth, NH: Heinemann.

Marshall, P., Smagorinsky, P., & Smith, M. (1995). *The language of interpretation: Patterns of discourse in discussions of literature* (NCTE Research Report No. 27). Urbana, IL. National Council of Teachers of English.

Maybin, J. (Ed.). (1994). *Language and literacy in social practice.* Clevedon, UK: Multilingual Matters in Association with the Open University.

McLaughlin, M., & DeVoogd, G. (2004). *Critical literacy: Enhancing students' comprehension of text.* New York: Scholastic.

McMahon, S., Raphael, T., Goatley, V., & Pardo, L. S. (1997). The book club program: Theoretical and research foundations. In S. McMahon & T. Raphael (Eds.), *The book club connection* (pp. 3–25) New York: Teachers College Press.

Mehan, H. (1979). "What time is it, Denise?": Asking known information questions in classroom discourse. *Theory into Practice, 18*(4), 285–294.

Mercer, N. (2002, Spring). The art of interthinking. *Teaching Thinking, (7)*, pp. 8–11.

Mercer, N., & Hodgkinson, S. (Eds.). (2008). *Exploring talk in schools*. Thousand Oaks, CA: Sage.

Mercer, N., Wegerif, R., & Dawes, L. (1999). Children's talk and the development of reasoning in the classroom. *British Educational Research Journal, 25*(1), 95–111.

Michaels, S., O'Connor, C., & Resnick, L. B. (2008). Deliberative discourse idealized and realized: Accountable talk in the classroom and in civic life. *Studies in Philosophy and Education, 27*, 283–297.

Mohr, K. J., & Mohr, E. S. (2007). Extending English-language learners' classroom interactions using the response protocol. *The Reading Teacher, 60*(7), 610–620.

Moll, L. (1992). Funds of knowledge for teaching: Using a qualitative research approach to connect homes and classrooms. *Theory into Practice, 31*(1), 132–141.

Morrow, L. (2009). *Literacy development in the early years: Helping children read and write* (6th ed.). Boston: Pearson.

Murphy, P. K., Wilkinson, I. A. G., & Soter, A. O. (2011). Instruction based on discussion. In R. E. Mayer & P. A. Alexander (Eds.), *Handbook of research on learning and instruction*. New York: Routledge.

Murphy, P. K., Wilkinson, I. A. G., Soter, A. O., Hennessey, M. N., & Alexander, J. F. (2009). Examining the effects of classroom discussion on students' high-level comprehension of text: A meta-analysis. *Journal of Educational Psychology, 101*, 740–764.

Nassaji, H., & Wells, G. (2000). What's the use of "triadic dialogue"?: An investigation of teacher student interaction. *Applied Linguistics, 21*(3), 376–406.

New York State Education Department. (1996, March). *Learning standards for English language arts. (ELA) Retrieved August 6, 2010, from www.emsc. nysed.gov/ciai/ela/pub/elalearn.pdf*

Nunan, D. (1996). Hidden voices: Insiders' perspectives on classroom interaction. In K. Bailey & D. Nunan (Eds.), *Voices from the language classroom* (pp. 15–41). Cambridge, UK: Cambridge University Press.

Nystrand, M. (1997). *Opening dialogue: Understanding the dynamics of language and learning in the English classroom*. New York: Teachers College Press.

Nystrand, M. (2006). Research on the role of classroom discourse as it affects reading comprehension. *Research in the Teaching of English, 40*(4), 392–412.

Nystrand, M., & Gamoran, A. (1991). Instructional discourse, student engagement, and literature achievement. *Research in the Teaching of English, 25*, 261–290.

Nystrand, M., Gamoran, A., & Heck, M. (1992). Using small groups for response to and thinking about literature. *The English Journal, 83*, 14–22.

Nystrand, M., Wu, A., Gamoran, A., Zeiser, S., & Long, D. A. (2003). Question in time: Investigating the structure and dynamics of unfolding class-room discourse. *Discourse Processes, 35*(3), 135–198.

Ochs, E., & Schiefflin, B. (1982). *Language acquisition and socialization: Three developmental stories and their implications* (Sociolinguistic Working Paper No. 105). Austin, TX: Southwest Educational Developmental Laboratory.

O'Connor, M. C., & Michaels, S. (1996). Shifting participants frameworks: Orchestrating thinking practices in group discussions. In D. Hicks (Ed.), *Discourse, learning, and schooling* (pp. 63–103). New York: Cambridge University Press.

O'Flahavan, J. F. (1995). Teacher role options in peer discussions about literature. *The Reading Teacher, 48,* 354–356.

Ogle, D. (1986). K-W-L: A teaching model that develops active reading of expository text. *The Reading Teacher, 39,* 564–570.

Olson, D. (1977). From utterance to text: The bias of language in speech and writing. *Harvard Educational Review, 47*(3), 257–281.

Oyler, C. (1996). *Making room for students: Sharing teacher authority in room 104.* New York: Teachers College Press.

Pearson, P. D., & Gallagher, M. C. (1983). The instruction of reading comprehension. *Contemporary Educational Psychology, 8,* 317–344.

Pellegrini, A., & Galda, L. (1998). *The development of school-based literacy: A social ecological perspective.* New York: Routledge.

Pennycook, A. (1994). *The cultural politics of English as an international language.* London: Longman.

Philips, S. U. (1982). *The invisible culture: Communication in classroom and community on the Warm Springs Indian Reservation.* New York: Longman.

Pressley, M. (2006). *Reading instruction that works: The case for balanced teaching* (3rd ed.). New York: Guilford Press.

Resnick, L. (2010). Nested learning systems for the thinking curriculum. *Educational Researcher, 39*(3), 183–197.

Rosenblatt, L. (1995). *Literature as exploration* (5th ed.). New York: Modern Language Association of America.

Rosenblatt, L. (1994). *The reader, the text, and the poem: A transactional theory of the literary work.* Carbondale: Southern Illinois University Press. (Original work published 1978)

Rubin, D. (1990). Introduction: Ways of talking about talking and learning. In S. Hynds & D. Rubin (Eds.), *Perspectives on talk and learning* (pp. 1–17). Urbana, IL: National Council of Teachers of English.

Santoro, L. E., Chard, D. J., Hoard, L., & Baker, S. K. (2008). Making the very most of classroom read-alouds to promote comprehension and vocabulary. *The Reading Teacher, 61*(5), 396–408.

Short, K. G., & Pierce, K. M. (1990). *Talking about books: Creating literature communities.* Portsmouth, NH: Heinemann.

Shulman, L. (1986). Those who understand: Knowledge growth in teaching. *Educational Researcher, 15*(2), 4–14.

Skidmore, D. (2000). From pedagogical dialogue to dialogical pedagogy. *Language and Education, 14*(4), 283–296.

Smith, H., & Higgins, S. (2006). Opening classroom interaction: The importance of feedback. *Cambridge Journal of Education, 36*(4), 485–502.

Snow, C. E. (1989). Understanding social interaction and language acquisition: Sentences are not enough. In M. Bornstein & J. S. Bruner (Eds.), *Interaction in human development* (pp. 83–103). Hillsdale, NJ: Erlbaum.

Soter, A., Wilkinson, I., Murphy, P. K., Rudge, L., Reninger, K., & Edwards, M. (2008). What the discourse tells us: Talk and indicators of high-level comprehension. *International Journal of Educational Research, 47*(6), 372–391.

Swain, M. (1995). Three functions of output in second language learning. In G. Cook & B. Seidlhofer (Eds.), *Principle and practice in applied linguistics: Studies in honour of H. G. Widdowson* (pp. 125–144). New York: Oxford University Press.

Thompson, P. (2008). Learning through extended talk. *Language and Education, 22*(3), 241–256.

Tomlinson, C., & McTighe, J. (2006). *Integrating differentiated instruction and understanding by design.* Alexandria, VA: Association for Supervision and Curriculum Development.

von Bertalanffy, L. (1968). *General system theory: Foundations, development, applications.* New York: George Braziller.

Vygotsky, L. (1986). *Thought and language.* Cambridge, MA: MIT Press.

Wells, G. (1993). Reevaluating the IRF sequence: A proposal for the articulation of theories of activity and discourse for analysis of teaching and learning in the classroom. *Linguistics and Education, 5,* 1–37.

Wells, G. (1999). *Dialogic inquiry: Towards a sociocultural practice and theory of education.* Cambridge, UK: Cambridge University Press.

Wells, G. (2001). The case for dialogic inquiry. In G. Wells (Ed.), *Action, talk and text* (pp. 171–194). New York: Teachers College Press.

Wells, G., & Chang-Wells, G.L. (1992). *Constructing knowledge together: Classrooms as centers of inquiry and literacy.* Portsmouth, NH: Heinnemann.

Wigfield, A., & Tonks, S. (2004). The development of motivation for reading and how it is influenced by CORI. In J. T. Guthrie, A. Wigfield, & K. C. Perencevich (Eds.), *Motivating reading comprehension: Concept-oriented reading instruction* (pp. 249–272). Mahwah, NJ: Erlbaum.

Wilkinson, A. (1970). The concept of oracy. *The English Journal, 59*(1), 71–77.

Wood, D., Bruner, J., & Ross, G. (1976). The role of tutoring in problem solving. *Journal of Child Psychology and Psychiatry, 17,* 89–100.

Children's Literature

Ahlberg, A. (1991). *The jolly Christmas postman* (Ill. J. Ahlberg) Boston: Little, Brown.

Armour, M. (1994). *Orca song* (Ill. K. Lee). Norwalk, CT: Second print.

Barron, T. A. (1996). *The lost years of Merlin.* New York: Philomel.

Collins, S. (2004). *Gregor the overlander.* New York: Scholastic.

Collins, S. (2005). *Gregor and the prophecy of Bane.* New York: Scholastic.

Crews, D. (1991). *Bigmama's* (Ill. by author). New York: Greenwillow Books.

Dahl, R. (1964). *Charlie and the chocolate factory* (Ill. J. Schindelman). New York: Knopf.

Dahl, R. (1975). *Danny, the champion of the world* (Ill. J. Bennett). New York: Knopf.

Dahl, R. (1983). *The witches* (Ill. Q. Blake). New York: Farrar, Straus, Giroux.

Dahl, R. (1988). *Matilda* (Ill. Q. Blake). New York: Viking Penguin.

Farmer, N. (2002). *The house of the scorpion.* New York: Atheneum Books for Young Readers.

Farmer, N. (2004). *The sea of trolls.* New York: Atheneum Books for Young Readers.

Fleischman, S. (1986). *The whipping boy* (Ill. P. Sis). New York: Greenwillow.

Flournoy, V. (1985). *The patchwork quilt* (Ill. J. Pinkney). New York: Dial Books for Young Readers.

Funke, C. (2004). *Dragon rider.* New York: Scholastic.

González, L. M. (1994). *The bossy gallito* (Ill. L. Delacre). New York: Scholastic.

Heinz, B. (1996). *Kayuktuk: An Arctic quest* (Ill. J. Van Zyle). San Francisco: Chronicle Books.

Hiaasen, C. (2002). *Hoot.* New York: Random House Children's Books.

James, S. (1991). *Dear Mr. Blueberry* (Ill. By author). New York: M. K. McElderry Books.

Juster, N. (1961). *The phantom tollbooth* (Ill. J. Feiffer). New York: Random House.

Kaufman Orloff, K. (2004). *I wanna iguana* (Ill. D. Catrow). New York: Putnam.

LeGuin, U. (1988). *Catwings* (Ill. S. Schlinder). New York: Scholastic.

Lewis, C. S. (1950). *The lion, the witch and the wardrobe* (Ill. P. Baynes). New York: Macmillan.

MacLachlan, P. (1980). *Arthur, for the very first time* (Ill. L. Bloom). New York: Harper & Row.

Nimmo, J. (2003). *Midnight for Charlie Bone.* New York: Scholastic.

Paolini, C. (2003). *Eragon.* New York: Knopf.

Pierce, T. (1997). *Circle of magic: Sandry's book.* New York: Scholastic.

Polacco, P. (1994). *Pink and Say* (Ill. P. Polacco). New York: Philomel.

Riordan, R. (2005). *The lightning thief.* New York: Hyperion Books for Children.

Rodda, E. (2001). *Rowan of Rin.* New York: Greenwillow.

Ryder, J. (1988). *The snail's spell* (Ill. L. Cherry). New York: Puffin Books.

Ryder, J. (1991). *Hello, tree!* (Ill. M. Hays). New York: Lodestar.

Rylant, C. (1989). *Henry and Mudge get the cold shivers* (Ill. S. Stevenson). New York: Bradbury Press.

Rylant, C. (1994). *Henry and Mudge and the careful cousin* (Ill. S. Stevenson). New York: Bradbury Press.

Rylant, C. (1996). *The whales* (Ill. By author). New York: Blue Sky Press.

Scholastic. (2001). *The magic school bus: Whales and dolphins* [Computer software]. New York: Author.

Scieszka, J. (1992). *The stinky cheese man and other fairly stupid tales* (Ill. L. Smith). New York: Viking Juvenile.

Seuss, Dr. [T. Geisel]. (1940). *Horton hatches the egg* (Ill. By author). New York: Random House.

Shaw, J. (1988). *Kirsten saves the day* (Ill. R. Graef). Middleton, WI: Pleasant.

Sheldon, D. (1991). *The whales' song* (Ill. G. Blythe). New York: Dial Books for Young Readers.

Woodson, J. (2005). *Show way* (Ill. H. Talbott). New York: Putnam.

Wrede, P. (1993). *Talking to dragons: The enchanted forest chronicles, book four.* (San Francisco: Harcourt Brace Jovanovich.

Yolen, J. (1996). Killer whales. In J. Yolen, *Sea watch* (Ill. T. Lewin). New York: Philomel.

Young, E. (1992). *Seven blind mice.* New York: Philomel.

Index